ROBERT SMITH
THE CURE & WISHFUL THINKING

RICHARD CARMAN

Published in 2005 by
INDEPENDENT MUSIC PRESS
Independent Music Press is an imprint of I.M. P. Publishing Limited
This Work is Copyright © I. M. P. Publishing Ltd 2005

Robert Smith: The Cure & Wishful Thinking
by Richard Carman

British Library Cataloguing-in-Publication Data.
A catalogue for this book is available from The British Library.

ISBN 0-9549704-1-1

Cover Design by Fresh Lemon.
Edited by Martin Roach.
Printed in the UK.

INDEPENDENT MUSIC PRESS
P.O. Box 69,
Church Stretton, Shropshire
SY6 6WZ

Visit us on the web at: www.impbooks.com

For a free catalogue, e-mail us at: info@impbooks.com
Fax: 01694 720049

ROBERT SMITH

THE CURE &
WISHFUL THINKING

by Richard Carman

Independent Music Press

CONTENTS

Acknowledgements

First and foremost, a thousand thanks to my publisher, editor and friend Martin Roach, for all his help and support, as well as a thankyou to Kaye and Alfie Blue. Thanks also to Clive Timperley, Lynda Moynihan, Mick Mercer and Stuart Dwyer.

Dedicated to my kids, Alex, Jamie and Tom, for coming down the stairs in the middle of the night on a regular basis and asking 'what are you doing?' ... and then going back to bed having broken my train of thought. And eternal thanks to Linda, my wife of twenty years, who likes 'Catch', and who catches me when nobody else would.

Foreword

The history of The Cure has been well-documented in parts, and in others very poorly so. There are innumerable websites dedicated to the band – some of them truly astonishing in their depth – as well as hundreds of magazine articles to trawl through, ranging from ten-word photo-shoots to extensive pieces in magazines such as *Record Collector, Uncut* and *Mojo*. Dig them all out – they make fascinating reading. I have researched a variety of sources, all of which – where possible – have been credited. At the time of writing, two seminal works on The Cure have both not been updated for a long time. *Ten Imaginary Years,* the excellent, official biography of the band, and *The Cure: A Visual Documentary,* a day-by day account of their early and mid-years development, are both essential reading for any Cure fan; second-hand copies are readily available if you dig deep enough. Both contain a wealth of personal reminiscences from all the band members and their associates, especially on The Cure's very early days. A number of websites contain more information on the band than any book of this nature could include, including set lists, ticket scans, gig reviews and so on. I highly recommend a visit to *www.afoolisharrangement.com* and to *www.picturesofyou.us* to any fan who has not visited these sites. Although in the past I have owned copies of both Jo Anne Greene's book *The Cure* and Darren Butler's superb visual collection of Cure artefacts *The Cure On Record*, these are both out of print too, and no longer on my book shelf, but they are worth digging out if you are lucky enough to find them.

In *Robert Smith: The Cure & Wishful Thinking* I have tried to do what no writer has done in book form for a long time, and that is to tell the whole story to date, through the early years and the days and nights of slogging around the UK, Belgium, Germany, Australia etc, up to the Nineties and into the new millennium with the *Live8* concerts of July, 2005. Inevitably there is more to come in the history of The Cure, as Robert

Smith, Simon Gallup *et al* approach their fiftieth birthdays in a few years time.

But for now, I hope you enjoy the ride …

Introduction

I was born within a year of Robert Smith. We were chucked into a world only fifteen years free of the Second World War. Our parents had lived through the most protracted, divisive of conflicts, and we were the result. Churchill was still alive, Kennedy was as yet un-elected. We came in after the best of Elvis and before The Beatles. The world has changed a lot in our lifetime: it was in a mess then – some would argue it's in a bigger mess now. For me, as for many of my generation, rock music mirrored both the mess we were in and offered release from it. It's a neat trick, and it's why rock is the greatest diversion of our time.

My own personal history of rock goes like this: Elvis shook the planet, but as I've said that was before I was born, so it didn't mean much to me. The Beatles turned that world on its head – and I was there to see it. Dylan made everything that had gone before him seem fit only for kids. Bowie was the next landmark. After Bowie there were no more pop stars, only 'pop stars.' Pop music was forever after aware of the inverted commas that kept it in place. Ziggy was the first post-modern icon of rock. In this edgy climate, punk shifted things again, and out of punk came a wealth of intelligent, unusual and truly worthwhile bands. Many of them lasted a single season and their drummers were back in the dole queue before their albums had even slipped off the chart. Some of them soldiered on and survived to the era of Eighties revival tours. A handful continued to contribute. One band outstripped them all.

I have always loved The Cure. For nearly thirty years, in a jaded, increasingly celebrity-driven world, they have genuinely *meant* something to their audience. That counts for a hell of a lot. To put their career in perspective, the entire recording career of The Beatles fits into the gap between *Three Imaginary Boys* and *The Head on the Door*. Twenty years after the latter album, The Cure are still at the top of the pile, still controversial, still relevant. Robert Smith has got stamina and so have the people who have stayed with him for so long. With an audience in the tens of millions worldwide, The Cure and Robert Smith are still a life-enhancing force for their fans. And I find that moving. And I like the fact that he genuinely appears to return the compliment by caring about his audience too.

In this book I have tried to do a very simple thing: tell the story. As a story. Signed for most of their career to a label named after inventive writing, and with a band leader who has at times revelled in intense mystique, story-telling seems a pertinent motif. And, like all good tales, it has plot twists that Mary Shelley would die for and more false endings than *The Sound of Music*. And it's not over yet.

At the age of sixteen I had a little band with my mate Phil. We were called First Page (though for a three-day period we had a violinist and were a hippy trio called Misty System). We were crap, but one day we were going to get decent gear and we were going to be good. We never did, and we never were. But when I listen to The Cure at their best I am still inspired to get my guitar out and plug a microphone in and have a crack at it. That's what Elvis did, it's what The Beatles, the Spiders and the Pistols did; it's what Green Day and Interpol do too. Listening to them all makes us want to go out and do it ourselves. The Cure still inspire.

And at the beating heart of The Cure is Robert Smith.

This is his story ...

Chapter 1: Malice Aforethought

Blackpool is Britain's ultimate seaside resort, a windy, grey town on the north-west coast of England. Cheap and cheerful – though often neither – Blackpool is where the northern working-classes have spent their grim, rain-swept holidays for a century or more. Lovers in search of privacy and saucy excitement go to Blackpool for 'dirty weekends.' Kids in d roves stalk the self-regarding 'Pleasure Beach' and ride the highest, fastest and longest rollercoaster in the country. The sea is the colour of granite and the castles of sand are washed away twice daily by a greasy tide. It could be Morrissey's 'seaside town they forgot to close down.' Suitably, it is where the story of Robert Smith and The Cure – the masters of gloomy rhetoric and pure pop fantasy – begins its incredible tale spanning three decades.

Like Blackpool, The Cure are a confusing gaggle of different things to different people. To some they are the classic goth band, to others the ultimate indie rock band. They remain merchants of some of the most shimmering, glorious pop of their generation. Stadium-filling internationalists, they occupy a place in the hearts of their audience, a fan base surprisingly swelled by the ranks of the Playstation generation, for whom pop and rock have often been overtaken by electronic games and the internet. The Cure were, and remain, a real band, notwithstanding their routine personnel changes and shifts of musical direction. Like the town of Blackpool, they are at times sensational, occasionally gloomy and overcast. Like Blackpool they can be pure showbiz, but they have their dark corners too, and the shifting tides of fashion have changed them little over the decades. The Cure – despite seeming to perennially change and re-invent themselves – fundamentally understand exactly what they are and what they represent, and they have never wavered from that course. And, like the town of his birth, in Robert Smith they have an institution that refuses to go away, refuses to compromise, and shows every intention of continuing his outstanding work well into a new era.

Robert James Smith was born in Blackpool on April 21, 1959, a birth date shared with the mighty Iggy Pop, twelve years his senior. He was the third-born of the Smith family children: older brother Richard was to be a big influence on Robert's musical tastes. A little over a year after Robert was born, he was joined in the junior ranks of the family by little sister Janet, who – along with older sister Margaret – brought the full complement of the Smith family to six. There was no evident classic rock and roll dysfunction in the Smith household: parents Alex and Rita raised a straightforward, liberal Catholic family, and Robert's early childhood was typical of the experience of tens of thousands of kids at the time. The children spent much of their early years on Blackpool's (occasionally) golden sands, living a normal and happy childhood along the edges of a slowly turning tide. In 1983 Robert described his first memory as the taste of the sand on Blackpool beach. Elsewhere he remembered pulling earthworms out of the ground, hoping to feed them to his sister.

In December 1962, when Robert was three, the family left Blackpool and the north-west of England and moved to Surrey. "My parents had no time to be sentimental," Robert told Dutch magazine *Hitkrant* in 1986. "Working was the only thing that mattered. My father worked hard to become a well-to-do-citizen and we were able to leave Blackpool. But even then, he stayed a modest person. He never looked down on the working-class. It's a lesson in life I've never forgotten." Initially they settled in Horley, a railway town nowadays in danger of toppling into the M23 motorway but then, as now, the nearest town to Gatwick, one of the UK's busiest holiday airports. Robert described his early childhood memories for *Smash Hits* in 1986, spending all day in the brambles in the garden, or dribbling on passers-by from the sweet chestnut tree at the front of the house.

Music was already creeping subtly into Robert's life

especially with older brothers and sisters playing the latest singles on their bedroom record players. Aged five when The Beatles released 'Help!', the song still moves the forty-something adult, bringing back memories of hearing the wonderful new sound spilling from under his sisters' bedroom door. It was a time of immense optimism and hope: we really were going somewhere new. Everything, after twenty years of post-war austerity, suddenly speeded up, became colourful, was imbued with youth and liberty. As our parents' generation benefited and felt the new wave rushing over society so we, the children of their optimism, benefited too. I can remember incredible excitement in my own house when – living near the brother of George Harrison – we caught occasional glimpses of a Beatle. When Robert spoke to Will Hodgkinson of *The Guardian* about 'Help!' he talked of how, for the first time as a child, it gave him a sense of something else happening outside of his immediate world. "I listen to 'Help!' and I'm filled with hope that the world could be a better place."

Robert was to tell French magazine *Rock and Folk* how, way back at the age of three, his father had made him read newspapers, pushing both him and Richard to read, read, read. Smith was a voracious and mature reader as a child, and his early love of literature was to be evident in many of the songs he went on to write for The Cure.

Robert attended St Francis' Primary School in Horley. Father Alex worked for Upjohn Pharmaceuticals in Crawley, and with Robert moving up to St Francis' Junior School the family made one last geographical hop, moving to Crawley when Robert was six years old. This was to become Robert's – and his family's – home town, the starting place for all Cure adventures. Crawley, like Horley, is a town owing its development to the railway running from London to Brighton, from which an offshoot runs through the town. Developed even more when Gatwick was opened just before the Second World War, Crawley grew quickly and became one of Britain's 'New Towns' – development initiatives aimed at providing much-needed housing in a number of areas around Britain in the post-war years. At the time that Robert's family moved in, Crawley was maturing as a New Town, its population reaching some 60,000. Many people moved into New Towns from elsewhere: the Smith family's experience was far from unique, but for many these were vibrant new centres designed to cater for the welfare of the population, meeting their professional and employment needs but also attempting to ensure that the burgeoning populations had adequate health and social care, leisure facilities and so on. Towns such as Crawley, or Swindon – where the young Andy Partridge would start The Cure's near-contemporaries XTC – were perfect breeding grounds for nascent rock bands.

One of the children with whom Robert shared the journey to and from school every day was a boy called Lawrence Tolhurst. 'Lol', as he has become known to millions of Cure fans worldwide, was born in Horley only a couple of months before Robert's own birthday, on February 3, 1959, one of six children born to parents William and Daphne. The boys didn't cement a relationship until later in their childhood, but – like Jagger and Richards before them – the relationship between these band-mates goes way back to the short-trouser days of the early Sixties. Dave Thompson and Jo-Ann Greene's book *The Cure: A Visual Documentary* quotes Robert as saying that his ambition at the time was to be the last human being in the world; not an unusual concept for a bright and deep-thinking child. Smith claims that he didn't try hard at school, aiming to get by on as little work as he possibly could. It was around this time that brother Richard, a confirmed Captain Beefheart fan, started to introduce Robert to the guitar.

It says a lot for Alex and Rita Smith's forward-thinking parenting, or perhaps their sons' fierce independence, that on the evening of Sunday, August 30, 1970, Robert found himself – at only eleven years of age – in a tent on the Isle of Wight. With his brother, Robert had made the seventy-five mile journey to the island off the south coast of England for what has gone down in legend as one of the greatest rock festivals of all-time. The 1970 spectacle was the third Isle of Wight Festival, boasting slots from dozens of major acts including Leonard Cohen, Joni Mitchell, The Who, Jethro Tull, Traffic, The Doors, Miles Davis (are you counting up in your head what this line-up – if it were possible – would cost today?) and more. One of the headline acts was Jimi Hendrix, whose Sunday night set was one of the last before his death in September that year. Hendrix seemed to be riding two rollercoasters at the same time, each pulling him in a different direction. With Mitch Mitchell on drums and Billy Cox on bass he was moving in deep waters musically, still searching for the perfect band sound but getting booed in Germany only a week after the IoW festival. He had just opened his own Electric Ladyland studio complex in New York and was still highly revered among the majority of rock fans, but a punishing schedule and a prodigious intake of pills was making him more and more vulnerable to the tragedy that soon overwhelmed him.

Jimi was to become a major influence on Smith and his music in The Cure, and to this day Robert counts him among his favourite ever acts: a shock-haired, theatrical guitar hero with a loving, cult audience. Jimi could do anything. What he played while he was singing was better than most guitarist's finest solos. When he let go and played for real he was the most remarkable musician I have ever seen play, a Picasso for the electric guitar. When he saw Hendrix for the first time Eric Clapton is reported to have stood with his mouth agape thinking, 'I can't do that!'

For some reason Robert did not actually get to see Hendrix himself at that festival. Nonetheless, the young Robert found a role model in Hendrix that – untimely death aside – was deeply important; a musician who took his craft seriously; who worked to develop his playing and his writing over years of patient study; private and quietly-spoken off-stage but mesmeric when stood before an audience. Hendrix's example taught the schoolboy Smith a lot. He told *Guitar* magazine in 2000 that Hendrix informed everything he had done as a guitarist: "Other kids at school were always learning Hendrix's solos, but I was much more interested in learning the way he put chords together. I thought the way he left notes ringing was really weird and sounded really good."

While Hendrix was struggling through the last few weeks of his chaotic life, a young guy in his early twenties was stoking the fire of a mighty ambition. A hit single from 1969 had introduced the young David Bowie to the charts, and the ethereal, unusual song – with its tragi-comic astronaut sitting in a tin can – lodged quietly in the minds of everybody who heard it that summer when Neil Armstrong and Buzz Aldrin became the first men to step upon the surface of the moon. I can remember that day as clearly as if it was yesterday, and remember Bowie's 'Space Oddity' drifting through the house from our aged radio in the kitchen. Three years later, his hair spookily spiked and his arm languorously draped around the body of another guy, this oddity re-appeared in our lives. He blew us away. Some gigs are legendary: The Beatles at Shea Stadium; Dylan at the Albert Hall; The Sex Pistols at Manchester's Lesser Free Trade Hall; David Bowie's appearance on *Top Of The Pops* on July 6, 1972 set the world on fire for so many of us. The latter remains one of the seminal moments in pop music on TV. Thirty-plus years later it is still one of the most exciting things I have ever seen on the box.

Marc Bolan had been glittering along just fine. T Rex were feminine but ballsy, camp but boogie-driven. Outside of Marc, most of the male pop stars around in the early Seventies were either largely inane, or sensitive singer-songwriters who could move you but not set your pulse a-racing, or just plain ugly plodders. And most of the women were much worse! Suddenly Bowie arrived, this beautiful, weird, reptilian creature in a coloured jump suit, clearly wearing make-up, with cheek bones you could line your books on, leering across our screens with a truly confusing sexual grace. He was the first pop star whose teeth you could spend an hour discussing at school the next day (except, perhaps, Ken Dodd and Tiny Tim). Bowie's smile was so wide that you just knew you could trust him. Wherever he was going, you knew instantly that you wanted to go with him. And you wanted *that* hair-cut. And all this was cemented in our brains before he'd even reached the first chorus.

The 1972 single 'Starman' is classic Bowie: a little reminiscent of 'Somewhere Over The Rainbow' in the chorus, a taste of The Supremes' 'You Keep Me Hanging On' in the staccato instrumental phrase that precedes it, and a whole bunch of hooks and 'come and get me' lyrics that are pure Bowie. Part-Hollywood, part-Motown, part-Bolan, the image hit us all between the eyes, but the song – so simple, so catchy – stuck between the ears. Bowie had it all. And we wanted some of it.

That summer 'Starman' was everywhere. I can remember my family's camping holiday in Scotland, where – in a disco on one camping ground – it was played alternately throughout the night: one record, then 'Starman', another record then 'Starman.' Only Alice Cooper's fantastic 'School's Out' came anywhere near it.

The Ziggy Stardust Companion (www.5years.com) summarises the impact of this TV appearance on the massed ranks of Britain's future rock and roll stars. Ian *McCulloch of Echo And The Bunnymen*: "As soon as I heard 'Starman' and saw him on *Top Of The Pops* I was hooked ... all my other mates at school would say, 'Did you see that bloke on *Top Of The Pops*? He's a right faggot, him!' And I remember thinking 'you pillocks,' as they'd all be buying their Elton John albums and all that crap. It made me feel cooler."

Gary Kemp, Spandau Ballet: "I watched it at a friend's council flat. My reality was so far removed from this guy's place, that my journey from that moment on was to get there."

Gary Numan: "I just thought, and still do to this day, that it was the greatest rock and roll star image that there has ever been."

Alan McGee (Creation Records): "The reason I got into rock and roll is because I saw David Bowie on *Top Of The Pops* with a bright blue acoustic guitar playing 'Starman' in July 1972 … I was gob-smacked."

Martin Fry, ABC: "I remember eating beans on toast, watching Bowie on television, and nearly spilling my dinner."

Boy George: "Everything changed, and that was basically the end of normality for me … I'd go to Beckenham on the bus and just stand outside his house and hang out with all the other fans … one day we were being quite noisy outside his home, and his wife, Angie, opened the window and shouted, 'Will you all fuck off!' It was the highlight of our year, we were all quite chuffed to be acknowledged."

Now that's what I call influential stuff. My own world changed that night. Bowie brought things into my little twelve-year-old world that might not have got there for another ten years, if ever. And two hundred and fifty miles away from my mum and dad's front room, the thirteen-year-old Robert Smith was watching too.

*

Robert had been listening, as had many like him, to the records in his brother and sister's collection. To his parents' consternation, by the age of seven or eight he was already smitten. We've established Hendrix was one mighty influence. Robert also loved the early Rolling Stones and their rhythmical R&B. It is interesting to note that when Smith talks about these early influences he often refers to the rhythm of the bands he cites as their major influence on him, The Stones included. Brother Richard also introduced him to bands such as Cream and Captain Beefheart. But that night in July 1972 changed everything for Robert. "I felt that [Bowie's] records had been made with me in mind," he told *The Guardian*'s Will Hodgkinson. "The school was divided between those who thought he was a queer and those who thought he was a genius. Immediately, I thought: this is it. This is the man I've been waiting for. He showed that you could do things on your own terms; that you could define your own genre and not worry about what anyone else is doing, which is I think the definition of a true artist."

Bowie certainly polarised the population. Earnest musos instantly dismissed him as a fraud, a triumph of 'style over content', as John Peel put it. Flared denim-ites, used to head-down, no-nonsense, mindless Quo and Purple, dismissed him as lightweight. Mum and dad (though not mine) threw their tea at the screen and shouted 'poof!' But in school on the morning of July 7, 1972 it was *the* big talking point. And if you got it, it stayed with you forever.

Up to this point Robert – still, of course, a young boy – had not discriminated between different types of celebrity. For him Mick Jagger and George Best were both out of the same barrel. A football fan too, for Smith these guys were simply celebrities: they were definitely not part of his world, but he also had no comprehension of the world which they inhabited. Bowie opened the door to another world and the first record that Smith bought for himself – as it was for me too – was the incomparable *The Rise And Fall Of Ziggy Stardust And The Spiders From Mars*. With the album having kicked rock music a few paces forwards, the convoluted, conceptual title itself said a lot about the changing times, when compared with that of the innocence of the era of The Beatles *Help!*

Soon, the young Robert was causing a bit of a sensation himself. According to the book *The Cure: A Visual Documentary* he claims to have been in trouble at school by the age of eleven for turning up wearing one of his mother's black velvet dresses, and getting beaten up on the way home into the bargain. Robert's parents encouraged his interest in all forms of music. It might have been the era of The Glitter Band and of Slade, but Mr and Mrs Smith ensured that Robert got a smattering of classical influence too, playing him records from their own collection. Robert and his class mates – by now at Notre Dame Middle School – began selling home-brew to raise money to buy records. Robert claims to have bought more than a hundred albums this way. He'd started experimenting with his sister's make-up bag too, locked away in the bathroom. Robert's school was perhaps not surprisingly unimpressed when he arrived sporting eyeliner, his hair now halfway down his back.

Another musical influence at the time – and one of Smith's favourite bands – was the Sensational Alex Harvey Band. Harvey was born the same week as Elvis Presley, albeit in Glasgow, Scotland. He'd been hailed 'The Scottish Tommy Steele' way back in the mid-Fifties. His Alex Harvey Soul Band was up and running by the end of that decade, but it took until the early Seventies before he enjoyed hit singles with 'Delilah' and 'Boston Tea Party' in 1976. Harvey came to the notice of a lot of Bowie fans because he covered Jacques Brel songs. Bowie's covers of Brel classics 'My Death' and – on the B-side of 'Sorrow' – 'Amsterdam' were favourites for fans, and Harvey made wonderful drama out of the French writer's 'Next.' But in guitarist Zal Cleminson, Harvey had a make-up wearing role model too, and although the tough soul rocking of the Sensational Alex Harvey Band was a long way away from Ziggy, here at least were two reasons for all Bowie fans to check them out. "Alex Harvey was the physical manifestation of what I thought I could be," Smith told *The Guardian* some thirty years later. "He had the persona of a victim, and you just sided with him against all that was going wrong."

Zal Cleminson's make-up was inspired by pierrot clowns. We were all tempted for half an hour or so by the 25-year-old Leo Sayer, who donned pierrot slap for his 1973 hit 'The Show Must Go On.' In America, Kiss – looking unnervingly like a Zal Cleminson tribute band – had started their own comic book career behind Max Factor masks. Rock and roll in the early and mid-Seventies was a made-up world, literally and figuratively, largely because of Ziggy.

Robert started to go to gigs on his own: his first solo flight was to a beery, bluesy Rory Gallagher show, and within weeks he had seen The Stones, Gallagher and Thin Lizzy. He told journalist Kirk Miller that he probably saw the latter ten times in two years. Robert has said that he originally took up the acoustic guitar at the age of nine, taught by a student of John Williams, the classical virtuoso. With a sister who was considered by many to be a 'piano prodigy', he picked the guitar to avoid sibling rivalry (although he did later achieve the heady heights of a Grade 3 qualification on the piano). By the age of 13 Robert had his first electric guitar. He never looked back.

Robert claims to have always bought guitars based upon what they look like. Image was as important as sound early on in his career. I can remember being lent a Futurama guitar by my Physics teacher, and when I spotted that Eno had one in his arms on the inner sleeve of the second Roxy Music album, I never wanted to give it back. Plugged into our old record player, it was a door into the most glamorous world I could ever imagine. Smith, too, was beginning to crystallize his first ideas for a band.

*

Chime bars gathered together on a table by the wall; a piano at an angle by the teacher's desk; musical instruments on torn posters lining the walls and the notes of the stave drawn out in chalk on the old-fashioned blackboard. By 1972 Robert was at Notre Dame Middle School, and it was in just such a music room that he started to play with long-time buddy Lol Tolhurst, fellow pupil Michael Dempsey and others, killing time and having fun. They played whatever instruments were lying around, teasing out dodgy versions of current hits. This soon crystallised into Robert's first formal group, the wonderfully-named Crawley Goat Band which included kid sister Janet, occasional member/permanent brother Richard and others. They would play together at Robert's parents' house until at the end of that school year they renamed themselves The Obelisk. The first incarnation of his future band played in front of the class at the end of the last school year. Robert was on piano, Lol on drums, Michael and Marc

Ceccagno both on guitars and another pupil called Alan Hill played bass.

As school-mate bands go, The Obelisk were nothing special, probably typical of a thousand similar outfits starting up at the time. Unknown to Smith, Tolhurst *et al*, the biggest shockwave to hit rock music since Bowie was bubbling under the surface all over Britain: punk. Bands were fermenting who would – over the next year – transform pop for decades to come. In London the Sex Pistols had already played their first gigs and were building a local following before any national press began to cover them. Other early bands like Chelsea – featuring Billy Idol – would soon emerge. In Manchester, Pete Shelly and Howard Devoto were weeks away from forming Buzzcocks. In the north-east, the Angelic Upstarts would come together, while scores of bands like The Nosebleeds, Slaughter And The Dogs, Penetration and X-Ray Spex began to see a way ahead. It was a heady time. A great time, indeed, to be forming your first band.

By the first few weeks of 1976, Robert's band was playing more formal rehearsals on a regular basis and even had a more stable line-up, consisting of Smith on guitar (his Woolworth Top 20 favourite), Dempsey on bass and Marc Ceccagno on guitar. After a spell with a drummer known only as 'Graham, Lol Tolhurst eventually settled in as the long-term sticksman. The band duly reinvented themselves, appropriately punkish, as Malice.

Locals remember that at some point in the late Seventies Robert's father built a 'studio' for the band to rehearse in at the side of the Smith home. 1976 was a long, hot summer, defined/maligned for teenagers the world over by the huge seasonal hit 'Don't Go Breaking My Heart' by Elton John and Kiki Dee. The biggest-selling chart singles in the UK were by the likes of Brotherhood of Man, Pussycat, Abba, Dr Hook and Chicago (long, slow-dance snogging at the school disco). It was a world waiting for something to happen.

Over the drought-stricken weeks, Malice became more and more serious about their business, and rehearsals became more frequent. Ceccagno left the band, replaced by local guitarist Porl Thompson, who Robert met in a record store. Thompson and Smith shared a particular taste in music, more and more developed by what they heard on John Peel's influential radio show. Malice played their first 'proper' gig at Worth Abbey on December 18, 1976. Porl would play a part in Robert's life, and the life of The Cure, for many years to come.

In the swing of things, they followed-up two days later with a gig at St Wilfred's Comprehensive School, which Smith was now attending, supporting Ceccagno's new band Amulet. They were joined by a local journalist on vocals. 'Martin' turned up wearing a motorcycle helmet and a Manchester United scarf, untroubled by having never even rehearsed with the group. The David Cassidy sound-alike struggled against the 'wall of feedback' that the group produced as they rampaged through songs such as Bowie's 'Suffragette City', Hendrix's 'Foxy Lady' and Thin Lizzy's 'Jailbreak'. Lol sang a version of 'Wild Thing', and the evening turned into something of a riot. More than half the audience left, most of the rest wound up on stage and singer Martin left the band, reportedly with the parting words, "This is shit!"

Up in London, punk was well and truly on the way. The summer sounds of The Wurzels typified the lack of energy and imagination in the pop charts at the time. When US visitors The Ramones played their first UK gig at The Roundhouse in July, they fanned the flames of a fire already ignited by the Sex Pistols' legendary show at St Martin's college in November 1975. The Ramones' rudimentary rock and roll was all that was needed to energise the ambitions of hundreds of would-be musicians who had searched hard to find guitar bands such as Dr Feelgood under the gooey fudge of Tina Charles and the ornate pomp of Queen's 'Bohemian Rhapsody'.

Punk historians will argue until 'Hell' freezes over about who invented/instigated the punk phenomenon, but in the UK, the influence of the Sex Pistols cannot be doubted. Malcolm McLaren brought together the Pistols via his clothes emporium on the King's Road, and by the winter of 1976 he had engineered them into the role of the UK's most hated foursome. Their legendary appearance on Bill Grundy's London show *Thames Today* is now promoted as an event that really shook the country. In fact it was a regional show that would have caused no more than a ripple if the London-centric journalists who picked up on it hadn't splashed it across the national press the following day. The pre-Sid Pistols – Johnny Rotten, Steve Jones, Paul Cook and Glen Matlock – with moral support from, amongst others, Siouxsie Sioux and Severin (members of the so-called 'Bromley Contingent') 'outraged' a nation already frustrated by high unemployment and economic impotence. When Grundy repeatedly goaded Jones into more and more explicit dialogue, to the point where the Pistol called him 'a dirty fucker' live on air, our parents' generation were only too willing to react. Trace the Richard Hell clothing and Jonathan Richman records back as far as you like: punk was born on December 1, 1976, the same month that The (yet-to-be-named) Cure were born.

It wasn't just the Pistols of course. The Damned – who can claim the first 'punk' single release with 'New Rose' – The Clash, Buzzocks up in Manchester, punk spread around the country like a rash. For many it was a social phenomenon as much as it was about the music. It was fun. It was nights out with the boys, or with the girls. Disaffected teenagers found a way to draw attention to themselves when nobody seemed to care, via uniquely new clothing styles (some fashion experts argue the safety pin came from New York rocker Richard Hell's 'I can't sew and I can't afford new clothes' ethos, others suggest it was Vivienne Westwood on the King's Road) and anti-social behaviour. BBC Radio DJ 'Diddy' David Hamilton – hardly a radical promoter of punk – recently recalled being gobbed on by audiences simply because he was the next act at a venue where a punk band had previously played a week before. You wore pins, you spiked your hair up, you left *Never Mind The Bollocks* lying around, you spat at things you liked, you were a punk. You probably got your head kicked in for being so, but on a Saturday night out in late '76 and early '77 there seemed nothing more fun and more radical than to wear this badge of social disquietude.

For many, what took over London in the mid-Seventies was initially merely a fashion trend which quickly aligned itself to a music trend that was evolving at the same time. In a fascinating interview for *Musician* magazine, Robert suggested that punk itself was borne out of educational experiments in the early Seventies that gave kids an overly liberal education, often literally without walls, that allowed them to wander between open-plan lessons at will. Smith recalled his own middle school following this route, and becoming, in his opinion, "the most fascist school I'd ever been in" as the staff tried to control the anarchy that often prevailed. "That bred a lot of resentment ... we felt we were used as guinea pigs," said Smith, accounting for the restless, rebellious nature of this same generation of kids three or four years on.

Musically, of course, the sparse, twelve-bar rocking of punk was nothing new. All The Ramones did – but how important that they did it – was to remind people of how great three-chord guitar pop was: to re-invent Chuck Berry and Phil Spector for the 1970s. Cranking up the volume, The Pistols made it more aggressive, but only in the same way that The Who had stirred up audiences nearly a decade before. I remember playing Bowie's 'Hang On To Yourself' to a friend around this time, and him starting to pogo around the lounge shouting 'Punk! Punk!' The song was four years old already. Punk in New York was *art*: Debbie Harry, David Byrne and The Ramones were embraced by the Warhol set and paraded as thinkers. In the UK punk was getting pissed on a Saturday night, getting into a fight, annoying mum and dad and generally having *fun*. Only in retrospect – and with lashings of journalistic hindsight – did it become such a force of social change.

But boy, was it fun. And – unlike the world in which

Freddie Mercury and the genteel Abba lived – *you could be involved*. Curled up in his bedroom, Robert Smith picked up on The Clash and all the other first-wave bands via John Peel's radio show. Smith recently spoke with *Rockstar* journalist Simona Orlando about the time he felt that first thrill of punk: "(It) was just born, and nobody was excluded from it. It influenced anyone in my generation in England." Smith could see a light at the end of the tunnel – somewhere where his band might go. "When we first started, I wanted to be in the Buzzcocks," Robert said in 2001. "I wanted us to be a pop group. I wanted us to be The Beatles without all the psychedelic stuff." Influenced by The Stranglers, Manchester's Buzzcocks and particularly by The Clash's 'White Riot', Robert cut his hair short and approached his own band one night in January 1977 with the idea that they should change their name and get moving. Named after one of Lol's songs, The Easy Cure was borne out of the ramshackle ashes of Malice.

Chapter 2: Becoming The Cure

The Easy Cure comprised Smith on vocals and guitar, Tolhurst on drums, Porl Thompson on guitar and Michael Dempsey on bass. With typical *élan*, Robert was suspended from St Wilfred's school soon after Christmas for being "an undesirable influence", but soon reinstated. Back to study his A-levels, he continued to lead his band onwards and upwards. For a few fleeting days in March 1977 they were supplemented by a new vocalist, the mysteriously named Gary X. Gary lasted little longer than Martin, and was replaced by Bowie fanatic Peter O'Toole on vocals. On the day after Robert's eighteenth birthday, the new singer played his first gig with The Easy Cure at St Edward's Hall.

In April, keenly scanning the music papers, Robert found an advert that in a roundabout way changed his life. "Wanna Be A Recording Star?" ran the headline, under which a brace of 'funky chicks' writhed gleefully over a drum kit and electric guitar. "Get your ass up! Take your chances!" entreated German record label Hansa. The advert asked for 'only experienced bands' or 'singer/songwriters' between fifteen and thirty years of age. At least The Easy Cure fitted that last condition.

"The pop label that brought you Boney M (in 2005 still one of the biggest-selling singles acts of all time) and Donna Summer" were looking for new talent. Aware that the disco boom wouldn't last for ever, Germany's biggest independent record label were searching for something to spice up their catalogue. The Easy Cure saw Hansa's ad in *Melody Maker*, and, chez Smith, recorded a rough tape, including Robert's compositions 'Killing An Arab', and '10:15 Saturday Night'.

As the advert had required, the band also submitted photos of themselves. Incredibly, they were selected as one of the five bands Hansa were interested in, and in May 1977 Robert received a telegram from Hansa asking the boys to call them "urgently." Robert later claimed that Hansa hadn't even listened to their tape but had selected them on the basis of their photos, but whatever grabbed the label they were keen to meet The Easy Cure.

Elated and excited, The Easy Cure played at The Rocket, a popular local pub in Crawley – their first 'real' gig – after Amulet couldn't make the gig. Smith simply called The Rocket and asked if his band could play instead. The venue became a staple local gig for the band, and they built up a modest but impressive following of a few hundred people, attracted by Porl's impressive rock guitar (the only thing, according to Smith, that most of the audience could hear).

A band shoot-out was organised by Hansa at Morgan Studios in Willesden, London. Robert, Michael, Lol and Porl made their way northwards a week later, to one of the capital's best sound studios. Lou Reed's *Berlin* had been recorded there, as had been sessions by The Kinks, Blind Faith and many others. Bowie had made one of his most unusual forays there a couple of years previously, playing alto sax on Steeleye Span's folk-rock album *Now We Are Six*. Wet behind the ears they may have been, but if the Crawley boys were intimidated by their surroundings and the implications that success or failure might have for them, they didn't show it. Performing three songs to a video camera, they came out winners of this national contest: serious recognition of both the quality of their material at the time and also of their potential.

The Easy Cure duly signed with Hansa on May 18, 1977, pocketing a thousand pounds from the deal, which they immediately spent on band equipment, clearly with an eye to their future career rather than simply blowing it in the pub. One of the runner-up bands was also signed as a result of the competition. Japan, who had been together for longer than The Cure, went on to have more success with Hansa than Smith & Co, following the New Romantic road while The Cure stayed closer to their new-found punk ideals.

June saw The Easy Cure playing a 'peace concert' in Queen's Square, Crawley. They received coverage in the local press, who bigged-up their deal with Hansa and pushed the fact that a single would be officially released by the band. A handful of gigs saw them through the local summer scene but in September O'Toole left, leaving Robert to take on vocals himself. It must have been a tough decision for Robert, moving from guitar to the (albeit still fairly dim) spotlight, a move that would ultimately change his life for ever. But it was an obvious move: if singers kept coming and going then one of the settled band members would have to take on the responsibility, and in doing so Robert signalled a leader's role in the band. "I was paralysed with fear before we went out," Robert was to say in later years, "I drank about six pints of beer ... I was singing the wrong song. Of the first three songs, I started on the second song. No-one even noticed. So I thought 'If I can get away with that I can be the singer.'"

In the autumn, The Easy Cure recorded two sessions at SAV studios in London for their new label, but as matters progressed it was increasingly likely that the relationship could lead nowhere. More than twenty years, later Robert admitted to *Uncut* magazine that Hansa were probably after the band's looks, not their sound, possibly wanting to craft them into a teenage boy band. A version of 'Killing An Arab' was dismissed as racist by the label. Other originals such as 'Meat Hook' and 'See The Children' were tried out, alongside versions of Bowie's 'Rebel Rebel', and Lennon & McCartney's 'I Saw Her Standing There.' But this was evidently not a band that Hansa would be able to sugar-up and aim at 'the kids.' They rejected suggestions of various covers from the label themselves and, not for the first time, stuck to their creative guns. Robert knew that Hansa weren't looking for left-field avant-gardists, but had thought that once the band were in the studio, with a contract under their belt, they would be able to steer their own ship and record the kind of material that they were developing for themselves. He was woefully wrong.

They were certainly not going to be the pretty-boy pop rock band that Hansa seemed to envisage. The contract with Hansa was dissolved on March 29, 1978, and the band walked away retaining the rights to all the sessions they had recorded: a valuable asset for the future. The experience strengthened Smith's resolve and tightened his concept of what his band was about.

Meanwhile, over the latter half of 1977, The Easy Cure had continued a pinball-like series of local gigs, bouncing between benefits for a teacher who had lost his job and gigs in the local hospital. Some of their gigs even attracted attention from the police when unwelcome National Front activists began harassing the band for their support of a gay local teacher friend.

By now Robert had a permanent girlfriend who would become one of the mainstays of his adult life. Mary Poole was a beautiful girl that Smith knew from St Wilfred's, and they started going out together in 1974, their first dance being to Bowie's 'Life On Mars'. In later years Robert would pay tribute to Mary on countless occasions and – apart from the occasional photograph of her that would surface on the internet around the time of their wedding – they have managed to keep their relationship largely out of the press. As the changes that beset The Cure's history in the coming years came and went, Mary was one constant in Robert's life: a friend, confidant, critic and lover who at any point could look beyond the rock star and beyond The Cure and understand the real Robert.

In the first few weeks of 1978 the band played more sessions for Hansa, but the message was clear for both parties that this was going nowhere. After their parting of the ways with Hansa in March, Robert made one final early decision that helped define the nature of the band: he dropped the 'Easy', and the band became known simply as The Cure. Short, conceptual names were still in vogue, and it seemed an appropriate change. 'The Easy Cure' could have meant anything; 'The Cure' positioned them clearly in the immediate post-punk scene. "It was with punk that I discovered my call and my voice," he told *Musica* more than twenty years later. Never a punk in the true sense of the word, the do-it-yourself ethos of the punk movement has lasted to this day within the largely democratic nature of the band. Despite the wealth and the fame and the immense public profile, The Cure is still, in many respects, a post-punk band.

In May, Porl became the first member to leave the newly re-christened band. Not for the first time, a member of the band left only to return later and establish his mark more than once on the band. At the time of writing, Porl is back with the band again. "He didn't actually like what we were doing," Robert told *Musician* in 1989. "We didn't really like what he was doing either ... eventually it just became absurd." Matters were made more convoluted by the fact that Porl was dating Robert's sister, but after a brief break from gigs The Cure reconvened without him as a trio. On a miniscule budget Smith, Tolhurst and Dempsey put together new demo material to start a fresh onslaught on larger record companies. More experienced in the recording studio and ever-more ambitious, the tape (that included 'Boys Don't Cry', 'It's Not You', '10:15 Saturday Night' and 'Fire in Cairo') was mailed out. A number of labels showed interest, including United Artists, but The Cure were not snapped up by anyone. If some labels recognised something in their sound, or immediately regretted their decision, only one person actually picked up their tape and did something with it.

Chris Parry was born in Upper Hutt, New Zealand, in 1949. At fifteen he joined local band The Sine Waves, taking over the drum stool when its former incumbent was pulled out of the group by his mom and dad. The Sine Waves went through a variety of names before becoming Fourmyula, and – in a manner spookily foretelling The Cure's early days – they won a series of Battle of the Bands competitions before getting a record contract with HMV and winning a trip to England. Between 1967 and 1969 Fourmyula became New Zealand's biggest pop act, and when Parry *et al* arrived in London, as the decade came to a close, they were on the crest of a wave.

London proved to Parry and his band mates just how distant New Zealand was both geographically and culturally. The band realised that, although they were big at home, they were far behind the rest of the world – and the UK and USA in particular. A radical re-think was necessary. Influenced by all the late-Sixties big names, most particularly Led Zep, and kitted out with new equipment, hip clothes and a heavier rock sound, Fourmyula nevertheless found it hard to take their new sound back to New Zealand. With studio time at Abbey Road under their belt, a return trip to Europe found them caught between two stools: too heavy for the home market, too provincial for the UK. They had a decent run in Scandinavia, but by 1970 they had split up.

Chris Parry married, became a father, and joined Phonogram as an International Manager in London. By 1974 he was settled in the A&R department at Polydor, and found himself perfectly placed, as punk and new wave hit, to sign John Otway, The Jam (tipped off to see the band by future Pogue Shane McGowan) and Siouxsie and The Banshees to the label. Parry was a fan of the Pistols, but was just beaten to the deal by EMI as Malcolm McLaren hyped his protégées around London. By the time he found The Cure's demo tape on his desk he was more than ready to consider another edgy, post-punk trio, in the hope of finding The Jam Mk II, and was already thinking of an escape from the corporate world with his own label.

The Cure's demo tape excited Parry's curiosity. '10:15 Saturday Night' was enough to make him want to meet with them and find out more: "the whole song was haunting," he told one reporter. Chris invited the band up to Polydor's Stratford Place offices. In the official Cure biography *Ten Imaginary Years*, Robert describes their first impression of him as an absent-minded, Italian-looking Colonel Gaddafi lookalike "with bird-shit on his shoulder." Parry, for his part, immediately took to the band, and especially to Robert. Each weighed up the other party, and it was agreed that rather than have the band play in London, Parry would journey out of town to see them play live on their home turf. Parry recounted his first impressions: "I instantly thought they could be successful," he said. "They had good tunes, and played in a quirky, different way." It was a significant night, introducing The Cure to the man who would become their manager and friend and, alongside Smith, the most consistent 'band member' for years to come. Within forty-eight hours Parry had offered to sign them to his new label, an imprint to be distributed via Polydor but independent of the major label. Fiction Records offered The Cure some hope of independence after their unpleasant experience with Hansa, and by the end of that summer they had signed an initial deal with Parry for six months. Things would never be the same again.

*

Parry put the boys back into the recording studio again, and a September 1978 session at Morgan produced five songs intended for their yet-to-be conceived album. 'Fire In Cairo', 'Killing An Arab', '10:15 Saturday Night', 'Plastic Passion' and 'Three Imaginary Boys' were very different to what Parry had produced with The Jam, his other legendary three-piece. The Cure had a withdrawn sound, spare, edgy. Listening to the early Jam, one can imagine the sweaty, beer-strewn floor of some rowdy cellar club – The Cure had something altogether different. As well as this initial recording session, Parry's next move was to get The Cure out and into the provinces, touring with the likes of The Press, Jerry Floyd, Wire and UK Subs. This was a training exercise for the threesome, getting fit for bigger things to come, sharing the limelight with recently established bands such as Chrysalis band Generation X, who had troubled the lower reaches of the Top 40 with 'Your Generation' a year or so earlier.

Used to playing familiar gigs in their local area, by early autumn The Cure were touring 'proper', playing Canterbury, Windsor Castle (supporting Electrotunes at the first gig, Young Ones later on in December), Hampstead's Moonlight

Club, Northampton Cricket Club and Cardiff's Top Rank – a notable punk venue for south Wales. Dates followed at Tiffany's in Halesowen, Birmingham, Cromer, Bristol, Dunstable and Oxford. In October a second session at Morgan put down enough tracks from which Parry could compile an album. There was tension almost from the start. Using late-night time allotted to The Jam, who were recording *All Mod Cons* in the same studio, they also borrowed that trio's kit. In the liner notes to the reissue of *Three Imaginary Boys* in 2005, Smith recalled how Tolhurst both borrowed and busted Rick Buckler's drum kit, which they tried to fix with chewing gum. Tolhurst's at times modest style as a drummer also made for a distinctive sound and so the pared-down, minimalist feel of the album was developed.

In less than a week, The Cure had over two dozen songs on tape, mainly their own compositions, which would be credited to the band as a whole and not to individual members. Parry insisted that Smith broaden his sound by buying the band new equipment rather than rely solely upon his Top 20 guitar, but as production went on Robert was concerned that the tracks simply did not sound like the band he had in his head. For a start, he felt there was too much reverb. Eventually, however, the record started to take shape – he would later reflect that it was very stark and didn't sound like any other band of the moment.

Robert had clear ideas of what he did not want the band to be; Parry however clearly had a profile in mind for the band, and was heavily involved in discussions about the album's production. If Smith had concerns that once again a third party was involved in the sound of the band, then to his credit Parry did not want his new signings to sound like anyone else, as Hansa had done. And it is from somewhere between these two ideals that the album was generated.

Robert was immediately faced with an age-old problem that newly-signed bands endure: many of the songs recorded were already a part of his past, written early in his teens (as he now approached the age of twenty) and thus didn't have the redolence that they once held for him. Six months after writing songs such as 'Winter', he felt they were already d readfully old-hat, and argued with Parry over the latter's insistence that the band play him everything they could. "I can remember thinking it was toe-curlingly awful and being angry that Parry would even consider including it on the album," he said in late 2003. Even the best amongst them, such as '10:15 Saturday Night' and 'Killing An Arab' went back to Robert's earlier teenage years when his youthful lack of life experiences meant he didn't have a lot to say about anything other than the books he was reading at the time.

Late in November, BBC producer John Walters went to see Generation X 'and support' at The Greyhound in Croydon. The support band was, of course, The Cure who were being paid a fiver for the gig whilst having to pay Generation X the princely sum of £10 for the use of lighting and sound gear. Suitably impressed, Walters booked the band to appear on John Peel's Radio One show, a substantial breakthrough. Early in December the band went into in Maida Vale Studio 4, recording their first ever Peel session. They taped 'Arab', '10:15 Saturday Night', 'Cairo' and 'Boys Don't Cry' for the first of their dozen or so sessions for the show. Most of the punk and new wave acts of note had debuted on Peel's p rogramme, including The Banshees, Generation X, Adam & The Ants and The Adverts. The experience of Siouxsie and The Banshees – signed by Parry to Polydor soon after it was declared that, post-Peel, the BBC would be releasing the unsigned band – had proved that major success could follow such an appearance, and although Peel himself wasn't present at the session, it lived up to the band's expectations. Dempsey described the night as capturing the sound of the early Cure better than their original demos had done, without adding the studio gloss that the album sessions had. The session was eventually released on the Strange Fruit label in 1988.

Working harder and harder, The Cure made a mighty journey four days later to Leeds (the night that the Peel session was broadcast), and rounded the year off with gigs at York, Colchester, Islington, Crawley and Newport then more in Plymouth and Bournemouth dragged them into the New Year. Inevitably, with Parry at the helm, their efforts began to bear fruit. Adrian Thrills of *New Musical Express* had already seen the band live back in September, but on December 16 *NME* published the first national press piece on The Cure under the unfeasibly witty headline 'Ain't No Blues For The Summertime Cure.' Thrills gave a summarised history of the band, led by "teenage lynchpin" Smith, praising their lack of sophistication and their "breath of fresh suburban air." He described their live act as "a triumph of impulse and spontaneity" and Robert talked in the piece of his own inspiration in pursuing The Cure. He compared them to all the bands playing "absolute rubbish and getting somewhere doing it," by acknowledging that his own band was "so much better." Smith also referred back to their deal with Hansa, and of how they had been pushed into a studio with "one of their soul producers" to try and come up with something that would make them into another Child.

Most tellingly, Thrills announced the release of The Cure's forthcoming single 'Killing An Arab', (which Robert cheekily dedicated to "all the Arabs who go to Crawley College discos to pick up the girls"). The single, from their Morgan sessions with Parry and engineer Mike Hedges at the helm, was to be the first release on Fiction, but given Polydor's understandable reluctance to promote it so close to the busy Christmas period, the track was initially licensed to Small Wonder Records, an independent label based in Walthamstow. The deal was an excellent first step for the band: under it, Small Wonder were licensed to print 15,000 copies maximum of the single, after which rights would revert to Fiction who – should the 15k sell out – would then have raised the funds to release it themselves in the new year. With impressive advance orders of 2,000 copies already under their belt, Small Wonder brilliantly achieved this, so demonstrating both The Cure's potential as a recording band

and Chris Parry's assured understanding of the record business. The first major leap forward for The Cure was under way.

'Killing An Arab' was released on Small Wonder on December 22, a little over a week after their first appearance on John Peel's show. Based on one of Robert's favourite novels, *L'Etranger* by Albert Camus, the song recounts the scene in the novel (set in Algeria) where the main character Meursault kills an Arab on the beach after attending his mother's funeral. Smith has often been called upon to answer the ludicrous and myopic indictment that the record was racist. Put simply in the context of the novel, only 'an Arab' could do. It was, of course, a nonsense and misinformed accusation.

The track was a monumental opener for The Cure's recording career. Launched by Lol's atmospheric, isolated cymbal hits, Robert's arabesque, descending riffs give the track a distinctly 'otherly' flavour, much as the oriental figures of Siouxsie and The Banshees' 'Hong Kong Garden' had declared 'the east' in their first hit earlier in the year. The song is medium paced – no helium-energy-Buzzcocks rush here – and underpinned by Tolhurst and Dempsey's uncomplicated rhythm section, it is Robert's accomplished guitar (part-Middle Eastern flourish, part-punchy rock annotation) that gives the track its guts. Smith's vocals are distracted, un-emotional and refreshingly free of rock and roll flourish: the lyrics speak of Camus' own 'absurdist' philosophy, based upon the concept that suicide is the most fundamentally pure human act, as everything else we do must be constructed to validate our existence via some religious 'meaning.' Only by ending it can our life be said to have been fulfilled without artifice. Robert's lyrics neatly define the simplicity of the decision that separates life from death, one condition from the other.

The B-side, '10:15 Saturday Night', was another instant Cure classic, much beloved by fans then and now. Like 'Arab', written when Robert was sixteen, the song is darker, more fashionably bleak and contemporary. Introduced by Lol's simple beats, Robert's guitar is again at the forefront alongside his sparse vocals, the production almost industrial in its thinness. This most certainly wasn't 'punk' – there was no social complaint or call to take arms against a sea of middle-class troubles. This was a bunch of middle-class lads working out a new way for music to go, a soon-to-be-fashionable austerity. On the day of the single's release they played two gigs – one at the Music Machine in Crawley and one, in the afternoon, at the Christmas party of Robert's dad's company.

Almost to a man (and a woman), the rock press loved the record. Remarkably, in January they appeared on the front cover of *Sounds* magazine, and inside the mag journalist Dave McCullough expressed sheer delight at having come across the single amongst all the dross on his desk in his role as singles reviewer for the paper. He'd favoured '10:15 Saturday Night' of the two tracks, loving the "bored, effortlessly tired vocals" and the pared-down "sparseness." McCullough met the band – at their suggestion – at London's Natural History Museum. Amazed at their youthfulness, he was particularly impressed with Smith's studied leadership, as Michael and Lol sat back and let Robert do most of the talking in the nearby pub. As a live outfit he was also impressed both by the band and by Parry, despite, by the journalist's own admission, having little time for managers and record company execs. McCullough recognised energy and hope in the band, and was convinced – as were nearly all the other reviewers of the single – that there were big things ahead for The Cure. *Sounds* claimed that the record sounded like "single of the year", a remarkable achievement.

Elsewhere, Ian Birch in *Melody Maker* implored readers to not let The Cure pass them by. They "showed a glorious potential," he wrote in the New Year's Day edition of the paper. Their material was a "plundering of classic Sixties pop rock with post-punk economy and drive ... considered, but on the right side of rough." Reviewing a gig at The Hope

& Anchor, *NME* writer Rick Joseph described 'Killing An Arab' as "a zany crossbreed of 4/4 thrash and Moorish bazoukie fever."

The band were back in Morgan studios by the second week in January for sessions to complete the forthcoming album. Gigs through January and February saw them on the road proper by March, and they were to rack up almost 120 gigs over the year ahead. Gobbed on at one gig by skinheads, uninvited and unwelcome members of the National Front turned up at another show in Kensington to hand out tasteless flyers in support of the notion of killing Arabs; and at a gig in Bournemouth the local press ran a feature about how a girl managed to pull off her boyfriend's ear during their set. Eight weeks after its release by Small Wonder, 'Killing An Arab' was re-released as FICS001, the first release on Fiction records.

In March the second official Cure release came about with their appearance on Polydor's sampler compilation *20 Of A Different Kind*. In attendance on the album were The Jam, 999, The Skids, Sham 69, The Adverts, The Stranglers: sixteen bands in all, most with a track each, but John Otway and Wild Willy Barrett merited four inclusions and both The Jam and 999 had two tracks listed. This is where I first heard The Cure, getting a copy of the album in order to hear The Jam's 'In The City'. I was immediately struck by 'Killing An Arab' – its one-guitar, keyboard-free simplicity and its menacing, uncertain narrative. The Cure were clearly walking down a different sidewalk than Jimmy Pursey, Billy Idol and the rest of the Polydor people. Sadly, the album left my hands a year later to help fund a holiday to Egypt, along with all my Hendrix and T Rex records, but – amidst the dubious quality of some of the songs (The Lurker's 'I'm On Heat' was, I remember, particularly irritating) – it was clear that The Cure were here for a reason. That was possibly more than might have been said for Belgian punk puppet Plastique Bertrand!

On Sundays in March, for the princely admission fee of £1, Cure fans could see the band during a four-week residency at

The Marquee in London. Under the banner 'A Dose of Sundays', amongst the support bands on the first weekend were the emergent Joy Division, still only just managing to fill their set without repeating songs. This was only Joy Division's third London gig. They had previously appeared twice at The Hope & Anchor: their first gig there in December attracted about thirty people and was the scene one of Ian Curtis' first epileptic fits. Those thirty people have probably dined out on the story ever since. By the time the two bands appeared at The Marquee almost one thousand people crammed into the Wardour Street venue. In *Ten Imaginary Years* Smith claimed not to remember Joy Division at all, though Tolhurst recalls a "sad aura" about Ian Curtis, whose suicide was less than a year away. The two bands played together again at Canterbury in June. Michael would remark, many years later, that it was the influence of Joy Division, along with that of Wire and The Banshees, that would eventually lead to his leaving the group. What is certain is that the Mancunians would become one of the most influential British bands of their generation, and one can't help feeling that the guys who invaded the stage on that first Cure/Joy Division gig had picked a cracking gig for their Sunday night out.

*

A vacuum cleaner. A standard lamp. A fridge. It's a long way from four loveable Liverpool moptops, but this was the image of the threesome with which Chris Parry chose to launch his protégés' first album. In retrospect it was a minor stroke of marketing genius to include no shots of the band on the album, no track listing, no nothing. By the end of March the single had been reviewed almost universally well and the band was building a growing audience due to heavy gigging. They'd had front-page features and Smith, Dempsey and Tolhurst were becoming increasingly recognisable. What better way to push them even further then, than to deny that they had an image at all? There were arguments over the presentation of the record as well as its actual recording, with Parry being heavily involved again.

In fairness to Parry, and in retrospect, his claim that he had a band with great music but no image is reasonable enough. It certainly didn't hurt the image that The Cure was to develop in the decade to come: they were always to be found standing slightly to one side of all their contemporaries, always 'outsiders' to some degree. In launching their album career this way, Parry made a definitive statement about the band – he set them apart from the start. Many 'alternative' bands took a similar route. Over in the US, the first two albums by Talking Heads had particularly dispassionate and 'arty' images, presenting the band either without images or with those images cut up into a series of Polaroid-like snaps. Their 1979 release *Fear Of Music* presented a black, industrial flooring design as the album cover. Jamie Reid's provocative designs for the Pistols' releases insisted on art and image rather than pictures of the band, and the ever-present Buzzcocks – helped by the classic graphic artwork of design legend Malcolm Garrett – resorted to Marcel Duchamp for their 'Ever Fallen In Love With …' one of the most influential punk singles of 1978. Joy Division launched their album career with a design based upon electromagnetic waves from a dying star. Images were increasingly functional, industrial, ego-less (no coincidence that Factory Records was so-named.) Compare this with the images of the ten best-selling UK albums of 1978 – all (save for Kate Bush's *The Kick Inside*) from mainstream acts – and the message is clear: established stars sold their wares via mug shots and soft focus lenses. Anything new had to find a new way of being (or not being) seen.

Robert was also unhappy with the sound of the album. Over the years he has claimed it to be his least favourite Cure album. Listening to live recordings from the period – in particular those released on the *Three Imaginary Boys* deluxe edition of 2005 – it is clear that the band certainly rocked harder on stage than on record. But the album defines a certain flavour of The Cure that has lasted to this day, and is evident in greater or lesser part throughout their career: dispassionate vocal arrangements; music pared down to its basic instrumentation; a mix of gloomy semi-despair and of pop joyfulness. And, for many long-term Cure fans, it remains a dear favourite, a first doorway into the world of The Cure that led to many journeys and discoveries later. In short, despite Robert's own public reservations, *Three Imaginary Boys* is a little gem of an album.

'10:15 Saturday Night' opens the album: domestic, bored, harsh strip-lit scenes, and the resonant dripping of that tap. This is the world, albeit it painted in a different palette of colours, that Joy Division inhabited, all misunderstood solitude and jaded observation. The poppy bass lines and simplistic drumming are perfectly patched up against Smith's guitar, which veers from clipped chord patterns to jarring and raucous annotations. For teenage listeners at the time this was a snapshot of their own domestic worlds, sat in front of *Dr Who* with kid sisters and brothers while wishing they were in The Banshees.

'Accuracy' picks up a bass-line that carries half the melody punctuated by Smith's restrained guitar. On 'Grinding Halt' it is Robert who opens the song, his single guitar note speeding up to tempo like a bouncing ball, and the little riff giving the song a Buzzock-lite feel. The song celebrates a world empty of everything – things, people, emotions.

Weeks away from the return of the Conservatives to Downing Street and to the election of Margaret Thatcher, this was pop soon to be defined by The Specials 'Ghost Town', a world still without a future, despite the Pistols' call to arms. The next track on the album, 'Another Day', was filled with jarring arpeggios and reverb guitar lines, finding Smith staring through the window, lost again in his insouciant sense of bleak, teenaged despair.

The tone, and Robert's vocals, pick up on 'Object', but lyrically this is as bleak as ever, with the subject of the song being reduced to an object, lifeless and worthless. But there's a little sexual wit and innuendo in there for the keen listener, the voice of the dazed and confused teenager: "there's nothing to say but I know I need to speak – there's nothing in my life but you need to know all the things in my life." It's a particularly late-Seventies/early-Eighties sentiment not found in Fifties and Sixties pop, and lost by the mid-Eighties 'me, me, me,' culture promoted by Thatcher's loadsamoney Conservatism.

'Subway Song' has a little of the urban decay of Barry Andrews' 'Rossmore Road' of the following year – a narrative song of fear and pursuance. Where Andrews' splendid single celebrated life above ground in the buzzing streets of London, Robert's haunting reverb is buried under an uninviting subway, an early piece of Smith fiction.

'Foxy Lady' – the only cover on the album – opens with the band's pre-take fiddling off-mic. Vocally and musically The Cure strip Hendrix's track down to basics: this was a live staple from The Easy Cure to date, and the recorded version both nods back at Smith's favourite guitar player and points the way to a functional future of clipped guitar and toy-shop drumming. Dempsey took over the vocals, and Smith has repeatedly dismissed the track over the years, calling it "my least favourite Cure song." 'Meat Hook' opens with s t rumming chords and descending bass lines, Robert's jazzy licks hanging over the thick, punchy bass. Lyrically, the song has a repetitive hook of its own in the repeated titular refrain. I've always liked the references to slaughterhouse art and the little reggae inferences throughout, just at a time when The Police were starting their rock/reggae fusion. The concept of 'So What' is slightly more entertaining than the track itself. One of the more plodding tracks on the album musically, the lyrics are largely taken from the back of a packet of sugar, an ad for a cake icing set no less (the band's own biography, *Ten Imaginary Years*, says Robert was drunk and couldn't think of any lyrics). The offer at least period-dates the recording, as all entries had to be with the manufacturer by the 31 December,

1979! Between the references to recommended retail prices, nozzles and decorating bags however, there is a tense, melodramatic little emotional drama going on.

'Fire In Cairo' was the second Cure track to wander into the sandy world of Arabia. Unlike 'Killing An Arab' however, this is a sultry, dusty, sensual track. Robert's distracted vocal hides away a delicate lyric. 'It's Not You' is a more straightforward punk song, tiredness, dismissive and petulant. But the last 'official' track on the album is another Cure gem.

'Three Imaginary Boys', like 'Arab', '10:15' and 'Fire In Cairo' is classic early Cure. Set in a desolate minor key, it recalls some of Bowie's darker, early tracks such as 'All The Madmen', a veritable *Blair Witch Project* for the punk generation. As The Cure would later become associated with the emerging goth movement, so this is a gothic horror movie writ small, set amongst statues in a threatening darkness.

Chilling and beautiful in its terse and abbreviated form, 'Three Imaginary Boys' officially closed down the album, but tucked in at the end lies a track, 'The Weedy Burton', a paean to guitar-wizard Bert Weedon, whose instructional guitar manuals set hundreds of thousands of pickers and strummers on their way. With walking bass and country-picked solos from Robert, the track recalls what all teenage bands sounded like as we tried to figure out how a band could work, with half a dozen covers under our belt and a Bert Weedon book under our desk.

*

Three Imaginary Boys was received with almost universal glee by reviewers already encouraged by the intriguing single. Further, John Peel's continued support of the band (he played the single almost nightly on Radio One) ensured the album a ready audience. Interestingly, Dave McCullough in *Sounds* laid the success of the album squarely with Parry, his packaging enhancing the "cheaper charms" of the "expressionistic" music. He noted that while providing something new, the band also stuck to their energy, drive and integrity: not "chic" but "workable", not "gross" but "intense". Mick Houghton wrote that The Cure were "out on their own," while Ian Birch described them as "accessible to everyone" in his review headlined 'The Eighties Start Here' for *Melody Maker*. The one dissenting voice came, unsurprisingly, from Paul Morley in *NME*, who described The Cure as "anguished young men ... not content to let ordinary songs die ordinary deaths.'" It was an unfair review in that it criticised the band for the packaging of the album trying to sell a concept "artificial" and "willowy," a premise that was not essentially of their own making. Ironically, though upset by the review in the main, Smith later admitted that he had agreed with some of Morley's comments. Twenty five years on, Robert told journalist Bill Crandall that "I decided from that day on (that) we would always pay for ourselves and therefore retain total control." Similarly, for the unofficial Cure documentary entitled *Out Of The Woods*, Morley was to sum up his original reaction to the album. "I hated the whole package," he said. "It seemed to me there was a concentration on trying to market mystery ... I had to review it on the night Margaret Thatcher got elected, and I was in a very bad mood. I really took it out somewhat on the album."

With apparently only this lone dissatisfied critic, The Cure had arrived as a viable recording band, rather than a curiosity. They received plaudits from almost every quarter for their live shows too, and they continued to court occasional controversy. The Thatcher years quickly split UK society in a bleak and aggravated way, with political factions amongst the young and not-so-young of Britain becoming more and more polarised. The more extreme edges such as skinheads, the National Front and the Anti-Nazi League might all turn up at a Cure gig, usually with the police in attendance (Smith's bands, of course, was not alone, with many bands being blighted by such crowds, Sham 69 and Madness being two more high profile examples). Police raided The Cure's hotel rooms in April, and though none of the threesome were found to have any illegal substances in their possession, one of their crew wound up in the dock for a stash of cannabis. Parry was booked for speeding en route to Middlesbrough and, after a gig in Cheltenham, was pulled over for driving the wrong way up a one-way street. Such were the every day hassles that beset The Cure's first major tour – relatively benign when compared to Sid Vicious's recent spiral of heroin abuse, his girlfriend's murder and ultimately his own death aged just 21.

'Grinding Halt' was prepared for release in May as the band's second single. The band returned to Maida Vale Studio 4 on May 16 for their second Peel session, Robert re-penning the lyrics to 'Grinding Halt' to parody Paul Morley's wrecking review of their album. As well as 'Plastic Passion', they also played 'Accuracy', and 'Subway Song'. Despite a thousand copies of the 12" being pressed and distributed to reviewers, the response to 'Grinding Halt' was not good and the idea was ditched in preference for the release on June 26 of 'Boys Don't Cry'. The song has become one of the best-loved Cure songs (it was re-mixed, re-recorded and re-released in 1986) but the single did nowhere near as well as expected first time around, despite the critical success of 'Killing An Arab' and an increasingly nationwide profile. Speaking in 1985, Robert admitted his disappointment that it wasn't a number one hit. It should have been.

The B-side 'Plastic Passion' opens with more clipped Smith guitar and economic bass and drums. Smith's vocal is increasingly mannered, his guitar solo terse and unemotional, but the jewel is on side A. Described by more than one reviewer as Beatle-like in its clear pop purity (*Record Mirror* called it "John Lennon at twelve or thirteen"), 'Boys Don't Cry' is sublime in its hookiness, the simple guitar riff and stuttering coda to each refrain of the title being irresistible, at least to this listener. Current popster darling Paul Young wanted to cover the song, but the record never came about, although Smith denied that he "refused" permission for it. Young had a run of good chart singles, but given the savaging he gave to Joy Division's 'Love Will Tear Us Apart' a lifetime later, it's probably better he steered clear of 'Boys Don't Cry'.

*

July 1979 saw cracks beginning to show in The Cure's make-up. Dempsey in particular was unhappy with the sound of the band and the direction in which they appeared to be moving. The first signs came about when Robert started a series of side-projects with a bunch of Crawley and Horley friends. First up were The Obtainers, a couple of kids who sent a tape of themselves banging away on Tupperware boxes, pots and pans to Robert.

Lockjaw were a local band who had already released a single and were described later by Robert as being "really hardcore … like The Clash." Their bass player, Simon Gallup, had known Lol Tolhurst from school days, and both they and The Cure played regularly at Crawley's favoured venue The Rocket. Robert and Simon became good friends, socialising around Crawley and Horley, and with Simon's brother Ric, Robert decided to invest fifty pounds in pressing up one hundred copies of The Obtainers' 'Yeah Yeah Yeah', on a label they called Dance Fools Dance (a title that would come back to Simon in later years). On the flip side they put Simon's then band The Magspies.

The next 'extra-Cure-icular' move by Robert was to bring Simon, along with Porl Thompson, sister Janet Smith and local postman Frank Bell into Morgan studios as the band Cult Hero. While The Obtainers sold the hundred copies of their 'Dance Fools Dance' single, Fiction released Cult Hero's 'I'm A Cult Hero' as Fics 005 (after releasing 'Boys Don't Cry' as Fics 002, the label's next two singles were by The Purple Hearts and Back To Zero respectively, both post-punk mod revivalists). In the UK, 'I'm A Cult Hero' didn't make many waves, but oddly was picked up in Canada where it was reported to have sold 35,000 copies.

The record is an unusual mix of disco, ska, Cure and John

Otway. Robert's reversed and heavily reverbed guitar gives interesting colour to the lengthy introduction, and when Frank The Postman comes in on vocals he is almost drowned by its sub-aquatic squelching. Sham 69-style backing vocals courtesy of Crawley's finest round the song off. 'I Dig You', the B-side, is more disco, more Otway – Estuary English with a self-conscious and ironic gormlessness to lyrics reminiscent of Otway and Barrett's single 'Really Free' (Polydor, 1977). Again Smith colours the track with some breezy guitar lines and Simon and Lol's rhythm, though unsophisticated, throbs along well – the first incarnation of what was to become a favourite Cure line-up of the future. Both sides of the single sound uncharacteristically *fun*.

In July, The Cure proper played a key gig at London's Lyceum, supported by The Ruts. To date they had already racked up over fifty gigs around the country since the New Year, ranging from Eric's in Liverpool and Barbarella's in Birmingham to Totnes Civic Hall and the Memorial Hall in Northwich, Cheshire (where both The Beatles and The Stones had played in their early days). At the end of the month a rainy outdoor festival in Holland was the band's first overseas gig, and they played a second impromptu gig that same evening. In August The Cure recorded another session for the BBC at Maida Vale, this time in Studio Five and not for Peel, instead for *The Kid Jensen Show*, broadcast late in the afternoon from Mondays to Fridays. They taped 'Boys Don't Cry', 'Do The Hansa', and 'Three Imaginary Boys'.

A round this time, at the YMCA off London's Tottenham Court Road, Smith was introduced by Chris Parry to Steve Severin of Siouxsie and The Banshees at a Throbbing Gristle gig. It was a meeting that would seal Robert and The Cure's fate for some time to come.

The Banshees had become darlings of the post-punk scene. They would soon become one of the most influential acts of the era, spawning much of what became known as the goth movement and influencing The Cure themselves a great deal. Severin and Smith got on well from the start, and when asked if The Cure would be interested in supporting The Banshees on their forthcoming tour, Robert jumped at the chance. Sometimes controversial – Siouxsie's one-time wearing of Nazi regalia still, thirty years on, incites debate despite her adamant defence that she had no Nazi leanings whatsoever but simply liked the visual imagery – the Banshees were exotic, uncompromisingly austere, enchanting and visually stunning. Their first single 'Hong Kong Garden' sold in droves, sufficiently enough to make the top ten in August 1978. And their live reputation was one of the best in the UK at the time. Joining The Banshees on tour could only be a good move for The Cure.

Maybe ...

Chapter 3: With The Banshees

Susan Dallion was born on May 27, 1957; Steven Bailey on September 25, 1955. As Siouxsie Sioux and Steve Severin they were amongst the first people in London to support The Sex Pistols, and can rightly claim to have been there at the very beginning of the punk movement. The 'Bromley Contingent', the group of friends who convened in London after an early Pistols gig at Orpington College, was a colourful collection of characters: Sue Catwoman, Billy Idol, Berlin etc. Described by Tony Parsons and Julie Burchill as "unrepentent poseurs, committed to attaining fame despite (their) paucity of talent," the Bromley Contingent was a group of fashion-conscious Bowie and Roxy fans, bored with their own elegance and looking for something new. Ready to shock, ready to parade, the Pistols offered them a peg to hang their plastic bin-sack hats on.

At the end of August 1976, Malcolm McLaren organised the first UK punk all-nighter at The Screen On The Green cinema in Islington, north London. The Clash, Buzzcocks and The Pistols played probably the purist of the early punk gigs of summer 1976. Siouxsie was famously photographed in the audience. A month later, the punk festival at the 100 Club (two nights of bands – some of whom, like The Banshees, formed specifically for the event – and also arranged by McLaren) was one of punk's most notorious early nights out. If all the singers and bands who claimed to have been there actually were, it would have been three times the size, but certainly Shane McGowan, Chrissie Hynde, Gaye Advert and TV Smith were in the audience. Siouxsie and The Banshees were Siouxsie on vocals, Severin on bass, Marco Pirroni on guitar and John Ritchie on drums. Pirroni went on to join Adam & The Ants, while Ritchie, of course, went on to form Sid Vicious! Punk legend has it that Sid also invented pogo-ing the same night.

The Banshees 20-minute version of 'The Lord's Prayer' has gone down in punk mythology too, Ritchie's unrehearsed d rumming setting a varied pace – occasionally even on the beat. Photographer Barry Plummer remembered Siouxsie as the most outlandishly dressed person there and of all the bands that appeared, The Banshees were one of the most memorable. TV Smith of The Adverts remembered it fondly: "It was a horrible racket. It seemed like some horrible sixth-form wind-up arty band. I know they were doing it with the intention of sounding terrible. But they really were terrible."

By 1979 The Banshees were tied to Polydor, had enjoyed a hit single, had an album released and – although they were one of the last punk bands to get signed to a major label – were set to become one of the most enduring acts of their generation. In Siouxsie herself the band had a fabulous, iconic front. Siouxsie's pencil-thin, elegant frame was topped off by one of punk's best hair styles, a spikey black thornbush of heroic proportions. Her dramatic make-up, dark eyes and doll-like lips, high cheek bones and heavy eyelids were almost as dramatic as Ziggy; she had certainly learned a lesson in presentation from Bowie's example. And the band looked serious. Although many a mug shot of the Bromley Contingent can be found showing high japes and fun to excess, on stage The Banshees were austere, in it for the real deal.

The Banshees had built up a serious following by the late summer of 1979, and The Cure would support them on tour f rom August up to October. Robert Smith led his own band onstage at the Reading Festival on August 24, sharing the bill with The Police, The Tourists, Wilko Johnson and Motorhead, with whom the band shared a dressing room. John Peel wrote of how much he enjoyed the set in *Sounds*, calling it a "compact and determined performance." He noted one corner of the crowd cavorting under a banner that read 'Crawley Heavy Metal Hep Kats' – the fans were out in force! For *Music Week* they were the first band of the festival to show "polish and professionalism." Between songs Robert introduced new items to a set list largely comprised of *Three Imaginary Boys* tracks, setting up early interest for the soon-to-be-conceived second album. At the same time everything in the garden of reviews was not all rosy: elsewhere *NME* said their set was "candy floss... with none of the sweetness," and described The Cure as "three infuriating berks." If a tide of critical opinion was going to turn against The Cure then what better time than just as they would begin to change themselves.

*

Five days after Reading, The Cure joined The Banshees at Bournemouth's Stateside Theatre. All went well. The next night they arrived at Friars in Aylesbury, after which they were again lambasted by *NME*, who thought that 'Killing An Arab' had been a fluke "not repeated in anything else The Cure have done." Belfast saw them on September 5, and by the following night the bands had ferried over to Scotland for a gig in Aberdeen. Due to appear in a local record store during the day to promote *Join Hands*, their new album, The Banshees ran into trouble when Polydor failed to supply sufficient stocks of the record to the shop to meet the demand of the gathered hoards. Nils Stevenson, the band's manager, had a pile of promo vinyl in the trunk of his car (for DJs and press), but after a disagreement with drummer Kenny Morris and guitarist John McKay, tension came to a head and events began to spiral. So sick of the situation were they that Morris and McKay took a taxi to the station and returned to London, their tour passes left stuck to their hotel bedroom pillows.

So it was that after four years of slog, four years of companionship and devotion to The Cure, Robert Smith joined The Banshees. Fortunately this did not mean he had to leave The Cure as well. The immediate problem was how to deal with that night's gig. Siouxsie offered explanations to the audience, telling the mystified crowd what had happened to the band. The Cure stepped in and played an extended set, and at the end Siouxsie and Severin joined them onstage for 'The Lord's Prayer'. Four forthcoming gigs were cancelled.

Robert offered to play in both bands to keep the tour together, and Lol offered to sit in on the drum stool. "I think he was more annoyed than we possibly were," Severin was to say many years later. "Because it was his first big tour, and these two people were pulling the rug out from under his feet."

Ironically, although it was the problems facing The Banshees that figured mostly in the press, reviewer Phil Sutcliffe chose the date to give The Cure another great review in *Sounds*. "To put it succinctly," he wrote, "they put it succinctly … reviving the ancient punk ethic of saying what you've got to say and then stopping." The band had included several songs not yet released, including 'Play For Today'.

While what was left of The Banshees licked their wounds and figured out their future, The Cure high-tailed it over to Rotterdam on September 10 for the New Music Festival. In the meantime, The Banshees advertised for replacements for McKay and Morris on John Peel's radio show, and auditioned a selection of entirely inappropriate hopefuls. The situation excited the music press, who were keen to watch from the sidelines. Meanwhile, back in London, The Cure headed into Morgan Studios again to start work on their next single, 'Jumping Someone Else's Train', for which Siouxsie appeared on backing vocals, a unique contribution to the track.

The tour with The Banshees was rescheduled. The first gig was in Leicester on September 18, with Robert confirmed on guitar and with Budgie – formerly of The Slits, and later to become Siouxsie's husband – on drums. Robert would play a full set with The Cure, and, without even a change of clothes to signify his move into his 'other job', would then join Severin and the band for a second set. "Smith has a task which would have daunted lesser players," wrote *NME*, but equipped with appropriate effects pedals to approximate McKay's playing, Robert put in astounding efforts to keep both bands rolling. Passions guitarist Clive Timperley rated Robert's performance in The Banshees very highly. An excellent guitarist himself, watching his stable-mates perform together he was in as good a position as anyone to judge. "I respected him for that because there was a lot of hard work, and I thought he was good with The Banshees. Probably better than he was with The Cure – because they were a better band, I think, at the time."

Severin too feels that Smith benefited in a number of ways from working so closely with The Banshees. "Robert learned quite a lot by being in the band," he told interviewers for the documentary *Out Of The Woods*. "I think he learned how to be a front person just by standing next to Siouxsie every night for a couple of months … He came out of his shell. I think he learned how to be a bit more flamboyant … a bit about stage craft, and learning to use the audience a bit more."

In truth, The Cure did suffer. Talking to *Uncut* magazine more than twenty years later, Smith admitted that "for the rest of that tour The Cure part of the show was always uncommunicative and teeth gritted." In a purely physical sense Robert was becoming more and more isolated from his own band, travelling with The Banshees rather than, as he had always done, with The Cure. From Severin's point of view it must have made more sense for Robert to travel with what he naturally would have considered the higher priority band: if The Cure's vehicle broke down at least Steve ran the risk of losing only his 'support' band, not his lead guitarist. "We would travel separately and endlessly," Dempsey told *MOJO*. "Robert in the air-conditioned tour bus, Lol and me in the Austin Maxi with our chain-smoking, Wolverhampton Wanderers-supporting sound engineer. I thought it was Robert's way of distancing himself from The Cure …" "As soon as I got in The Banshees van," Robert was to tell *Uncut* in 2000, "it was all over." Robert added. "I found … that I was enjoying playing with The Banshees more than with The Cure."

It's easy to imagine how resentments can set in on tour. *NME* journalist Deanne Pearson observed that Michael was becoming more disillusioned with his position: when he denied that he and Lol were the "Bruce Foxton and Rick Buckler of the band," was he acknowledging that that was exactly how he felt – distanced from the focal point of the band as they had been from Paul Weller in The Jam?

Severin was becoming more of an active influence on Smith too. During the sessions for 'Jumping Someone Else's Train' he had advised Robert specifically that the darker, more radical sound of songs like 'I'm Cold' were where The Cure should be going, away from the pop-edginess of their work to date. The tour came to an end at London's Hammersmith Odeon on October 15. Within days Michael Dempsey had ceased to be a member of The Cure.

Tensions between Michael and Robert had reached a point of no return. Lol was a lifelong friend to Robert and Dempsey was not. Tolhurst and Smith shared many likes and dislikes: Dempsey was often on the outside, even when there were only three of them. Michael eventually found another gig, happily, with The Associates, who became more and more of a revered studio band. 'Jumping Someone Else's Train'/'I'm Cold' was eventually released on November 2.

Cult Hero became Cure Hero when Simon Gallup officially joined The Cure on Dempsey's departure. With him came Matthieu Hartley, Magspies' keyboardist (and trained hairdresser), so turning The Cure into a four-piece band. The new-look band began rehearsing immediately and – along with The Passions (who would have a hit eighteen months later with 'I'm In Love With A German Film Star') and The Associates – played its first gig at Eric's in Liverpool on November 16. About one hundred people were still in Eric's by the time the band arrived for their first four-piece gig, their vehicle causing problems on the drive up from the South East, but Robert described it as the best gig he had done. An opinion, no doubt, partly provoked by the tumultuous six months preceding it.

The Future Pastimes tour, with The Passions and The Associates on board, occupied the rest of 1979 for The Cure, coming to a grinding halt on December 7. The final date was, of course, back in Crawley, where once again skinheads crashed the gig. Clive Timperley, guitarist with The Passions, remembers the tour well. The Passions were half a generation older than The Cure – either pushing thirty or, in the case of drummer Richard Williams, their mid-thirties. "We got on with them fine, but they were much younger than us … and a couple of us had mortgages," Timperley told me. "They were still living at home, still living with their parents." The age difference meant that not everybody in The Passions got on well with The Cure. "We took the piss out of them and they took the piss out of us because we were all old … There was some friendly banter and some slightly bitter banter as well … we thought, 'Oh crikey – they're just school boys. We've been doing this for bloody years.' We weren't saying we were better than them – I think we resented the fact that they were so young and doing so well!"

Timperley, a veteran of some ten years in bands already, had been in the 101ers with Joe Strummer, and, after the dissolution of that band and the formation of The Clash, had joined a nascent Ladbroke Grove band called The Youngstars. Becoming The Passions, they were spotted at a gig at Hammersmith's Moonlight and were signed by Chris Parry to Fiction. Clive remembers playing many gigs in the UK and Europe with The Cure – as many as fifty. In Holland the Dutch punters would occasionally get confused and think that the two bands on the bill were just one – 'The Cure And The Passions.'

"We all travelled in a minibus," Timperley remembers. "And the equipment travelled separately." Smith had a neat little headphones-amplifier set up, so that he would practice on the tour bus with the sounds going straight to the headphones. The bands didn't socialise too much on the tour. Lol used to do Tom Waits impressions to entertain the troops. Timperley found The Cure quite insular: "They were all very kind of self-possessed as a band. They believed in what they were doing so much that they were a pretty tight unit. We didn't see them socially much on tour." They did an awful lot of gigs, a hard-working band. "[The idea was] to saturate the live circuit anywhere in the world … Chris Parry himself is a Kiwi and he made sure they played Australia and New Zealand. He made sure they did loads of world tours, and he really worked them hard actually. We just came in on a little bit of that, basically, and it was good for us because he got us to do lots of gigs in quite nice places. And we got a lot of our exposure from that, from fans who liked The Cure, and they liked us as well."

Clive remembers a feeling within The Passions that Parry was concentrating on The Cure at their expense. Having formed Fiction and taken The Cure with him as his first signing, it seems that the band were Parry's first priority, perhaps understandably so. Eventually, the emphasis given to The Cure forced The Passions to move to Polydor, feeling that they were potentially compromised. And it was with Polydor that they enjoyed their biggest successes. Closing an eventful 1979, The Cure were in Holland for the Dutch TV show *Countdown,* and some more gigs there, followed by a trip to Paris and Belgium a couple of nights before Christmas.

*

And so the Seventies came to a close. It had been a heady decade for all of us. When it began The Beatles were still in the charts with new material. Robert Smith had gone from primary school to the primary colours of headline stages around the UK and Europe. The Cure had evolved from nowhere. They'd had a record deal – then another one, a handful of well-received singles, a good album under their belt, a growing live audience.

What more could four imaginary boys want …?

Chapter 4: Into The Forest

A few weeks' break over Christmas gave Smith, Tolhurst, Hartley and Gallup a breather before heading back into Morgan Studios to record the follow up to *Three Imaginary Boys*. 1980 was the year of Bowie's *Scary Monsters*, one of his most creative and inventive albums. It was the year of Joy Division's *Closer* and the titanic 'Love Will Tear Us Apart.' 1980 was the year of Ian Curtis' death and of the birth of New Order. Adam Ant went Apache on us and The Police courted Top Ten controversy with their Lolita-like 'Don't Stand So Close To Me.' The Banshees would release *Kaleidoscope*, U2's first album *Boy* unleashed Bono and friends on an unsuspecting world, and for every imminent Duran Duran and Hazel O'Connor there was Elvis Costello's *Get Happy* or –if so inclined – *Sandinista!* by The Clash.

It was an exciting time. If we didn't sport too many safety pins any more, we still had lapel badges crying out the names of our favourite bands of the moment. In one direction we were eight years past Ziggy, and, in the other, only eight years away from Kurt Cobain. In the decade that brought us goth, new romanticism, Wham! and Boy George – but also The Smiths, The Fall, Echo & The Bunnymen and REM – The Cure would release what many (themselves included) would often judge to be their best work. Throughout the Eighties The Cure were *the* developing band. It is rare for anyone in rock to successfully reinvent themselves over and over again: Bowie was the past-master, but even his chameleon juice ran out eventually. Madonna made it happen, but within 'serious' rock it is a rare feat, and The Cure carried it off in spades over the coming years. Of all the bands to come careering out of punk with a future, The Cure were perhaps the least likely of all, but a future they certainly had.

With Mike Hedges in the control booth with him, Smith decided to produce the new Cure album himself (Parry was credited as "assisting"). Smith knew clearly what he wanted the next work to sound like. At the same time, he was learning to use the studio as an instrument. This next album would be darker, more atmospheric, less poppy, more coherent. Many of the songs had already been written by the time the band hit Morgan and several had been played on the Banshees tour. Smith had played his demos to Michael Dempsey, who was shocked. Smith thought they were "the final straw" for Dempsey. "He wanted us to be XTC part 2 … I wanted us to be The Banshees part 2."

Clive Timperley remembers being at some of the sessions for what would become the album *Seventeen Seconds*, as The Passions recorded at Morgan themselves. He recalls Mike Hedges' ingenuity in the process that created the burgeoning Cure sound. "He was a great engineer," says Clive. He remembers how Hedges created the drum sound by taping field-effect microphones inside the rim of each individual drum, so that each drum sound was recorded on a separate channel. The 'backward' effect within the drum sound was achieved because each drum within the kit could be treated separately, and with little spillage, creating the 'dryness' of the sound.

As a guitar player, what Timperley recognised early on with Robert was not necessarily his technical proficiency, but the atmosphere and emotional effect that he could create on the guitar: he was always impressed by the sound that he created within The Cure. "He had that Roland amplifier sound … we both had the same," remembers Timperley. "He's got a good jangly (sic) sound and it's basically that Roland JC120 that he used. That's what gives him the sound, and the Fender Jazz (guitar). It's all a bit kind of clangey and echoey – which is nice. It suited their bleak presentation."

There was an odd blend of influences to hand. Robert was listening almost compulsively to a handful of tapes: Bowie's *Low* from 1977, dark and swirling colour fields on one side, breezy Kraut-rock on the other; Nick Drake's *Five Leaves Left*, languid, articulate, breathtakingly beautiful; Van Morrison's *Astral Weeks*, sensual, warm and earthbound; Hendrix's *Isle Of Wight*. Pure nostalgia and perfect craftsmanship. It might seem odd to note that these are very 'Seventies' sounds, given that that decade was only days behind Robert, but none of these influences are anything like contemporary to what was going on elsewhere. Robert was clearly looking for something in which he was more rooted. Bowie and Hendrix were life-long favourites, Drake and Morrison sublime and traditional songwriters. *Low* – although three years old – was the most recent release, and its shadow was to loom large over the new Cure album.

Sessions lasted less than two weeks – one for recording and one for mixing. The band worked incessantly, refining songs that had been played into shape on the road, or – as with 'A Forest' – finishing the track in the studio, where they often slept after long early-hours sessions. From the opening chords of 'A Reflection' it is clear that the band were somewhere other than *Imaginary Boys* territory. The song is slow, simple, Eno-esque in production; piano chords recall Bowie's 'Subterraneans' from *Low*, reminiscent of Erik Satie or Debussy preludes more than Hendrix's 'All Along The Watchtower'. What this reminds me of most are Brian Eno's instrumental passages from his beautiful and whimsical album *Another Green World*. 'Play For Today', the second track, has more the flavour of the earlier album, but the sound of The Cure is much more accomplished – warmer, precise, the echoing, industrial drum beats recalling side one of *Low*. Smith's chorused guitar is precise and articulate – this is one of the things I liked most about The Cure then, and what I still rate today. Robert sounds as though the part is simple, almost simplistic at times. In fact, the picking is curiously florid, the colour of the guitar passages changes throughout the song. It's clearly influenced by the clipped, rhythmic new wave sound of the moment, but there are the sophisticated scents of guitar heroes Hendrix and Drake in the understated sound.

'Secrets' is slower again, its discreet piano chords filling the spaces that might have been left bare a year earlier. The single-note guitar runs nod just a little to Bowie's 'Andy

Warhol', but they have a more sombre flavour than that particular flourishing celebration. Lyrically the song is simple, sparse, yearning and touching, a paean to missed chances and lost opportunity. The unhurried measure of the album is continued with 'In Your House', one of my favourites from the collection: cyclical arpeggios on the guitar, relentless bass, and sparse drums stained with keyboard washes, and troubled, uncertain lyrics. 'In Your House' is another mini Cure horror movie, uncomfortable and disarming.

The air of suspense is maintained perfectly in 'Three', a collage of effects and soundscapes, and of largely indecipherable lyrics. This is The Cure painting pictures, far removed from the teen boredom of *Three Imaginary Boys*, a mature work again clearly influenced by Bowie's instrumental work on *Low* and *"Heroes,"* with perhaps a little Pink Floyd for good measure? The juxtaposition of an assertive beat with dissonant piano notes floating through an echoing fog is quite gripping, and the sense of uncertainty and discord is repeated on 'The Final Sound', less than a minute of gently disturbing non-melody.

As though ushered back in after 'The Final Sound', the cautious, wandering opening notes of 'A Forest' introduce one of the band's all-time finest songs. The increased maturity and studio-awareness is evident in spades. Where the track could have been a thrash a year previously, it is instead a careful jigsaw of sounds and observations, a nightmare vision neatly rounded by the now-trademark Cure beat and Gallup's efficient bass lines. Robert's voice has acquired more of its increasingly pleading, helpless tone, slightly wasted, no longer bored but just a little despairing. 'A Forest' was to be released as the first single off the album.

'M' opens on Smith's chorused strumming, another song in a minor key, and there is less of his distinctive, arithmetic picking, the song played on a guitar slightly off concert tuning. More industrial, 'At Night' mixes Smith's vocal way behind the beat, a track based upon Franz Kafka's short story of the same name, another song contrasting the uncertain 'otherworld' ('A Forest', 'In Your House') with a sense of safety and recluse. The track repeats Smith's guitar phrases under Matthieu's keyboard drone and fades gently into 'Seventeen Seconds', the final cut on the album.

'Seventeen Seconds' slows the pace of the album down to its end. Simon's bass is lyrical, the guitar again economical and sparse, yet its tone so much richer than on the previous album. It takes a minute for the drums to kick in properly, and another half minute for Robert's vocal to enter – plaintive, measuring out time in another wasteland of tentative touches on the bass and guitar. *Seventeen Seconds* fades out almost as it had begun, gently, the spaces between the notes as important as the sounds themselves, leaving the listener slightly disturbed.

The album has a distinct palette of sounds, a clearly defined tone. It is quintessentially a night-time collection: reflective, uncertain, pensive. I love it. "Producing's easy," Robert told *Trouser Press* later in the year. "People draw a line between experimental and acceptable music. I don't see why you can't combine the two." *Seventeen Seconds* is still a fine album to listen to, a quarter of a century after its release, a guitarist's album despite the washes of Hartley's keyboard. Where its predecessor was essentially urban in tone – suburban even – *Seventeen Seconds* has a distinctly pastoral tone: forests, reflections, night-time. It is the sound of drops of music splashing into a pool. Late at night, the windscreen wipers washing the black rain from the windshield ...

*

A gig outside Paris and a third BBC Radio session were followed, on the 18 March by a home-town date in Crawley, whence Porl Thompson joined them for a rendition of 'I'm A Cult Hero'. The Peel show featured four songs from the forthcoming album: 'Seventeen Seconds', 'M', 'A Forest' and 'Play For Today'. It was Gallup and Hartley's first session at Maida Vale. On March 23, Cult Hero appeared as a band supporting The Passions at The Marquee, an apparent 'one-off' sideline for The Cure that hadn't quite run its course. To play up the 'ironic' nature of Cult Hero, the band – with original postman vocalist Frank Bell – played a selection of songs that Robert had on an old cassette from 1973, including songs by Gary Glitter ('Do You Wanna Touch Me There?'), Thin Lizzy ('Whiskey In The Jar'), 'Blockbuster' by The Sweet and so on; a veritable cornucopia of early Seventies kitsch pop.

Activities with The Banshees temporarily suspended, Robert played one more celebrity gig in March when he appeared on guitar with The Stranglers. Finsbury Park Rainbow was taken over for a benefit for Hugh Cornwell who had been busted for possession and sent down to London's Pentonville prison. The line-up was a wonderful snapshot of London pop around the turn of the decade, and The Stranglers never looked more at odds as they were joined by, amongst others Toyah Wilcox, Steve Hillage (Gong), Wilko Johnson (Dr Feelgood), Robert Fripp (King Crimson and, latterly, husband of Toyah), Hazel O'Connor (sometime girlfriend to Cornwell), the resplendent Peter Hammill (Van Der Graaf Generator) and others including Ian Dury and Phil Daniels.

Robert played on '(Get A) Grip (On Yourself)' and 'Hanging Around' (sung by O'Connor) and Matthieu played on 'Peaches' and 'Bear Cage' (both presented vocally by the elegant Ms Wilcox). Both Cure members joined The Stranglers on 'Down In The Sewer'. Earlier in the evening, fans enjoyed what turned out to be one of the last chances to see Joy Division, who were amongst the support bands.

Over the same couple of days Robert also sang backing vocals with Fiction cohorts The Associates. Billy MacKenzie was one of the most talented, mannered and wonderful vocalists around, like Robert a singer of great individual charm and instantly recognisable. Like Smith, MacKenzie was also a big Bowie fan, and The Associates' first release had been a self-funded version of Bowie's 'Boys Keep Swinging', released only a few weeks after David's own. On 'The Affectionate Punch', Smith can be heard behind Billy's ba rgain-Bowie lead vocal – a cracking record then and now. Billy's suicide in 1997 touched many of us for whom 'Party Fears Two' remains one of the greatest singles of all time: insane, joyous, exuberant and unbridled pop joy. RIP BM.

*

'A Forest' was released as FICS 10 in the first week of April. *Sounds* said that, like The Banshees' 'Happy House' it "leaps over trivia into the Eighties," while *Trouser Press* felt it was "no more than excellent background music." The single was to prove the breakthrough track The Cure had deserved with 'Boys Don't Cry'. It was their first chart entry, reaching a creditable number thirty-one the week after release and staying in the charts for a total of eight weeks. During this year, 'alternative' bands would continue the onslaught on the mainstream chart that had begun in 1979. Blondie, The Pretenders, The Police, The Specials, The Jam and Dexy's Midnight Runners would occupy the number one slot for nineteen weeks between them, and David Bowie would spend a fortnight there with 'Ashes To Ashes' – ironically pe rhaps the most alternative single of the year. Putting this achievement in perspective, 1980 still saw acts like Olivia Newton John, Johnny Logan and Kenny Rogers up at the top, and – lest we forget – Christmas of 1980 had the recently murdered John Lennon's '(Just Like) Starting Over' at number one. Murder of a different kind was committed when that re co rd was toppled by the St Winifred's School Choir with 'There's No One Quite Like Grandma!' But such joys were months away for us all. On the B-side of 'A Forest' was 'Another Journey By Train'.

A one-off gig in Derby the day after the single's release prepared The Cure for their first trip to the United States, a market where they would ultimately become huge, one of the most successful British bands of the era. *Boys Don't Cry* – their first US album – had been released in the States in November and had built up a small but meaningful audience in anticipation of their first gigs. The album was effectively a compilation of works to date: from *Three Imaginary Boys* they had dropped 'Meat Hook', 'Foxy Lady', 'So What' and 'It's Not You' (few punters would have turned up to Hurrah's expecting Hendrix covers) and in their place were inserted 'Boys Don't Cry', 'Plastic Passion', 'Jumping Someone Else's Train', and 'Killing An Arab'. This neatly gave the expectant Americans a flavour of the kitchen sink Cure but also of the aspiring singles band.

Rip It Up described the UK singles on the album as "enlightened," and the album was generally well received. It became the point of entry in the USA for all early Cure fans. The band's first gig was at Cherry Hill, Emerald City, New Jersey (to me that somehow sounds more romantic than The Assembly Rooms, Derby) playing a set comprising most of the songs from their two UK albums to date. They then played three nights at Hurrah's, New York. *Melody Maker* described the band as "more than a little jet-lagged but seemingly quite sure of themselves." Phil Sutcliffe of *Sounds* and *Record Mirror* recounted tales of how the band tried their best to avoid the rock and roll clichés and handshakes, preferring Brits-abroad capers to rock and roll ligging, while in *Ten Imaginary Years* Smith tells tales of crazy car drives, drug use and of getting lost in Cape Cod on the way back to New York from Boston (again, better than being lost in Swindon perhaps).

Momentum was building nicely both in the US and at home. Within hours of touching down back in the UK, The Cure were to appear on BBC TV's *Top Of The Pops*, still – though Eighties cheese was beginning to sour its effect on the nation's youth – the most important pop programme in Europe. To this viewer at least, Robert appeared bored by the whole event, glancing off stage distractedly and just keeping his lip-synched vocals in time with the recorded track. Black-shirted and buttoned up to the neck, Smith's thumb was heavily bandaged after he had tried to repair a car wheel before they left America. With DJ Steve Wright managing to fluff his introduction to the band, the appearance had a profound effect on the UK record-buying public; bucking the trend that a *Top of the Pops* appearance would enhance any band's chart position, The Cure promptly dropped down the chart the following week.

The day after their main UK TV debut, The Cure took off on a tour of the UK that would promote *Seventeen Seconds*. The album was released to mixed reviews. *Sounds* found it filled with contradictions: less poppy than *Three Imaginary Boys* but perhaps more likely to be commercial. Phil Sutcliffe noted the isolation and loneliness of the album, mystified that the claustrophobic single should have hit where 'Boys Don't Cry' failed. Tellingly, he noted that despite their "occult-horror-movie-Gothic, Hammer when they should be Hitchcock" nature, The Cure nevertheless seemed intent on sticking with rhythmic, poppy structures at the same time.

Writing in *NME*, Nick Kent felt that it was impossible to find a thread that linked all their work to date. He noted "Robert Smith's pleading whine of a voice," and the band's ability to maintain a distance between themselves, their material and by implication their audience. As with the previous album, the artwork denied easy access to the personalities of the foursome. Although the kitchen appliances had been dumped, The Cure were represented by blurred, out-of-focus photographs. Clearly there was a move to retain privacy and individuality at the same time as building up a recognisable profile. Kent noted the Eno-esque nature of some of the instrumental passages. Finding the whole package "regressive", he nevertheless looked forward to their next release "with interest." Elsewhere reviews were similarly confused. *Record Mirror* asked "why don't The Cure come out to play," and described the collection as reclusive and disturbed. In fact, what most reviewers had inevitably latched on to was the change that Smith had imposed upon the production values and the sense of tone that he wished the band to present. However much their off-stage antics were fun and high jinks, the band was professionally heading down a darkened street that would produce darker and more serious pop than most reviewers could have expected from their first batch of releases. While their studio sessions may have been becoming more intense, they were hardly stretched out to *Dark Side Of The Moon* proportions time-wise, and The Cure were very much visible as a touring live band rather than studio boffins like Eno. The irony building up around the band was that they were accessible on one front to paying punters on the live circuit, but increasingly inaccessible artistically as the waters of their music darkened. Thus are born mythical bands.

The *Seventeen Seconds* tour kicked off in Cromer, Norfolk. Over the next few weeks they would glide through Manchester, Bristol, Bournemouth, Coventry, Brighton, some seventy-five more dates before the end of the year. The first UK leg came to a standstill in May at The Rainbow in London, where The Passions and The Fall were among the support bands. Johnny Waller reviewed the Edinburgh gig in early May for *Sounds,* and described Smith as "unruffled … taking everything in his stride as would a man on a Sunday afternoon stroll." Here too, the reviewer was confused by The Cure. Were they "the new Genesis?" Alternative and intriguing but destined to become bland mainstream? Waller noted their listlessness – Hartley wandering off for a fag when he had nothing to play – as well as Gallup's apparent dedication to the cause. The band clearly had set a confusing agenda for the supposed cognoscenti.

By the middle of the month they were back in Europe, this time on a fully scheduled tour for the first time. Brussels and Turnhout in Belgium were followed by gigs in Holland where the band narrowly escaped arrest following an early morning dip in The Channel at Rotterdam – a local resident called the police when Smith and one of the crew rounded off a night out by taking to the waters. On May 18 they played in Utrecht. That morning, back in Macclesfield in Cheshire,

Deborah Curtis had woken to find her husband, Ian, hanging by his neck in their family kitchen.

Increasing ill-health and personal problems had driven the Joy Division singer to a tragic suicide. The Manchester band cast a long shadow over pop for the rest of the year, as album *Closer* and single 'Love Will Tear Us Apart' became benchmarks for any serious act to follow. The Cure – like any other contemporary band – were affected by the death and indeed by Joy Division/New Order's rise to popularity. Certainly darker issues were at hand for Smith as a writer, and in the coming year those colours would fill his work more and more.

In terms of the current tour, Germany and France were next up: a session for RTL in Luxembourg was recorded before the band joined The Clash for the Rettel festival, north of Metz. After a string of gigs back in Scotland the band headed for their furthest trip to date: Australia and New Zealand, booked first into the Mainstreet Cabaret on Auckland's Queen St, one of the country's most notorious venues. Wellington, Palmerston, Christchurch – The Cure began a long and meaningful relationship with the Antipodes before scooting into Sydney and Melbourne for their very first Australian gigs. Increasingly mystical they may have become to the rock press, but ever-available to the paying punter, two days after leaving Australia they were in Sweden for a one-off gig in Stockholm, then back to Koln, Wiesbaden, Bremen and a string of German, Dutch and Belgian dates through the summer and autumn. It was relentless.

But all was not well. Again. The relationships between Matthieu Hartley and the rest of the band got increasingly strained in Australia, where the threesome of Lol, Robert and Simon continued to get on well but Hartley became increasingly distanced from the band both musically and socially. Four young men on the wrong side of the world, drained of all energies at one moment and pumped up with adrenalin the next, on the one hand free to do as they please but yet having to share rooms and live in one another's pockets. It can be tense for any band. There were media reports of damaged hotel rooms. Matthieu flew home from the tour early, and after the rest of the band returned to the UK he telephoned Robert to resign his position in the band.

Chapter 5: Faith and Pornography

The Cure's third album, *Faith*, was to be a career-confirming record for the band and Smith. It cemented their profile after *Seventeen Seconds* and pointed in the direction that they would follow for the coming few years, as they became one of the decade-defining acts of the Eighties. Their second album – morose and atmospheric rather than the bubbly pop that *Three Imaginary Boys* might have presaged – had been more successful than the reviewers expected, reaching the top twenty in the UK album charts. After Matthieu Hartley left the band in the summer, the newly reconvened threesome began rehearsals for a follow-up album in between European dates.

From the start nothing ran smoothly. Smith was keen to maintain the sombre textures of the previous album and to extend them further with songs that had originally been demoed in Mr and Mrs Smith's dining room. Within days the sessions ground to a halt. The cavalry came in the resumption of the never-ending tour, taking the boys out of the studio and back on the road. Throughout October, Lol, Simon and Robert crawled around north-west Europe again: Berlin, Brussells, Bordeaux and other cities and towns around Holland, France and Germany. 'Seventeen Seconds' hit the Top Ten in both Holland and Belgium, and – as in Australia and New Zealand – it was clear that The Cure were a band with international appeal. In November they were back in the UK. Reading, Leicester, Lancaster and Cardiff, my own very first Cure gig in the university student's union. I wish I could remember more about it. I recall having too many pints of Brain's Dark in the Senghennydd Bar beforehand, passing pint glasses over heads for what seemed like an hour before we went into the hall. By the time we got into the place we were as pissed as farts, and the friends that I went with, who'd been listening to a lot of King Crimson lately, heckled more than they should have done. But if I can't remember every moment of the set, I do have a distinct memory of a noisy and energetic night. I remember how edgy the band were compared with some of the more plodding acts that came through: punk was rife in Cardiff still, and any band vaguely aligned got a rousing, pogo-friendly welcome. We were into Talking Heads and Debbie Harry, and we liked our punks arch and arty, and The Cure was definitely in there with us and for us.

They wound up live activity for the year in London at a party the week before Christmas, as The Associates, Banshees and others joined the band at play.

After a session recorded for John Peel's show a week into the New Year (playing 'Holy Hour', 'Forever', 'All Cats Are Grey' and 'Primary' – early excursions for new songs) The Cure moved back into Morgan to work on the new album in February with Mike Hedges co-producing again with Robert. The vibes were not good. "I was OK on my own with the words and music," Smith explained. "But when I was with the others it was wrong. It was too happy." "It was a very difficult and cranky atmosphere," he told *Uncut*'s James Oldham in 2000. "I remember finishing the vocals off at Abbey Road and just feeling incredibly empty." This was the beginning of what Robert later called "an ever-downward spiral," that was to last for at least the next two albums. Stylistically, dark was currently 'the new black.' Joy Division's *Closer* had made it to number six in the UK album charts the previous summer. 'Love Will Tear Us Apart' had almost made the top ten singles chart (in 2003 *NME* voted it "the greatest single of all time"). The 'darkness' that became *Faith* was both from within and without: whether Robert deliberately felt drawn into an increasing trend for a more morbid tone amongst contemporary acts or whether it was coincidence that his own band followed similar inner journeys doesn't matter. What mattered was that The Cure were getting *really* serious.

When Morgan didn't work for Robert, he moved from studio to studio to find the right place for *Faith* to be born. Within the month they tried out Trident (off Soho's Wardour

Street, where *Ziggy* had been recorded), Red Bus (recently the birthing room to Duran Duran's first album) and Abbey Road (the world's most famous recording studio). By the time Chris Parry came down to see what was going on, the sessions had all but come to a grinding halt. As Pat Gilbert noted in a piece for *Record Collector* in August 2003, it reportedly took Parry's diplomatic and persuasive skills to get Smith and Hedges back on the same track after they had almost fallen out over the sessions. While Lol's mother was seriously ill at the time, and Robert's grandmother had recently died, Smith had turned very much towards his Catholic faith; not for its support or its comfort, but to look deeply within himself to establish whether he had any faith. The music became more and more a means of exploring the nature of faith itself. Robert took to observing people in churches, watching behaviour and trying to figure out the motivation of faith and its meaning for different people. Particularly for himself. "Both myself and Robert went to Catholic school, and were very heavily immersed in religion up until our teens," Tolhurst told *Record Collector.* " ... there were a lot of personal things that went into that album." Smith has spoken at length over the years about how he had more or less given up on the Catholic faith by the age of eight. "They let me alone after that," he told *Sassy* in 1990. Talking of his brother Richard's trip to India when Robert himself was still a child, he spoke of how he "came back with lots of pictures of women with eight arms to stick on my bedroom wall and upset my little sister. He used to tell us about reincarnation. I don't have any of the guilt problems that most Catholics have."

'Funeral Party', 'A Drowning Man', (sic) 'and 'Faith' were premiered on Richard Skinner's Radio One evening show in a session broadcast in early March. A 'fashion shoot' for *Record Mirror* at the end of the month showed a tired-looking yet smiling Robert 'relaxing' in his old school blazer. The magazine announced the dates for the forthcoming tour, highlighting the fact that a movie would replace the conventional support band at all the gigs except Brighton, where there were no facilities to show the film. Robert listed his top ten favourite records for a magazine at the time, quoting Frank Sinatra, Erik Satie, The Banshees, And Also The Trees, Brian Eno, Hendrix, The Psychedelic Furs, 13:13, Nico and Joy Division as his 'Fallout Favourites'.

The first single from the album sessions, 'Primary', was released on the 27 March. The emphatic bass line, moving in and out of phase, and the increasingly industrial drum sound suggested no more Buzzcocks riffs for the time being. Lyrically the song is more obscure than previous singles. Images of sleeping children, dressed in white, their innocence contrasting with the wasting of another relationship. In 1991 in *Cure News*, Robert described the song being about the idea "that it might be better to die very young, innocent and dreaming." His vocal is as trenchant and direct as the music – an increasingly typical trait in Cure songs for difficult subject matter to contrast against misleadingly simple sounds.

The album was released on April 11, 1981. The opening track, 'The Holy Hour' opens in sombre tone. Keyboard washed over bass and drums, cyclical phrases with meandering, pensive overtones. Robert claimed to have written the lyrics during a catholic mass in Crawley, trying to "make sense" of the communion: kneeling; prayer; silence; salvation – images of the holy ritual are the mainstay of the song that ends on a sobering bell ring.

'Primary' was the second track on the album. Despite another *Top Of The Pops* appearance on April 16 – this time introduced by Peter Powell, who at least got their name right – the single failed to trouble the top ten, but got as far as number forty three before slipping out of the chart altogether six weeks later. It would be more than two years before the band would appear on the nation's favourite pop programme again. 'Other Voices', its title coming from the novel *Other Voices, Other Rooms* by US novelist Truman Capote, is another repetitive series of bass lines and guitar, Robert's multi-tracked and echoing vocals building up a dark atmosphere around the whole track. The tasting of illicit pleasures;

sensual, tactile lyrics – Smith was becoming more and more proficient as a poet, able to hang his heart out for all to see but to retain secrets where need be.

'All Cats Are Grey' might be the first 'beautiful' Cure song. Setting a pace and a tone that The Blue Nile would later similarly make much use of, the sense of isolation is tangible. The feel of the track is almost as though it has had its top layer of skin removed to expose nerves never before able to feel. The lyrics are quite surreal. Where The Blue Nile would paint beautiful sound pictures of city landscape and lost love, here Smith's lyrics point deeply inwards, towards a dream-like world. Images appear fundamentally symbolic, creating wonderfully ambiguous mood. 'All Cats Are Grey' bears much of the Eno/*Low* influence that was all over *Seventeen Seconds*. The next track, 'The Funeral Party', again has heavy smudges of *Another Green World* dragged across its musical tones. Like the preceding track, 'The Funeral Party' is a beautiful thing, lyrically and musically. The deaths of Robert's grandparents were the starting points for the song and the images of a couple buried side by side, of their observer, and of children dreaming create a perfect triangle of reflection beneath a subtle series of synth and guitar chords and funereal drum beats. By now, anyone unsure of where The Cure were heading musically must surely have had their eyes opened: this is beautiful, serious, simple and affecting. Robert listened to a lot of Gregorian chants at the time, and the gentle motion of the track arguably suggests their influence here.

The tempo of the album picks up with 'Doubt' – more Clash than *Canto Gregoriano*. The lyrics seem again confounded by contradiction, balancing violence, rage and anger against kisses, and the 'holding tight' of the object of out-of-control violence. 'The Drowning Man' is the third title to sound like a painting or a short story ('*The* Funeral Party', '*The* Holy Hour') Taken from the cult classic (well – just 'classic') *Gormenghast* novels by Mervyn Peake, the imagery of the song measures that of Peake's writing well and points a finger at much of Robert Smith's own work. Peake's books are fantasy, but without the element of quest so prevalent elsewhere in the genre. Instead, Peake's fantasy is the fantasy of language, a rich and varied journey through wonderful words and writing as rich as a medieval tapestry. Uncluttered by ever-involving plot, Peake nevertheless creates a world that the reader can explore her/himself through the language and texture of the book, and this seems to me a good mirror on Smith's lyrics too. Throughout their career, every Cure album creates a point of entry into The Cure-world: explore it on your own or with others; let it carry you where it will. Smith and the band won't necessarily be there with you all the time, and often you won't know where you are, but being there is worth the journey in itself ...

And so to 'Faith', perhaps the raison-d'être for the album and certainly its core concept. Robert offers hope at last. Amidst the death and the loss and the solitude and the emptiness there is always faith. When we fall, when we lose our grip, there is faith. When 'Faith' fails, there is 'faith' with a small 'f' – hope in hope itself. Robert described this song as being "as optimistic as I could get," yet its slow-burn, minimalist guitar, drum and bass retain all the sobriety of the rest of a fantastic album. For 'All Cats Are Grey' and 'The Funeral Party' alone, the album is worth its weight in gold. That the two songs were written on the same day makes them even more stunning.

Reviewers were again unsure. Twenty-plus years later Pat Gilbert called it "an understated masterpiece" in *Record Collector*. At the time, Adam Sweeting (writing for *Melody Maker*) noted that on the evidence of their previous releases, no-one could have predicted the richness and deceptive power of *Faith*, "the desperately atmospheric keyboards and inexplicable melancholy" of the piece. "You may not love it," wrote Sweeting, "but you'll become addicted to it." *Sounds* pointed out similarities to Joy Division and noted that – aside from the fashionable sweep towards the Mancunians – The Cure had been there first. "It swings like a warm summer night," wrote John G. "This is life and I want more of it."

NME voiced concerns: "This album ... says absolutely nothing meaningful in a fairly depressing way," and signposted the peculiarly English attitude in contemporary pop, described as "grammar school angst." *Record Mirror* went further: "Hollow, shallow, pretentious, meaningless, self-important and bereft of any real heart and soul." *Flexipop* said "pass me the razor Robert," but called the album their "most fascinating so far." Countering accusations of self-indulgence, Smith talked of the opposite, the very brevity of the sessions. Unhappy with the album's production himself, and with the fact that the sessions hadn't really allowed the band to work the songs to their ultimate potential (they'd spent less than a month on it) he told Jim Green at *Trouser Press* that "if we'd taken longer, *that* would've been self-indulgent, (but) we kept getting thrown out of studios in favour of 'more important' people, and once we lost the mood we never quite got back the atmosphere we wanted."

In fact, *Faith* was almost perfect. What it achieved was something that few other guitar bands of the period managed, except perhaps Joy Division: deep, intense, personal, emotional mini-dramas. But not for pose, not for effect, but because these things somehow had to be said. *Faith* was a clarion call to disaffected teenagers of a certain sensitivity. Here was a band who knew what it felt like to be alone, to be lost, to be unsure, to doubt, to wonder. Not writing songs about The Cure's loneliness, or Robert Smith's sense of estrangement, but about the fundamental nature of solitude or loss itself. That was the key to The Cure beginning to open up to a very wide audience. If we'd all woken up to the fact that the punk bubble had been and gone and burst on us, and yet we still had no future; if we were a little bit older and a little less sure, where could we go? We could enter the increasingly baffling theme park of Cureland.

The packaging was designed to keep punters guessing. Like with Wire, like with Joy Division, there was an increased distancing of the band members' personalities from the fans.

This sense of withdrawal mirrors the content of the songs – this was difficult music to write, painful at times to play, and personality is not the issue, so why portray the band on the album's front cover? Both the album sleeve and that for the single 'Primary' (which, backed with 'Descent', was also the band's first 12" single), were designed by Porl Thompson, the album showing a solarized photo of Bolton Abbey, near Skipton, Yorkshire. Porl had been studying design, graphics and photography at West Sussex College, and would go on to design packaging for scores of Cure products through into the Nineties. Under the name of his design company, Parched Art, and with brother Andy (aka 'Undy Vella') as partner, Porl continued to work closely with his former band mates who included – in Robert – his future brother-in-law. The cassette version of *Faith* supplemented the eight vinyl tracks with an extra instrumental. 'Carnage Visors' (a pun on the antithesis of 'rose-coloured spectacles') was the twenty-seven minute-long soundtrack to the movie of the same name made by Simon's brother Ric, which would be played during the forthcoming tour for the album.

Initially, the band told John Gill for *Sounds* that the plan was to commission a film student to make a movie for them, that they would use instead of a support band. When no interest could be excited amongst the student world, the band approached professional film makers, but found that their idea of budgeting around £2,500 would be increased twenty-fold if they went this route. Enter Ric Gallup. Ric's first efforts had to be discarded right at the last minute when problems with the lighting of the project became evident. The film appeared virtually pitch black throughout. In order to stay on track for the tour, the whole animation had to be re-shot in only three days – a fraction of the time that Gallup had spent initially. The soundtrack to *Carnage Visors* is a gently disturbing, repetitive instrumental, where layers of instrumentation build up over a basic drum track. Smith played bass on the original track, over which Simon overdubbed later, and it is the bass that leads the track. Like so many Cure songs, guitars provide a context but the bass is the 'poppiest' instrument on the cut.

With the album out there for the world to love or loathe, The Cure did what they did now as a matter of course: they went on tour. The *Picture* tour boasted a lavish 16-page booklet that mixed black and white shots of the guys with stills from *Carnage Visors*, as well – of course – boasting a name for the tour itself, and from this time onwards each Cure tour would be 'named,' like a hurricane or a cyclone. In keeping with their increasing profile, the band hired Pink Floyd's PA system for the tour, which kicked off at Friar's, Aylesbury on April 18 and ran almost uninterrupted until the end of August. Mick Duffy reviewed the Manchester Apollo date in May for *NME*. "Smith possesses those intangible qualities that make him A (potential) Star," wrote Duffy. "Immediately he has assumed total control, is in complete command. He is the archetypal modern romantic, a cynical lover, the ultimate hero for this dour age of gloomy imperfection." Duffy noted the sense of "uncheery pessimism" and observed dryly that there was an air of gloomy hopelessness that "seems to be sucking The Cure dry." *Melody Maker*, reviewing the Hammersmith Odeon gig on May 4 described them as more "anaesthetic" than cure, their stage show "a pretty pointless exercise." The audience was a mixture of mature listeners and teenage fans. The encore of 'Killing An Arab' pleased the latter, while the increasing air of doom gave food for thought for others. With *Carnage Visors* replacing the traditional support act, the evening was spent entirely in the company of The Cure.

The band headed into Europe in late May, playing in a circus tent as well as more traditional venues through Holland, Belgium and Germany. Tragedy struck in late June when Lol's mother died. The night of June 24 they were booked in Sittard, Holland. Robert described in *Ten Imaginary Years* the experience, as Tolhurst was informed of his mother's death between songs. They went back on stage and Lol bravely tried to continue, lasting only a minute before he could only sit there, not moving (they later played a cassette recording of that gig at his mother's funeral).

Almost immediately the gigs resumed – Vlissingen, Rotterdam, The Hague ... relentless. At one, appearing with Robert Palmer, The Cure were told to stop playing or Palmer's roadies would pull the plug. Undeterred, the band launched into an incredibly slow version of 'A Forest' which lasted about fifteen minutes.

In mid-July a break came in the stressful, seemingly endless tour of the *Faith* songs, in the shape of a two-day session at the new Playground Studios in Camden, recording the follow-up single to 'Primary' with Mike Hedges. On 'Charlotte Sometimes' Robert sounds at the very end of his tether. Although failing to reach the heady heights that 'Primary' achieved (the single stalled at number 44 and lasted barely a month in the charts as a whole when released in October), I think 'Charlotte Sometimes' is by far the best Cure single to date: the vocals are split in a similar way to many of Bowie's most manic songs, moving around an octave higher than the lead. The drums continue to set a heavy, monotonous tone right at the front of the track; the guitar is subtle and lyrical. Lyrically, the song is inspired by the children's book *Charlotte Sometimes* by Penelope Farmer, the story of a little girl sent to boarding school, who wakes to find that she is suddenly someone else, living in a different time, surrounded by different children to the ones she went to sleep with the night before. Robert's plaintive yells and the repeated phrases of the title are particularly affecting. Robert told *Flexipop* magazine that he read the story as being that of an outsider, someone "who has to come to terms with an unfamiliar society," something that everybody has to do as they grow up. 'Charlotte Sometimes' should have been a top ten hit had there been any justice in the charts, but it was not to be The Cure's breakthrough single. The song reminds me of The Velvet Underground's 'All Tomorrow's Parties', it describes self-absorption, loneliness and solitude, but never with a sense of pity. Depiction, not morbidity. A goth signpost?

The cover of the single release featured a rare public profile of Robert's girlfriend Mary, a blurred photograph taken on holiday in Scotland – not of course that you could recognise her from the heavily disguised design.

'Charlotte Sometimes' was the inspiration for Eric Byler's 2001 movie of the same name. Kind of. A Cure fan in his teens, Byler says that although the song was not the direct inspiration for the film he could not believe the coincidence between the lyrics of the song and the movie that he had made about a group of Asian Americans. "It wasn't until after I shot the movie and began editing it," said Byler to Minnie Chin, "that I realized I needed to call it 'Charlotte Sometimes …' When I read the lyrics, it looked as if someone had taken this screenplay I had already written and made it into a poem. It was so … uncanny."

More dates followed. By the time they reached America they were playing what Steve Sutherland, in an excellent article for *Melody Maker* later described as "the worst ever" gigs they had played. Fights were reported between the band and the audience. Repeating the songs from *Faith* sapped them in every emotional way possible. Smith told journalist Bill Crandall that the band were "reliving a really bad time, night after night, and it got incredibly depressing … we would just drink ourselves into oblivion, and play these songs." They were becoming exhausted too. Robert managed to rack up a hotel telephone bill of nearly $500 in New Zealand as he fell asleep during a call to Steve Severin back in the UK. From Australia they headed on into Canada, and – after a break of only a few weeks – were back in Europe by early October. Between Rouen on October 1 and Toulon on the 23 they only had three nights off.

While 'Charlotte Sometimes' appeared in the UK, in America a new album was released to capitalise on the tour and the interest shown in their debut. *Happily Ever After* was essentially a double set of *Seventeen Seconds* and *Faith* released in new packaging, which cleverly developed the interest for the time being for those who had been intrigued by *Boys*

Don't Cry. The UK dates for the tour resumed in a chilly November: Sheffield, Edinburgh, Glasgow, Bradford, Coventry, Brighton and an end-of-tour show at London's Hammersmith Palais. The support for these gigs came from Lydia Lunch backed by Steve Severin, trading as 13:13. Lydia, whose nightmarish, claustrophobic material aptly suited the current state of mind of The Cure tour, asked Severin if he would work with her live, as she had supported the Banshees' first American tour. Worcestershire's And Also The Trees – who Robert would claim to be among his top ten favourite bands – were also on the tour, and would develop a good relationship with The Cure over the coming year.

The Cure were glad to see the back of 1981. A Boxing Day gig in Leeds rounded the year off but with the emotional stress of *Faith* and The Picture Tour behind them, it was time to get back in the studio. "We weren't in the best of health mentally,' Smith told Alexis Petridis for *Mojo* in 2003. "I thought we should have been making music that was on a par with Mahler symphonies, not pop music."

*

Mike Hedges' work on The Banshees forthcoming 1982 album *A Kiss In The Dreamhouse*, combined with The Cure's decision to bring in a new producer for the follow-up to *Faith* saw Phil Thornally on board in late December as initial demos were begun for the album that was to become *Pornography*. Smith had started fiddling with drum lines in September in a gap between the Canadian and French Picture Tour gigs, venting some of the *Faith* frustration on complex rhythm tracks. Over Christmas Smith took a break with Steve Severin, a holiday of sorts in which Severin tried to tempt Smith out of The Cure. "I used to either steal Lol's drinks or spike them when he was playing" he told *Mojo*. "I was always asking Robert to disband The Cure and join the Banshees. I was definitely sowing the seeds of discontent."

A Surrey windmill proved to be Smith's bolt-hole when the

studio sessions didn't work out, and he penned the lyrics to much of *Pornography* there. "I wanted to make the ultimate fuck-off record, then The Cure would stop," he remembered for *Mojo* in 2003. Severin was putting pressure on Smith to join The Banshees permanently and, given the already fractious atmosphere, matters got worse. "I was on a crusade", Smith told *Sounds* in 1987. "Against myself, and everything else that was going on."

Thornally, who had worked previously with Duran Duran, could not see eye to eye with Robert over the production. The band legendarily took to sleeping on the floor of the Fiction office, a mountain of beer cans growing around them as their lifestyle deteriorated, passing pop princess Kim Wilde at the studio door each day as she was leaving and they were coming to work in the dark. Although he would describe elements of the sessions as 'good crack' (as in 'fun' not drugs!), tension mounted. It wasn't just Robert. "After (*Faith*) there was obviously a conscious decision by Fiction to push me a little bit more," Smith told *Mojo*. "Simon took it very badly." Musically the band was finding darker and darker corners to inhabit. "The end had started for that line-up ..." said Robert later.

After a Peel session in early January, where they played four tracks off the forthcoming album ('Figurehead', 'One Hundred Years' and 'Siamese Twins' were broadcast, but 'Hanging Garden' was not) and with the album wrapped and ready for April release, 1982's *Fourteen Explicit Moments* tour was announced to the press in March.

On its release, The Cure's fourth album *Pornography* confused and delighted, depending on which side of the raincoat fence you sat. *Trouser Press* called it "turgid *pop noir* thematicism." For *Melody Maker* it was "downhill all the way, into ever-darkening shadows." *Sounds* were less ambiguous: "While Cure fans are insidiously locked in The Cure (otherwise this musical crap wouldn't exist), Robert Smith seems locked in himself, a spiralling nightmare that leaves The Cure making pompous sounding music that is, when all's said and done, dryly meaningless." *Record Mirror* had this to say: "predictable, but still worth a listen." *NME* were less critical: "as a piece of craftsmanship in expressive sound, it is a very big, very harrowing achievement." Dave Hill in *NME* got nearer than most reviewers to the core of the album: "*Pornography* was not designed to be objectified or probed, but taken *en bloc* as a very dense wash of emotional colour, portraying one soul on a leash, fighting back the panic in the dark." Hill went on to warn readers "don't have too much fun now." Smith himself told Italian magazine *Rockerilla* the following year that "*Pornography* is the best album The Cure have made, the most powerful: it started like the other ones, but then grew into something different; it turned into a kind of animal, while the others hadn't gone that far ..."

The opening track 'One Hundred Years' declared a new territory for The Cure immediately. Reflective and aggressive at the same time, the unrelenting rhythm spoke of an uncompromising genie at work. If the opening line suggested a woeful pessimism, then the rest of the collection at least took the question of dying seriously and explored it thoroughly. Almost seven minutes later, anyone expecting the album to be a return to *Seventeen Seconds* was undoubtedly reminded of the direction that *Faith* had pointed The Cure in: self-dissection; diagnosis; despair. *Rolling Stone* described the song as The Cure's 'My Generation' – if it doesn't matter whether we die before we get old, at least if we question the fact that we will *all* die at some point we might find some meaning, something worthwhile in the search itself. Speaking in 1989, on the subject of whether he still felt the same, Robert was more accepting: "If you hold that sense of futility in your head for too long, it can begin to eat into you," he said.

'Short Term Effect' picked up where the opener started. Dying birds, rotten atmospheres, sickness, madness and derangement. A hallucinogenic nightmare of grand proportions. 'Siamese Twins' followed the single, 'Hanging Garden', with a tribal drum beat and slowly-drawn picture of some kind of love act in which passion and cruelty combine.

Smith's lyrics again tempt responses from the audience that inevitably make the listener to The Cure write their own songs as they listen. For me, this is one of Robert's greatest gifts: like his early hero Bowie, in his best writing he draws abstracts with just a hint of the real, so suggesting a direction for the listener but leaving doors open everywhere for him or her to wander at will. 'The Figurehead' seemingly referred to the red and black packaging of the album which certainly implied a mourning process of some kind. The song contains statuary, pain, visions of hell and an eternity of corruption. 'Strange Days' evokes blindness, drowning, eyes closed, dust – the song filtering in slowly through myopic keyboard tones until, again, that relentless drum marks out solitude and drifting. Smith told Johnny Black for the liner notes to the album's re-release in 2005, that "I wanted it to be virtually unbearable," but instead the album proceeds with an inevitable force towards its conclusion. Like a good novel or a breath-taking movie, we couldn't wait to hear what the next chapter contained. On 'Cold', a deep, cello-like tone is even colder still, a chilling lyric of screaming.

And so to 'Pornography', the album's closing track. After the iced-silver of 'Cold' shimmers to a close, was redemption to hand? Clipped vocals in reverse and a chilly keyboard note introduced the track, the titanic and gloomy rhythms, keyboard sounds and disjointed guitar. "There was one particularly long row (with producer Thornally) over a guitar sound," Smith remembered for Johnny Black's liner notes. "He thought it was horrible ... and couldn't see that (that) was a good thing."

It was a remarkable, confounding release – one of the most significant albums, and one of the most consistently well-written song-cycles of the era. For the album sleeve and publicity shots the band wore specially designed masks. Robert described the concept to *Smash Hits* in May 1986. "We were photographed in Marilyn Monroe positions. It was supposed to be like Marilyn Monroe would have looked if she'd been left on her satin sheet for a number of years, decomposing." Now there's a cheery thought.

The *Fourteen Explicit Moments* tour kicked off in France on April 10. By the end of the year Smith admitted that he had "completely lost track of the central core of The Cure."

"We were cracking up," Robert told *Flexipop*. "So the people off-stage began to fall apart as well. Twenty-three people reverting to primitives is not a pretty sight; we were more like a rugby tour than a Cure tour ..." The number of gigs and the amount of travelling over the last two years had left Smith feeling like a "doddery old rock and roller" and this time around the schedule was drastically reduced. The Cure played fewer than fifty gigs over the entire year. UK dates occupied the band up to early May, and they headed back into Europe for the remainder of the month. If the psychological make-up of the band was getting messy, on Robert physically it was getting messier still: he had started painting lipstick around his eyes, and under the glare of stage lighting, as well as the sweat trickling down Robert's face so the lipstick would smear too. The effect – of blood dripping down – was startling.

Robert's appearance is one of the key traits of The Cure. It has merited almost as many column inches as his music over the years, and – like the loveable mop-top Beatle-cut or Ziggy's crimson bog-brush – has become almost a trade-mark for the band. The blend of make-up, lipstick and wild, ecstatic hair is so easily recognised but rarely copied to good effect elsewhere in rock. Early photos of Robert in the first incarnations of the band show a traditional, shiny-haired, almost schoolboy cut. This evolved into the spikey, punky, razor-cut look of the early Cure, before Robert's hair started to get longer and more straggly in the early-to-mid-Nineties (clearly influenced by Siouxsie's magnificent style). But where Siouxsie retained a very ordered appearance – sharp lips, clearly defined eyebrows – Robert has over the years allowed the lines of his lipstick and make-up to vary from blurred and smeared to neat and tidy, let his hair spike proudly or languish with abandon. In his forties at the time of writing, it impresses me that Robert has never cast the image aside. It may have evolved or changed over the years, but – like Alice Cooper – he has rarely allowed the mask to slip.

Back on that tour in the early Eighties, nobody appeared to fully understand the experience of watching this once so frisky, post-punk outfit wading now through deep, deep waters. Reviewing an early Brighton show, Richard Cook could not get to grips with the performance: "I found it impossible to distinguish lyric structure in the current Cure song cycle," he wrote in *NME*, but nevertheless recognised that something of note was on the boil: "By the time they reach Hammersmith there'll be few groups this live or this powerful." For *Melody Maker* a few weeks later, Steve Sutherland dismissed that May Day Hammersmith gig as "(senselessly) cyclical self-examination," while elsewhere another reviewer described the same gig as "a cross between a poor man's Human League and a bunch of Kraftwerk extras." *Sounds'* reviewer felt a "feeling of absurdity" as the crowd rushed to their feet when The Cure took the stage in Bristol. "Here we all stood like tombstones," the review continued, "… like extras in *Doctor Who*, hypnotised by this week's bad guy and unable to give up the illusion – trapped."

This was not your usual tour. "Me and Simon would jump into the audience and fight people. It was so out of character," Smith was to recall in *Mojo*. The decision to record and release *Pornography* so soon after the *Faith* tour was probably the worst decision the band could have made given the state of mind they were in, but these were the years when chart bands did not habitually leave four years between albums to soak up the Caribbean sun and search for that elusive bass sound. In 1982, bands still recorded singles that did not appear on their albums, rather than releasing every track as a single, and bands toured after every record was released to promote their product to a pre-MTV generation. This was the job description for would-be rock stars.

Another job description might have included 'must be prepared for in-house fights.' Right on cue, in a Strasburg bar,

Gallup and Smith amazed all present by going at one another hammer and tongue. "It was because of a misunderstanding," Robert told *Musikexpress* in Germany many years later. "Because we were dumb kids," was Gallup's reasoning. After two years of that it was inevitable that the climate within the band would change. After this extraordinary incident, the following morning both guys had quit the tour and quit the band, but Robert's father took matters in hand by turning his rock and roll son around and shoving him back onto the next flight back. Gallup rejoined the carnival too, but by the time they arrived in Brussels it was clear that Simon and Robert were not going to heal these wounds easily. "It got like when you really want to finish a chapter (in a book) but your eyes keep closing ..." Smith said of the whole tour. "I despaired about the whole business, being in a band, being involved in the music ..." So bad was the atmosphere, by the time the tour ended at that Belgian gig Smith insisted on playing the drums on stage for the first time in his life, Lol took to the (never-before-handled) bass and Gallup played the guitar. It was a holy fuck up, with a roadie shouting obscenities down the mic. A fight broke out on stage, and another in the audience. "I remember sitting in the dressing room thinking, 'Oh well – that's the end of the band then,'" Tolhurst told *Mojo*.

If increased favour in the singles chart might have helped the band stay together, it didn't show. 'Hanging Garden' fared better than before, reaching the more creditable heights of number thirty-four and staying around for a month in total. Of the accompanying video, Robert told Vicky Bogle in 1984 that "we got the two people who did Madness videos but it was a really awful video. They wanted to make us look serious, and we wanted them to make us look like Madness." It could quite easily have been the end of The Cure. By the close of the year the band had become – if it was anything at all – a duo.

And in interviews Smith was referring to The Cure in the past tense ...

Chapter 6: Darkness

Immediately after Brussells, The Cure limped home. It would be almost two years before Gallup and Smith worked together again. Contradictory sources suggest that Simon was sacked, others that he left of his own accord. Meanwhile, Lol decided to leave the drum stool and began taking keyboard lessons from "an old lady in Maida Vale." Smith and long-time girlfriend Mary disappeared from view on a camping holiday in the UK, while some magazines reported Smith to be very fragile. "It's important to me to have a sense of myself … outside of all of this, a sense of myself as a person not just a member of the group," Robert said. If the band was finished, what next? Over the years Smith has consistently referred to solo projects that he intends to fulfil outside of The Cure, and in July one such sideline appeared in the form of 'Lament'. A single-sided green flexi-disc released as a freebie with *Flexipop* magazine, Smith worked with Steve Severin on the track (another version without Severin appeared later in 1983 on *Japanese Whispers*) – evidence for the keen-eyed that maybe The Cure now existed in name only? The magazine had asked the band for an exclusive track, and promoted it as a Cure single, but the disc itself credited only Smith.

The summer drifted into autumn, and Parry – presumably as aware as anyone that his protégées were possibly disappearing into oblivion – asked 'The Cure' (ie. Robert and Lol) for a new single. The result was astonishing. 'Let's Go To Bed' is pure pop Cure. "When I took 'Let's Go to Bed' to Fiction and played it to them, it was like silence," Robert told Bill Crandall. "They looked at me, like, 'This is it. He's really lost it.' They said, 'You can't be serious. Your fans are gonna hate it.'" There was no sign of the gloom of the previous year, nor indeed of Gallup: Lol moved on to keyboards, session drummer Steve Goulding took Tolhurst's place behind the kit, and the two-some/three-some Cure made another attempt on the charts with as upbeat a number as they had ever released. Robert didn't see it as a Cure single – he would have preferred to release it under another name as Cult Hero had done, but admitted to journalists that he had let it go as a Cure single "to get major daytime radio play." "'Let's Go To Bed' was probably the only contrived record we ever made – and ever *will* make," he was to say later. "It was designed to completely break the mould of what The Cure had become, which I thought was very static and almost very stable. We've never acceded to business demands ... never really compromised our attitude to what we do."

True to form, the record made the mid-forties of the charts and then promptly wandered back to whence it had come. Robert was clearly under some pressure to deliver something in the name of The Cure. As he told *Flexipop*, "At first [the record company] respected me for not wanting to write hits, then they saw me as some kind of halfwit, and now they're trying to goad me by saying I can't do it anyway. I suppose I've let them get to me with 'Let's Go To Bed'. As you can see from the video, I don't take the song seriously and that's its saving grace. If I took it seriously, that would make it even more gross."

He also admitted at the time that if it somehow did get them into the top five he would have great pleasure in never attempting to get there again. "I don't despair about losing touch with The Cure. It's more despairing that I'll never attain the heights of a Bach or a Prokofiev," he said towards the end of the year. Despite the attempts to push The Cure (the single was released as a twelve-inch as well as a seven-inch single) nothing was moving – except on the west coast of America, where the record was a hit in California. The Tim Pope-directed video did little to help the single's progress other than to introduce the band to the man who would make some of the Eighties' best pop videos with them.

Meanwhile the bat-like wings of The Banshees began to open over Robert's head once more. Smith's friendship with Severin was firmly rooted since their Banshee-rescuing gigs. "The two groups that I aspired to be like were the Banshees and the Buzzcocks," he told *Uncut* in 2000. In 1982, he added the Bunnymen and New Order to that pairing. Tellingly, the bands he would play for did not seem – at that time – to include The Cure. Although under pressure to deliver Cure success, Smith accepted Severin's request that he join the live Banshees once again, after John McGeoch, who had replaced Smith in the Banshees after leaving Magazine, suffered health problems after a series of gigs in Spain.

"The reason why I joined (The Banshees) for a while was because I got fed up with being the singer in The Cure and nothing else," Smith told Ro Newton for *The Hit* in 1985. "But eventually I became frustrated because I couldn't have the same control over what they were doing." After appearing with them on BBC TV's *The Old Grey Whistle Test*, Robert joined the Banshees tour that opened in Birmingham, and which, through Glasgow and Edinburgh onwards, came into London's Hammersmith Odeon at the end of November. Prior to Robert's joining them, the Banshees had already seen off much of Europe and Japan, and it had been a punishing schedule already. Another TV appearance on *The Oxford Road Show* and an interview with Radio One's Peter Powell were dealt with in early December, and then off to Germany, Belgium, Holland and France. Two more dates at Hammersmith were played between Christmas and the New Year.

The tour headed out east after a break during January to Japan, where a feature in the magazine *Music Life* showed a handsome, winsome Smith staring into space. Then on to New Zealand and Australia. Robert was interviewed a number of times, and it appears that he considered himself a true-blue (black?) Banshee. Visually, Smith was certainly beginning to develop the look that would cement both him and The Cure in people's minds: clearly growing out to meet Siouxsie's electric busby, Robert's hair was longer and increasingly dishevelled, bearing a goth chic all of its own. Coming back to the UK in March after the last gig in Sydney, Robert was involved in a project to score a ballet. The concept resulted in the track 'Siamese Twins', featuring Tolhurst and

Severin and The Venomettes on backing vocals, who had joined The Banshees dates. Siouxsie and Budgie, meanwhile, set off on their own side-project, The Creatures, which would over the years produce some of their very best work and would rank for some time alongside The Banshees as a fabulous band. Elsewhere, Simon Gallup joined forces with Matthieu Hartley and formed a band called Cry which evolved into Fools Dance. Harshly criticised for their "Cure-like sound" but with a number of EPs and live gigs in the UK and Europe, the band retain a modest following even now, though of course Gallup was due to return to pastures Cure before long.

*

By 1983 there was clear water between the rush of new bands that had followed punk's first surge and the old wave that had been pure punk. Punk had hit Britain like a freight train. Since the heady days of The Osmonds, Bay City Rollers and glam, the UK media had almost forgotten its youth. Punk reminded everyone that there was an army of young people in London and the provinces who had a voice, a life-style and an ethos way beyond that of their parents' generation. Once punk hit, every newspaper in the land ran articles on the scene, increasing the profile of the 'movement' and claiming surges in their readership into the bargain.

By the early Eighties that same media was hungry for new styles to despise, celebrate, fete and deride. Out of punk came a number of movements: Oi, 2-Tone, new romanticism – a plethora of easily-defined, visible tribes, each of whom had its fair share of gurus ready to give column inches and pose for photographs. One of these was goth, with whom The Cure would be forever linked. Debates have run for many years over whether The Cure are, or indeed ever were, a goth band. Rarely does a reviewer or interviewer write on the subject without referring to the movement or using 'goth' as an adjective to describe The Cure. At the same time Robert has repeatedly denied that the band was ever goth at all. Goths themselves will either embrace the band or deny them a place in the goth canon according to the darkness of their own particular vision of what that perennially unfashionable subculture is about. So, to try and get to the bottom of what goth *is* about, it is necessary to go back in time.

The movement exists on different levels: music; fashion; lifestyle. 'Goth Rock' does not necessarily mean an abiding interest in Edgar Allen Poe, and dressing like Marilyn Manson doesn't mean you don't listen to Eminem or Nelly.

First of all – where does the word 'goth' come from? "Gothic" was largely a late-eighteenth century and Victorian concept of art – in particular literature, but equally applicable to architecture or painting – based upon a historic sense of the grandly medieval. The great gothic architecture of Europe – Notre Dame in Paris being the most notorious and perhaps the most fantastical – was part of the inspiration for writers such as Mary Shelley, Bram Stoker, Matthew Lewis, Edgar Allen Poe and others to create works of fiction defined by darkness and the grotesque. Sensational, melodramatic and above all *dark*, the gothic novel has remained one of the most popular formats in all of Western literature. In *Frankenstein* and *Dracula*, Mary Shelley and Bram Stoker created characters that have informed everyone from Darth Vader to Dave Vanian. Edgar Allen Poe's work – in particular *The Raven* – continues to influence writers and artists from all walks of life (see Lou Reed's album of the same name). *Dracula* has been made into more feature films than almost any other story (Andy Warhol's nickname 'Drella' defined him as half-Dracula, half-Cinderella). It was largely the movie representation of gothic that set the course for many bands and fans who adopted the term in future years: vampires, werewolves and hideous monsters from the crypt rarely appeared in the movies dressed like Barbie and singing like Doris Day. The children of the gothic night owe much to the atmospheric movies of Bela Lugosi and Lon Chaney Jr, and film makers still dig deep into the atmosphere of the gothic novel and the great gothic movies of the Thirties to create the darkness and unease of the modern horror movie.

Goth has its visual roots way back in rock and roll. If it was something new, it was born of something not so new: like most youth cultures it splintered partly from last year's model, and the model before that. Punk was a catalyst, but goth went right back to the Fifties and Sixties, before most of its leading lights were born. Like punk, it started out as much a fashion culture as a musical one. Deadpan make-up, spiked hair and mohawks, black leather and above all darkness. Stilettos or a pair of Doc Martens 1460s, all picked up from Symphony of Shadows in Kensington High Street, or charity shops, jumble sales: dyed, painted, cut. Torn, black denims, with fishnet showing through. Calf-length leather coats, velvet, lace and PVC, biker jackets, dark tattoos and eyeliner.

Darkness is, of course, the very shade that illuminates the corners of all great rock and roll. Way back in the fifties Elvis was initially considered dangerous: leather-clad and moody, his hair dyed black *á la* Tony Curtis and a whisper of make-up around the eyes. With songs about Lonely Street, desolation and heartache and a resolutely black image, Elvis – were he still with us – could claim "Uh-huh – I was the first goth rock and roller." Little Richard, who appropriated make-up from country blues singer Bill Wight, was another early rock and roller who developed in his image one of the visual basics of rock culture that became one of goth's key characteristics: an asexual use of make-up and adornment.

Leap on half a decade to the early Beatles in Hamburg: George Harrison just out of short trousers and Stuart Sutcliffe as cool and as beatnik as you could get. Part-Fifties rockers, part-arty poseurs, The Beatles – under the pre-Epstein influence of friends Jurgen Vollmer and Astrid Kirchherr – were distracted in black, echoes of Jimmy Dean and more than a little Brando. Dark, serious, leather-clad and very much lost in their own image world. Before the booze and the cakes filled out their chubby Liverpudlian cheeks, The Beatles in Germany were early, moody lords of their own pill-popping obscurity. Looking for visual role-models who defined 'dark and moody' the early Fabs were as cool as you could get.

Two Sixties bands laid down a template from which much of later goth culture was devised. Jim Morrison (born James Douglas Morrison, Melbourne, Florida in 1943) was a middle-class kid from a military family: intelligent, confident, restless and screwed up. Constantly relocating around the United States as his Navy-officer father moved with work, and living with his grandparents for a time, Morrison was a voracious reader, ploughing through Nietzsche, Rimbaud, Joyce and the Beat Poets, and was writing his own self-absorbed poetry by his teenage years. A fan of blues music, he wound up studying theatre at Florida State University before moving on again to study film at UCLA. Doped-up on Venice Beach, Morrison met the members of the band who would go on to form The Doors, namely Ray Manzarek, John Densmore and Robby Krieger. The Doors were possibly the first true goth band. With Morrison's obsession with poetic darkness, his wasted good looks and leather-clad snake-thin hips, and the band's 'like no-one else' sound, they were unique at the time. In a United States ever-troubled by Vietnam, and watching the dream of California pop turning sour, The Doors were a perfect alternative for deeper thinking pop fans. The fact is though that after a shimmering debut with 'Light My Fire' they never achieved a great deal musically. Great singles such as 'Riders On The Storm' and albums such as *LA Woman* were cut short by Jim's addictions to alcohol and drugs, and by the time of his Rimbaud-inspired move to Paris his days were running out. Jim Morrisson died a miserable death in a Paris bath tub in July 1971 leaving behind some awful poetry, some great records and an image to die for.

Meanwhile, on the other side of the nation, a bunch of leather-clad arty types were working under the aegis of painter Andy Warhol to create another enduring and mythical band equally able to lay claim to a branch on the family tree of goth.

Lou Reed met John Cale at Pickwick Records, where Reed was working as a songwriter. Reed has spoken as recently as the summer of 2005 of how becoming a songwriter was a natural progression from his deep love of music, and although his posting at Pickwick seems inappropriate in retrospect, it did get him his first foothold in the business. With Cale – who had come to the States from Wales in 1963 on a music scholarship, and who had been working with avant-garde composer John Cage – Reed formed a series of bands that quietly evolved into The Velvet Underground. Reed and Cale were joined by drummer Maureen Tucker and guitarist Sterling Morrison and – later – the German model and occasional movie star Nico. Under Warhol's guidance they became one of the most influential bands of the era. Once again the signs of early goth are there: dark, moody songs with esoteric lyrics often influenced by symbolism, erotica and sado-masochism; unusual instrumentation, with Tucker's drumming and Cale's viola being unique; a blackness to almost everything they did (an early song 'The Black Angel's Death Song' was responsible for their being fired from one of their earliest club residencies in New York); cool, leather gear. And shades.

In Lou Reed they had a genre-spanning leading light, the godfather of glam and the grandfather of punk and maybe the retired uncle of goth. With shining irony, his *Transformer* was one of the best and most-loved albums of the early Seventies while *Metal Machine Music* has been hailed one of the least accessible of all experimental pieces. Reed's influence can be heard in nearly all half-decent post-Velvet guitar bands, including all the punk bands who evolved into goth. But in Nico, their complicated, Teutonic, junkie-chanteuse, they had the genre's true maiden aunt.

Nico was a tragic figure in many respects, incredibly beautiful and seemingly doomed. The sometime lover of Alain Delon, Dylan, Jim Morrison and Brian Jones amongst others, she was born Christa Päffgen in Berlin in 1938. After modelling jobs in Germany, she appeared in Fellini's legendary movie *La Dolce Vita* in 1959, moving to New York in 1960. Her recordings with The Velvet Underground remain amongst the most loved of their work and demonstrate some of Reed's best songwriting exercises, in particular 'All Tomorrow's Parties', and 'Femme Fatale'. After the Velvets she started on a string of albums – *Chelsea Girls, The Marble Index, Desertshore, The End* – which define her goth credentials. Dark and troubling, instrumentally obscure (she preferred the harmonium as her instrument of torture) and tinged with Eastern influence, they are works of immense depth and well worthy of investigation. Sadly, she also started on a course of self-destruction via heroin and a life of small-time gigs around Europe to fund a prodigious habit. I remember watching her proudly at her harmonium in support of Buzzcocks in the late Seventies, singing Jim Morrison's 'The End' while being gobbed on by the front five rows of an audience of Cardiff punks. In later years she moved to Manchester, then a den of heroin availability, and her years there have been superbly chronicled in a book by her keyboard player James Young in *Songs They Never Play on the Radio*.

I lived around the corner from Nico at this time, and saw her play regularly in and around Manchester. Always funny (she would play 'Deutschland Uber Alles' in all seriousness, and beautifully, then denounce it as "a loooodicrous song"), she knocked out fantastic renditions of Bowie's 'Heroes' with her backing band The Blue Orchids, and would play all of her Lou Reed Velvets tracks, sometimes denouncing Lou as a fool, sometimes calling him her favourite-ever songwriter. She was tall, over six feet in her habitual biker boots, smelled of incense and unspoken other things, and dressed fabulously in dusty black rags, her dark, henna-streaked hair long down her shoulders. The dark side of the beauty of Julie Christie. Goth.

A few times I chatted with her at gigs, and bought her a drink on more than one occasion. The first time we met I was stood at a bus stop in the late-night Manchester rain, and she stepped out of a VW Beetle that had stopped opposite. I crossed the road and introduced myself as a fan.

"Hoooow deeeeed you recognise me?" she asked in her outrageously German drone. "You're fucking *NICO!*" I thought, but instead pulled out the copy of her recent single that I had been given by a friend the previous day, on the cover of which she was wearing exactly the same clothes in which she stood before me now. She laughed and disappeared into the night. In 1988 she died of a brain haemorrhage after falling from her bicycle in Ibiza. She was wonderful, though I think – from everyone who knew her well – impossible to deal with. Among the last to see her alive were the various members of New Order, on the island themselves, a little Manchester reunion in the sun. Ironically, they too have a story to tell in the birth of the goth tradition.

Before God cast his great shadow of gloom across the waters and created goth, other early motivators were already at work. David Bowie described his 1974 masterpiece *Diamond Dogs* as "gothic" at the time. Its sprawling, wonderful series of songs on side one – 'Sweet Thing', 'Candidate' and 'Sweet Thing (Reprise)' do, indeed, have a magnificent sense of gothic doom.

"*Diamond Dogs* was quite a key thing," says Paul Morley. "I think that all that was the seed of The Cure." Claustrophobic, outside the normal social mores, it is the tale of characters on the edge of society trying to find means of coping, of staying alive. The line "we'll buy some drugs and watch a band/and jump in the river, holding hands" carried a message of romantic, dark defiance to us all: it's our world, let's live in it as we will. "*Diamond Dogs* was almost ground zero (for goth)," said Morley. Bowie's own drug-addled darkness has been well-documented. Prodigious ingestion of cocaine and repeated attempts to escape its control led Bowie into some dark music and some of God's darkest corners. *Station To Station* was, in part, as glum as it gets, and after the soul-cleansing plastic soul of *Young Americans*, Bowie sought refuge in Berlin where he worked on two albums that again shone a narrow beam at the future that was goth rock: *Low* – solemn un-rock instrumentals – and *"Heroes"* (with its

Germanic lyrical style) were beacons to everyone coming out of punk. Bearing more Germanic influence in the electro-pop of much of both albums' songs, the records introduced many bands to the synthetic sounds of European pop and the drum beats of Kraftwerk and Can. The Cure were amongst many bands who by the early Eighties were experimenting – if not totally relying – upon synth-drum techniques in the studio.

Joy Division were one of the best of the bands to pick up the darkened torch of *Diamond Dogs, Low* and *'Heroes'* and run with it. Their world was deathly, cold, industrial and detached. The suicide of Ian Curtis unavoidably gave them a mystical level of notoriety. By the time the flag of goth was flying high from the turrets of Castle Rock, Curtis was long dead and of course New Order – born of the ashes of Joy Division – were the best contemporary electro pop band ... but by no means goths. But if Joy Division themselves were one of the first big indie bands rather than a purely goth band, musically they must be considered one of the early templates. The term 'gothic' was even used in a TV interview by manager Tony Wilson to describe them as far back as 1979. Jon Savage, the author of *England's Dreaming*, commented that "Joy Division were incredibly important because of their doomy, even suicidal lyrics against music that really rocked."

Writer Mick Mercer – a long-time advocate and supporter of all things truly gothic – was twenty-years-old when goth struck him like a lightening bolt. "Goth changed my life and I knew it straight away," says Mercer. "It was so obvious." Mick recalls seeing The Cure at The Marquee "(when) Robert Smith looked as though he was bunking off school. They were a really good, punky pop band," Mercer continues, "... and then they grew up. *Faith* and *Pornography* was a band growing up."

Visually, the scene grew out of punk organically. Siouxsie Sioux's astonishing appearance – at once aggressive and intimidating yet feminine and refined – is clearly the starting point of the true goth scene. Mick Mercer disputes whether The Banshees were a goth band in much the same way that he doubts The Cure's credentials, but visually there was quite obviously a link. "So many girls ripped off Siouxsie's image, which is understandable because it was a classic image," he says. "Not that many actually ripped off Robert Smith's image – they just said 'that's a goth image: look – he's been dragged through a hedge backwards, or fallen asleep at a party and someone's put lipstick on him.' And (as a result) people think 'that looks really gothic.' It's an iconic image with him because his face would always be quite blank."

Elsewhere, Dave Vanian of The Damned can lay claim to helping promote the early, vampiric, tombstone death look. Richard O'Brien's *The Rocky Horror Show* was fast becoming one of the world's most popular stage shows: camp, gothic melodrama of the highest order. Its own influence on the look of goth can't be overestimated either. Elsewhere, before Mike Mansfield's mini-drama videos turned Adam & the Ants into mainstream superstars, their early look was particularly influential around the live scene in London, all arty, death-like make-up and cheekbones to die for.

"That's where the first audience came from," Mick Mercer says of The Ants, recognising them as perhaps the very first goth reference. "It was the audience before the bands in many ways: they came from the Adam & The Ants audience." Mercer describes a gradual coalescence of groups into the earliest goth audiences: "Its not like all the audiences came from nowhere: (goth) came from the followers of quite a few bands." Gloria Mundi, a very shrill and theatrical band, were the first that Mercer himself identified as something special after the Ants. "If you showed somebody film of them, and said 'what genre do you think this band belonged to?' it would just be goth. With a noose hanging from the stage, looking like Victorian beggars – there's nothing else it could be."

Before Midge Ure would transport them – via a trip to 'Vienna' – to the top of the singles charts, Ultravox were another keen influence in the early scene. "I saw Ultravox when John Foxx was with them," recalls Mercer. "They were playing with Gloria Mundi. I thought this is just as exciting – but it was actually more vicious than any of the punk bands. The sheer venom that was coming off the guitarist was stunning – it created a different atmosphere completely. They were quite creepy, quite decadent, but also quite emotional. And that's the thing that goth always had – it's got this central emotional content: if it's not got that, it's not really goth."

Musically, the beginnings were equally varied. As The Banshees' appearance attracted attention, so their first album *The Scream* (November 1978) offered up a prototype sound that resurfaced quickly, washed even darker, on Joy Division's *Unknown Pleasures*. Hollowed-out rhythms took the place of chainsaw punk, the listener left alone to figure the landscape, not invited in for a pogo and a punch-up. While *The Scream* can also easily be classed as a punk album, and Joy Division were hardly goths themselves, it fell to Bauhaus to release the first records that yelled something new.

Bauhaus hailed from Northamptonshire, England, originally known as Bauhaus 1919. Vocalist Peter Murphy's performance on their first single, the wonderfully dark 'Bela Lugosi's Dead' was one of the first notably public goth dreams, recorded before the band were even two months old. The band played the song live in the club Heaven for the Bowie movie *The Hunger*, itself a goth reference point. Appealing to punks, Bowie-freaks, and everyone with an ear for the unusual, Bauhaus had great style and, in Murphy, a fantastic, iconic frontman. The band recorded four albums in four years, reaching number fifteen in the UK charts with a version of Bowie's 'Ziggy Stardust', a fab pastiche/homage to the most influential artist of their era. After disbanding in 1983, Murphy went on to join Dali's Car with Mick Karn of Japan, made a famous series of TV adverts for Maxell tapes, and developed a well-supported solo career. Murphy's high cheekbones, hollowed-out eyes and all-round spookiness were an important part of that early goth image, his vocals sufficiently nightly to once again help set the blueprint.

Murphy – like so many characters on the nascent scene – would later deny that the band were goths themselves. "Goth was a myth dreamt up by journalists sometime back in the Eighties," he told one interviewer, and still – in 2005 – he was claiming that Bauhaus was more glam than goth.

"Bauhaus were a goth band!" insists Mick Mercer. "They were basically dark, bleak and theatrical with one spotlight on them: you could not possibly have a less 'glam' glam band. (It was) just handy for them to bat away the goth tag when they realised it might be an impediment ... what surprises me more is that they haven't used it more to become really big again."

Murphy's claim that goth was the invention of journalists certainly carries some weight, and it can't be denied that many of the bands who have been associated with the genre have denied ever having been really involved, including, of course, The Cure. Labels are easily attached. Semantics and music do not make comfortable bedfellows. The Beatles can be said to have been the leading Merseybeat band, but they never (as far as I know) cut a commercial record within thirty miles of Liverpool. Likewise, The Stranglers were one of punk's leading lights, but had punk never dawned it is probable that their mix of pub rock and artful sidelong glances would have found them a market anywhere: they were not a 'punk' band *per se*.

The term 'goth' in the sense that it has become regularly used was probably coined in an interview with The Cult's singer, Ian Astbury. The dole queue became the favoured meeting place of Thatcher's lost children, and Brixton, south London, a den of cheap accommodation and arts activity. "Thatcher's Britain," said Ian Astbury in 1997, "was horrible and oppressive. Unemployment was very high, and it was very Orwellian... it was almost like the youth were in mourning." Sex Gang Children, a Brixton-based band, were among the early-Eighties groups of influence. Leader Andi Sex Gang's domicile was nicknamed 'Visigoth Towers' by the group of friends who congregated there. Andi himself nicknamed 'The Gothic Goblin', and his acolytes were grouped together under the affectionate nickname of 'goths'. It was Astbury, leader of Southern Death Cult, who referenced them as such in an interview with journalist David Dorrell. Dorrell, like so many others, is loathed to admit that he was to blame for goth. But inevitably the phrase stuck. "As a journalist," Dorrell said in 1997, "I noticed that the end of punk was starting to get darker." The increasing darkness of John Lydon's work with PiL, and the death of Ian Curtis were two instances that, according to Dorrell "allowed a vacuum to occur, into which all of these other bands scurried."

"Punk no longer resembled what they (people who had been involved since the start) had originally intended it to be," Astbury told *Details* in 1997. Goth was the opportunity for them to find a new platform of their own. "But people have been dressing like this for tens of thousand of years. Primal man used to take the ashes out of the fire and rub it in his eyes and hair to emulate a skull." "It's like a tribal mentality," Robert Smith agreed in the same article. "The Banshees used to give me so much grief about how I looked in The Cure – we were a raincoat band, but we were never goth."

As 'Di Fever' took over the media in the build-up to the Royal Wedding of Prince Charles and Lady Diana Spencer in summer 1981, so the Di-lookalikes of New Romanticism took over pop in their frilly big shirts and flicked-back hair. Duran Duran and Spandau Ballet were the leading lights, and, in their ever-hungry surge for publicity, courted the mainstream press with enormous success. Journalists were aware that youth culture had some new post-punk icons, and were keen to identify any other media-friendly movements where they could. The opening of a new Wednesday night club in London's Dean Street in 1982 opened the floodgates. Over time The Batcave moved around different venues in town – ironically sharing a venue with the New Romantics' hot spot Gossips, but was always a magnet for goths and other post-punks looking for something new. When it was based in

Leicester Square an army jeep was positioned at the bar. Initially Batcave nights were Bowie-orientated, glam affairs, but gradually the style gurus injected more leather and lace than glam rock, and members of all the emerging goth bands could be seen there regularly, including members of The Cure. The media picked up on the scene quickly, and a whole raft of new magazines and style papers – most notably *The Face* – began to glamorise and internationalise the look. "(Batcave) was run by Ollie Wisdon, who was in Specimen," Ian Astbury recalled in 1997. "It wasn't just this dark, deathrock club. Specimen was the house band and they were very dark ... like a Death Bowie."

Amongst the other bands that defined the early goth movement were Southern Death Cult. Originally from Bradford, Yorkshire, they joined Bauhaus on tour in 1983 before becoming Death Cult and – of course – ultimately *The Cult*. Sisters of Mercy built their audience up through the early Eighties, until their first album was released in 1984, evolving circuitously into The Mission (through former member and future goth icon, Wayne Hussey). Sex Gang Children, Gloria Mundi, Ausgang, UK Decay, Danse Society and ruralists such as And Also The Trees all had their part to play. As John Peel supported many of these bands on his radio show, helping develop their audience in the provinces, so The Batcave itself toured Britain, establishing goth outposts throughout the country's major cities. By the middle of the decade the style and the sound of goth had become recognised everywhere, and bands such as The Cure and All About Eve were easily tagged on to the culture, often reluctantly so. Mick Mercer won't accept that The Cure is a goth band: "It's not like any of the original goth bands would have been influenced by The Cure, because they were (all) forming their own bands and feeding off the energy of punk and bringing out their own ideas."

Punk had been an attempt to do something new: goth was a means to something newer. Inevitably, the influence of goth seeped into the mainstream just as punk had done, and a backlash of independent, clipped guitar, danceable bands rose against the indulgence of goth and goth-influenced rock. The wheel of pop fashion turned again, and goth became a watchword for indulgent fantasists, a solipsistic isolationism. If goth was pushed back underground in the UK, overseas it developed healthy audiences in Japan, Germany and the United States.

A number of people kept the flame alive. With goth back in the crypt, the culture was ripe for new growth. Mercer, who has over the years written extensively on goth culture, notes in his excellent 2002 publication *21st Century Goth* how many factions now exist within the culture. With pseudo-goths like Marilyn Manson reaching huge new audiences there has been a resurgence in goth culture over the first five years of the new Millennium. Bands such as Evanescence have promoted a gothic image and been hugely successful in terms of chart success. Mercer points to the fact that while this development pleases some, there are still thousands of old-fashioned goths who resent the popularisation of their cult and even those who resent his own writings for helping keep that flame alive.

Evanescence have declared themselves goths, but Manson has been defined as gothic by others who ought to know better. People like Nick Cave and bands like The Cure have been victims of the same fate, according to Mercer: "People want their lifestyle validated. There are no bands getting big that really tie in with goth, so they (the contemporary goth audience) just appropriate someone because it suits them ... What they want is someone who is quite arrogant and cocky, or really high-presence. So Marilyn Manson will do. The Cure are huge, have (an) enormous back-catalogue, and they're clearly a respected band, so that suits (the goth audience) as well ... it's obviously a need."

So what part do The Cure play in all this? Are they a goth band? Were they a goth band? Does it matter? Evidently, the answer to the last question is "of course not," but debate has been heated over the years as to their goth credentials. Certainly they retain an element of the goth audience.

One major goth website polled its readership in 2005, asking for votes for the all-time favourite goth band. The Cure won. This, on a website where all manner of things *newly* gothic are promoted and discussed. Clearly amongst that contemporary congregation there is still a great wave of goth affection for the band.

Mercer believes that the contemporary goth audience is quite far removed from the original template of the movement. "The problem is that if as many goths were as seriously into goth music as they profess to be, then the majority of the goth scene would be people in their thirties or older," he suggests. "And (that's) simply not the case. Goth is *still* probably eighteen to twenty-five-year olds. The majority of people are just passing through, and so they're not actually taking it that seriously – it's more of a lifestyle thing." The modern audience – for whom there is little or no real history of goth evident in the media – pick and choose according to their needs but without a clear understanding of the background. Marilyn Manson is Bowie-meets-Heavy-Metal, but there's enough goth paraphernalia around his image to add him to the nebulous contemporary goth culture.

There are many minor factions that distil the scene even further: "The blinkers come down in lots of little sub-genres," Mick Mercer says, as we discuss the similarity between the arguments over goth and those of our parents' generation over jazz. "They don't know what 'goth' is: people have said '(a particular music) is goth, I like it, and I don't really care.'" The fragmented cyber-goth and techno-goth scenes are, for Mick, not goth scenes at all. "Most goths who go to clubs (nowadays) probably rarely hear an actual goth band. They're listening to all this dance stuff, thinking yes – this is goth!" But they're wrong.

The Cure appear to have been tagged onto goth initially because of their association with The Banshees. Without that link they may have escaped the tag in those early days. If The Banshees were responsible for the initial visual aesthetic of goth then The Cure were simply alongside them – both spiritually and literally. While the rest of the band over the years have sported a variety of rock and roll hairstyles, Robert has taken his barnet on a rollercoaster ride of dishevelled excess. As his hair became longer and more vertically inclined, this one image has remained in people's minds. Siouxsie's hair was one of the first iconic goth images. Robert's looked similar, but was more eccentric, less aggressive, more achievable for copyists. More contemporary bands favour the long, straight-haired (*a la* Wayne Hussey) model, but I'm sure that if you stopped one hundred people in the street and asked for a hair style that defined the gothic look most (if they didn't just stare at you blindly and walk away) would cite Robert Smith.

The historic record doesn't remember The Cure as a goth band either. Photos of their early years portray a band clearly not long out of pure punk: school blazers, trainers, drainpipes. As the Eighties developed – by which time their reputation was becoming well established – there were endless colourful pop promo shoots done for the likes of *Record Mirror*. "You can't stylize history," said Robert in 1997. "If the photos show you wearing ... the accoutrements of goth, you're a goth band. The thing is – it never happened with The Cure. There are no photos." The Cure weren't a goth band. Period.

Mick Mercer believes that the reason why The Cure are still so big in the hearts of the gothic audience is a misreading of the fact that their audience across *all* genres of pop and rock is so huge. There are other genres, besides goth, the fans of which are also big Cure fans. Because The Cure became so huge, across all continents and over such a long period of time, there is quite possibly a bigger following in terms of actual numbers among – say – metal fans than amongst the goth audience, but no-one would claim they are actually a metal band. Likewise, music fans who do not follow a specific code, who have not adopted a lifestyle to ape their chosen music, are Cure fans simply because The Cure have made such fantastic pop singles. But The Cure are not defined as a pop group in the way Kajagoogoo or Wham! clearly were. It seems to me that The Cure became visible at the same time as goth bands did, and – like those goth bands – they were clearly different from what was considered mainstream at the time. They associated with bands who *were* influential in the goth movement, and because their lead singer had a hairstyle that fitted the bill, they became tagged on to the goth thing. And for me, that's all there is to say about whether the band were a goth band themselves.

"People find an empathy with The Cure," says Mick, "which a lot of people *should*. A lot of the lyrical concerns and musical atmospheres are similar to what goes on in goth ... (but) there's a lot of ignorance around. If people can't be bothered to look into what The Cure *are* and listen to what The Cure actually *say*, and work out that The Cure *aren't* a goth band, then that's where ignorance becomes stupidity."

Goth is on the outside looking in; darkness illuminated by scented candles; all tomorrow's parties when tomorrow never comes; mine, not yours, ours – not theirs. Goth is the radiant, bejewelled wasteland in the corner of a Pre-Raphaelite painting, the cold stasis of Celtic ritual sites abandoned in a modern world, the washing of the waves and the blowing of the trees through a dark winter window. The Cure, too, have sat outside pop's mainstream for ever, looking in whilst also looking out, lighting the way with pinpricks of light, not great searchlights in the sky. Between the bleak albums of despair and contraction are bejewelled gems of gorgeous colour and celebration. The Cure have inhabited their own private world for so long, in a way that few bands have ever done.

Today goth is whatever you want it to be: literature, photography, fashion design, jewellery, make-up, music, sculpture, poetry, erotica, witchcraft, clubs, interior design – the list is endless. Type 'goth' into *Google* and you will come up with nearly three million hits. Goth seems to get reborn every few years, before disappearing back into the crypt again: kind of appropriate for such a vampiric concept.

In 1997, Robert said "The goth scene has never been a part

of The Cure." I think that's true. The Cure were not then, nor are they currently a goth band. But, rightly or wrongly, The Cure have been a part of the goth scene in the minds and hearts of many of the people who have maintained it. On the main streets of London, Berlin, Seattle or Buenos Aires boys and girls walk with their heads held high and their blackened hair falling down their dusty black gear. Death-white faces squint bravely against the daytime sun, their leathers and fish-nets, their boots and belts, jangling in the breeze ...

You can guarantee that whether they are nearly twenty or pushing fifty, they will have a private little part of their blackened gothic hearts dedicated to The Cure.

Chapter 7: Glovecats

Back from more live commitments with The Banshees, Smith and Severin began to realise a project that had been bubbling under for some time. With The Banshees sidelined while Siouxsie and Budgie engineered the dawn of The Creatures in Hawaii, the remaining pair were in the studio from March onwards laying down tracks for what would become The Glove. The Cult Hero project aside, this was Robert's first true creative work outside of The Cure. The sessions lasted weeks, but only about five days were actually spent recording. The rest was spent partying – "an endless party to which we invited a succession of people," as Smith told Ro Newton a couple of years later. "It was like a station – once they got really out of it, they'd be moved on and the next batch brought in. In between all this we'd record a piece of piano or drum." The entire experience didn't help Robert's psyche at all. Severin described the period succinctly: "He just used to turn up on my doorstep, Friday night, with a crate of different beverages. We'd sit there making cocktails."

Overloaded, the pair kept the new project confined to the studio: "That's one reason why we're not going to play live," Severin explained in an interview with Paul Bursche at the time. "There's no way that we can hope to recreate some of those moments on stage. No way." The Glove were named after the sadistic, psychedelic character in The Beatles' *Yellow Submarine* cartoon, and while The Glove's album *Blue Sunshine* was named after a cult 1977 murder movie, in which the main character goes on an extended killing spree after ingesting too much of a drug of the same name, the title also suggests an ironic brighter side to *Yellow Submarine's* Blue Meanie characters. In fact many of the songs on the album were inspired by movies watched by the pair as they crawled home in the early hours of the morning, stuck a video in the machine and chilled out. In 1984 Smith admitted that *Blue Sunshine* was one film he had never actually seen, but was aware of its reputation. 'Sex-Eye-Makeup', for instance, was based upon Nic Roeg's 1980 movie *Bad Timing*, described at the time by its own distributors as "sick, sick, sick" (a movie of sexual obsession, rape and tracheotomy!) "The next day, of course, when we went in to record, the film would still be in our minds," said Severin. *Blue Sunshine* remained unreleased in America until 1990, when it was put out on CD by Rough Trade.

Spring, finally, brought some new life to the relatively static Cure. *The Oxford Road Show*, BBC 2's Manchester-based TV programme, requested a two-song session from the band, and Robert – by now a member of three groups – agreed. On board came Andy Anderson from Brilliant – he had also played with Hawkwind – who had been adding drums to *Blue Sunshine*, and Derek Thompson from SPK. Born on New Year's Day, 1951, Anderson was significantly older than the other members of the band, but fitted in immediately. The Cure agreed to appear on Peter Powell's show, and played two songs from *Pornography*. It appeared that to be back behind a microphone with The Cure was what Robert really needed to fire some kind of new focus in his career. While The Glove was no doubt a serious concern for Smith and Severin, at the same time it couldn't have had too much of a future while The Banshees and The Cure still pulled at its two members. Re-energised, after appearing on the programme it was decided that The Cure would go back into the studio.

The resultant single 'The Walk' was compared by some reviewers to New Order's seminal 'Blue Monday', which had been released in March. Produced by Steve Nye, who had recently worked on Japan's *Tin Drum*, the distinctive keyboard hook, however, strongly distinguishes The Cure single from that of New Order. The accompanying Tim Pope video showed Robert smeared with finger paint – artistically, of course. "(Pope) thought that we should be more surreal, and a little ... *disturbed*," Smith was to say. It was an original and gripping song.

At the beginning of July, while overseas with The Banshees,

Robert was called back to the UK as the single began to get serious airplay. Astonishingly, whereas the band's attempts at single success consistently got them only into the mid-forties chart placings, 'The Walk' was a big hit, even playlisted on Radio One. The band reluctantly aired the song on *Top Of The Pops* on its July release, the show introduced by the ever-supportive John Peel. Two weeks later they were on again, and the song eventually made it to number twelve, a major success aided by Tim Pope's witty and entertaining video. Fiction released a number of different formats for The Cure collector, including picture disk and twelve-inch versions. *Melody Maker* noted that the single proved "a timely reminder that, even off-beam, Smith still figures among our acutest sensory autobiographers."

"We had this agreement with our record company," Robert told *No. 1.* "If our single was a hit then we'd agree to do all the various things that it entails .... so we've had to do promotional work, and *Top Of The Pops* and so on." He continued, "I don't like doing any of those chores. I'd sooner be getting on with more important work." For the second appearance on *Top Of The Pops*, Robert had brought in *Faith* producer Phil Thornally on bass (Porl Thompson stood in on the first appearance). Robert talked to *Record Mirror* about the expected pressure from the record company to "follow through" with more commercial singles. Despite reservations about such talk, little did he know how much the next single would follow through!

At the end of the month the band – with Thornally and Anderson on board – convened for one of 1983's rare live appearances at the Elephant Fayre festival in Cornwall. They played 'secret' warm-up gigs in Bath and Bristol before the festival, which helped root the new boys into the band. *Melody Maker* reviewed the Elephant Fayre and noted that "the new recruits, drummer Andy Anderson and bassist Phil Thornally, have added a much needed zip and punch, which gives a freshness to the group that transcends the … cocoon of numbness that afflicts some Cure recordings." Writer Dave

Massey noted how the development of The Cure mirrored the process of Joy Division becoming New Order, and called them "a group at ease with themselves." Finally?

The gig was possibly the longest set the band had ever played, including tracks right back to *Three Imaginary Boys* f rom right across the career to date. Anderson's drumming and Thornally's "nervous" bass impressed Steve Sutherland for *Melody Maker*, but it was Smith, "flirting with disaster and coming through smiling" who impressed the most. Robert's work rate was increasing now that both The Cure and The Banshees pulled on his resources. Recording for The Banshees album *Hyena* was underway. The Glove's album was released in August, to mixed reviews. *Sounds* called it "a work of privilege" and "abject baloney." Dave McCullough, who had followed The Cure right from the beginning, went on to write that "Smith has either lost his mind, is having a privileged joke at his fans' expense, or drug abuse of the headier kind really has come into mode … Tiny Tim meets Magnus Pike." Jeanette Landray's vocals – Budgie's girlfriend joined them to avoid Robert's vocals sounding too much like The Cure – were also the subject of somewhat harsh criticism, as were the psychedelic, abstract lyrics. 'Like An Animal', the first single from the album released in August betrays a rather thin vocal from Landray, a fast moving, nervy track filled with keyboard and a bass line that *Trouser Press* described as "busy." Impressively, the song reached a creditable fifty two on the UK singles chart.

As if there wasn't enough to do, in August a handful of gigs took the new line-up Cure over to the States and Canada, and back to London for a session for Radio One's Kid Jensen. In America, Lol noted how the exposure on MTV enjoyed by 'Let's Go To Bed' had introduced screaming teenage girls to their gigs. MTV had been launched in 1981 to great success, but in 1983 – the era of The Cure's great leap forward – the station became available in Los Angeles and New York, and thus began a rapid increase in the influence it had over the music business.

MTV effectively broke bands like Duran Duran in the States, and a whole generation, from U2 to Prince and Madonna rode the MTV wave as it beamed increasingly sophisticated (and often increasingly naff) videos into the heartland of America.

Back in London on Kid Jensen's radio show, The Cure aired a new song, 'The Lovecats', which would become the next single. The Banshees took Robert overseas again in September, including gigs in Israel and at the Modena festival in Italy, while two dates back in London's Albert Hall were filmed and eventually released on the album *Nocturne*. Of the trip to Israel, Robert was to say later that he found the people there very defensive and closed: "You can ask for something in a shop and people will stare at you ... no reaction at all. I mean – I was there with the Banshees, and if they walked into anywhere they'd get *some* kind of reaction!" Also in September The Banshees released a wonderful version of The Beatles' 'Dear Prudence' as a single, putting extra pressure on Robert as he was forced into another *Top Of The Pops* appearance. Three bands, two singles, two albums, two tours, recording sessions ...

... and suddenly, a top ten hit. 'The Lovecats' changed everything for The Cure. From being an interesting band with a cult audience, to an intriguing band with a growing audience, they suddenly became a huge band with a screaming teen audience. Witty, absurd, irritating, catchy, singalong – 'The Lovecats' had everything that a hit single should have and more. It betrayed Smith's instinctively poppy nature, hidden long beneath the veneer of 'serious' Cure: "Even before The Cure," Robert said to Dutch magazine *Oor*, "I used to always write things like 'The Walk' or 'The Lovecats'. I just couldn't be bothered recording them. Why? Because it didn't meet our image," he said. For many established Cure fans 'The Walk' and 'Let's Go To Bed' had been poppy but not sufficiently different from their regular sound to really grab their hearts. 'The Lovecats', however, with its accompanying video, was sufficiently nuts to pull in the regular fans but also open the door to thousands of record buyers who had never heard the band but couldn't resist the single. It's not often that a song inspired by a novel and ostensibly about drowning kittens can be so effective!

'The Lovecats' merited three *Top Of The Pops* appearances over the coming weeks, during at least one of which Robert appeared to miss the words. The single reached number seven, and spent eleven weeks in the charts. From its jaunty, simplistic piano riff, squalling feline yelps, echoing claustrophobia and impossibly finger-clicking bass lines, it is an irresistible oddity. Keyboard stabs, gormless backing vocals: Robert's customary sob has a lightness of tone that is much more accessible than on previous singles. 'The Lovecats' is silly and quirky, it made you stop and turn the radio up or stop what you were doing to listen. And that hissing little chorus ... fantastic. The phrase 'The Lovecats' came from Patrick White's novel *The Cockatoos,* amongst Smith's current reading matter. "We put the love cats in a sack and threw them in the lake" goes the reference to the illegitimate kittys of the novel. Always ready to undermine his own efforts and achievements, Smith called the three singles up to 'The Lovecats' "fantasy" singles which "have got absolutely nothing to do with The Cure or with me. Except of course for the fact that I actually wrote them ... Usually I write about stuff that moves me, whereas these three singles are about nothing really. Especially 'Let's Go To Bed' ... I wrote that song to be the dumbest poppy tune ever!"

Ambivalent as usual, Robert tried to avoid publicity for 'The Lovecats' where he could. "In the UK, I cancelled virtually every interview, and turned down an offer from some primetime talk show," he told *Oor.* "The people at Polydor went crazy! Supposedly seven million people watch that show. But I don't want to be known as the guy who invented that catchy tune ... I have done way more and way better than that." "All the singles we've done are odd things we've thought of. Dumb singles. That's all we've done since *Pornography* – dumb singles," he told Pennie Smith for *NME.*

For some it was the single of the week, for others the single of the year, but 'The Lovecats' was the breakthrough that Chris Parry had for so long hoped The Cure would have. It remained their highest UK chart entry for six years and – despite the band's continuous ambivalence towards it over the years – remains a great pop record. As Smith told one journalist, "suddenly everything we did started to sell ..."

Chapter 8: Staring At The Sea

The compilation 'mini-album' *Japanese Whispers* was originally intended to make singles released in one market available in another via a different format. The record contained the A- and B-sides of the last three singles and was, on the back of 'The Lovecats', made available in the UK too. Smith was now clearly involved in an improbable quantity of music. Sessions for The Banshees' *Hyena* were becoming more and more protracted, and Smith's ability to be in the studio for the band at the right time was compromised by his increased interest in The Cure. Sessions for the next Cure album had started alongside *Hyena*, and yet Robert was obliged to go promote 'Swimming Horses', the new Banshees single.

"I ended up having a kind of breakdown," Smith told *Mojo* much later. "I used to do the Banshees' album at Eel Pie in Richmond, then travel out to Genetic Studios in Reading in a taxi. We were all staying in a pub, so I'd meet up with the others … I'd have a few drinks then go into the studio. We'd start recording at 2am. Someone would make a pot of magic mushroom tea. Then I'd go back to Eel Pie. I used to sleep in the taxi, so I'd have about four hours' sleep a day. I did that for about six weeks." While still officially living 'at home' in Crawley, Smith had now become a virtual itinerant, staying in whatever place he found himself when he needed to sleep. The perfectionist was increasingly demanding of himself. Chris Parry was particularly worried about his charge. As he told *Q* magazine's Robert Sandall in 1989, "(Those sessions were) a struggle. Robert looked terrible, puffy-faced, eyes bleary, sores on his lips. He was always listless. I was worried that he was going to have a heart attack … I told him after we'd finished, driving back home in the car, 'You know there are a finite number of records we can make in this way.'" Sandall reports that Robert took the warnings to heart.

After a session for Channel 4's *The Tube* in the New Year, and a *Top Of The Pops* appearance, The Banshees headed off into Europe, playing Lille, Rouen, Lyon and Paris in France, then following up in Italy at Bologna and Milan. Immediately before this, The Cure had played in Munich and Zurich and recorded sessions in London for Richard Skinner and Kid Jensen. A prodigious work load. With white bows in his increasingly deranged hair, blue eye shadow, red lips and a black business suit, Robert's presentation inevitably drew more and more attention. Germany's *Bravo* magazine described their effect on a Munich cab driver under the line "from die-hard punk to witty dance band," as their European profile continued to increase. With his buttoned-up oversize white shirts, rosaries and leather trousers, Robert cut a dashing figure – darker and more refined than any New Romantic, the look of The Cure nevertheless fitted well in mid-Eighties chart pop despite a lifestyle that could challenge the hardiest of rock bands.

While the Banshees gigs took Smith up to the end of March, dates for the forthcoming Cure tour were announced too – almost sixty gigs that would span the UK, Europe, Australasia and the United States. "Sometimes I feel I'm on a computer adventure game, with all these people moving me around on a gigantic chess board," he told Paul Bursche for *No 1* magazine. Bursche's article – conducted at one in the morning while Robert continued to flit between sessions – was under the title 'The Elusive Butterfly' – a perfect snapshot of Smith's chaotic lifestyle in early 1984. Bursche noted Robert's propensity to take on too much work while at the same time refusing to commit to it officially. The article analogised this with Robert's private life. Having been boyfriend to Mary Poole since his early teens he still, at the age of twenty five, felt no need to marry. "It doesn't make any difference to whether you love someone," he rightly pointed out. "It's just a form of security, and I like to shy away from security." Bursche noted that Smith's contracts with both Fiction Records and The Banshees were 'verbal' agreements. Robert spoke of The Cure not being 'a proper group' anymore, and of how he liked it that way: "I prefer commitments that are left unsaid."

'The Caterpillar', the follow-up to 'The Lovecats', was released in March, a track from the forthcoming album. Smith told Paul Bursche how he had tried to lose the 'whine' in his voice. "My voice is better than it was," he said, "but it's still a struggle to make it sound at all different." Certainly Robert seems richer in vocal on the track, which opens with the unnerving chaos of random piano arpeggios and his own absurd violin scrathes, but of course the track was instantly recognisable Cure. As the bass and drums come in so begins another breezy pop anthem: as different to 'The Lovecats' as it could be, but helplessly catchy stuff. Wonderful lyrics and funky backing vocals. Throughout the sessions for the new album, Robert had played many of the instruments himself, as Phil Thornally was in Australia working on the Duran Duran album *Seven And The Ragged Tiger* Smith played bass, bringing Porl Thompson back into the studio to play saxophone. He stayed. Lol was also credited with multi-instrumentation on the album, and Andy Anderson stayed on board on drums.

The tour opened in Newcastle late in April and ran through twelve dates in the UK, the most visible the band had been on the UK live scene in two years. As it plundered Europe the tour demonstrated that a new audience was discovering the band. Robert was concerned that new fans, lured in by the pop sheen of 'The Lovecats' would miss the point of what the band was about. *ME Sounds*, reviewing the Newcastle gig for their German readership, noted how "the girls pounce on Robert like a swarm of bees." While most British bees probably 'pounce' only rarely in comparison with their Teutonic cousins, it does give a clear indication of the teen-angst hordes taking the band to their hearts. Like Bowie in the early Seventies and – more presciently with the rise to the number one hit status of Culture Club a year or so before – something strange happens to an audience when its stars don make-up. The female teenage market takes Max Factor bands to its heart more than any other. Duran Duran, Japan and latterly Marilyn Manson: something happens with these bands where a clear use of make-up defines the image. Glam metal – taking over from the Deep Purple-inspired original heavy metal – had the same effect. Soften the hair up, slap a bit of eyeliner on, and the girls join the boys in the audience. There's a barrier of masculinity crossed, and – almost like finding a new doll to cuddle – an embracing. This was never more clear than when Boy George dolls were marketed – more than a quarter of a century on it will still cost you twenty bucks for such a treasure. And in Robert I am sure the same iconic embrace was at large.

NME reviewed the Glasgow gig, unhappy at what they saw as a cynical undertone to the band's performance. "When you really get down to it the most irritating thing about The Cure is that *they know*. They know they can afford to indulge themselves in nonsense … and still send the fans home happy …they've got a sense of humour but are so arrogant that the joke can only be on the ticket buying public," wrote Andrea Miller.

ME Sounds, who accompanied the band for the duration of the tour, noted that "half of England" seemed, if not obsessed by, then at least acutely aware of The Cure. 'The Black Devil' – the band's Volkswagen tour bus – carried them over to another gig in Brussells after three at Hammersmith Odeon. Then 6,500 French fans lit up the Zenith with their fag lighters during 'A Forest'. Following this, the band made its first trip to Italy, where a thousand Milanese fans stormed the gig early to escape a rainstorm, cancelling out the sound check. In Dusseldorf, where 800 locals had constituted the band's audience only two years before, now well over four thousand crammed into the Phillipshalle. Reviewing the Dutch gigs, *Oor* magazine in Holland noted that Robert was restless and introverted both on and off stage. His troubles weren't over yet.

In May the next album, entitled *The* Top, was released. The opening track 'Shake Dog Shake' enters on heavy duty drumming and phased, open-tuned guitar, with Smith's vocal stronger than ever before, a valiant, spitting rant. The track bears much of the flavour that would entertain Cure fans right up to their 2004 album *The Cure*. If the tales of Robert's health were to believed (he told one interviewer of how his skin had been peeling off during the *Top/Hyena* sessions) then he certainly seemed to have exorcised some of the demons here, with images of sick dogs, new blood, coughing, shaking and razor blades. Track two, 'Birdmad Girl' is lighter, poppy, annotated with piano and electric guitar. Lyrically though the song is no lighter, contrasting the passion and heat of the girl with flight. The track reminds the listener of The Associates in the backing vocals, a tightness in the drumming, and as it halts suddenly, there's a feeling of the opportunity of another single release from the album missed.

'Wailing Wall' ushered in with more abstract sonics, Fripp-like guitar surges and Levantine swirls, inspired by Robert's trip to Israel with The Banshees. As with 'Killing An Arab' so long ago, Robert appropriates sound textures from the culture of his subject, and intersperses them with Banshee-like rhythms and percussion. This is intriguing stuff – a long way from what new fans would have expected from The Cure of 'The Lovecats'. 'Give Me It', opening with a love cat howl, has the urgency of some of Bowie's work on *Lodger*, the drumming reminiscent of tracks such as 'Look Back In Anger', while Smith's guitar has a flavour of Fripp's flailing guitar work on Bowie's late Seventies albums. But lyrically, far from Bowie's dramatic crooning, 'Give It Me' is again loaded with hysteria, bile, panic and an unremitting abandon. 'Dressing Up' – a song about performance, according to *Cure News* in December 1990 – was originally marked out for The Glove, but Smith kept it for *The Top*. "I liked it too much," he told a journalist later. The song slows the pace of the album down, a mixture of keyboards in dreamy sequences and an uneasy pop rhythm. Robert wavers in and out of tune on this wistful and reflective track with its 'caught you napping' ending. Poor old Robert sounds almost deranged on 'Piggy In The Mirror', which follows the single 'Caterpillar', torn between grand-goth vocals and disturbed yelps.

The military snare beats and oblique, poetic lyrics of 'The Empty World' pull this strange little piece in different directions. If the percussion is reminiscent of Kate Bush's 'Army Dreamers' then the bass reminds me of her *Hounds Of Love* (still a year away). After 'Bananafishbones', its title inspired famously by JD Salinger's ensnaring short story 'A Perfect Day For Bananafish', the title track rounds off a strange collection of songs. Back in the gothic dark rooms of *Faith* for a few minutes, 'The Top' sounds more like 'The Cure of Old' than 'The Cure of The Future'. The guitar and bass sound deliberately – not inadvertently – turgid. Where the song sounds as though it may suddenly open up into a great swathe of chorus and tunefulness, Robert pulls it back to the claustrophobic opening. The lyrics, like so many of Smith's songs, hint at a short story never written. And is that a snatch of off-key Glen Miller towards the end?

Speaking to *Melody Maker* in 1989, Robert called the album "a muddled disappointment, largely compromised." His work rate and conditions of work were perhaps largely to blame: "I didn't have the mental strength to communicate what I wanted to anyone else … I was ill for months between *Pornography* and *The Top*." Smith later told journalist Bill Crandall that "when I listen back to the album, I have a strange image of me sitting in the middle of the studio floor surrounded by little bongos and spoons and things … it dented my confidence in that way of working, and I put a stop to it."

Nevertheless, the album was by far The Cure's biggest-selling original album to date. *Debrett's Peerage* – that yardstick of rock and roll excess – quoted world sales figures of Cure albums to date in 1991. Paul Gambaccini apparently nominated Smith for entry in the publication and Robert saw it as "the perfect Christmas present for my mum and dad!" Robert teased readers by listing his hobbies as deep-sea diving, hot-air ballooning and – more realistically – reading and writing. And "looking into space." The first album (including, somewhat misleadingly, the sales for *Boys Don't Cry* within the figure) was listed as having sold some 850,000 copies. *Seventeen Seconds'* sales fell to around 650k. *Faith* dropped another 100k, and it was only with *Pornography* – which sold over 800k that things rapidly improved. The mini *Japanese Whispers* sold over a million, and *The Top* sold almost one and three-quarter million copies worldwide: a significant achievement. But with a cost. Smith described the period after *The Top* as his only "serious breakdown." Something had to give.

Robert eventually cut his links with The Banshees. By early in the New Year The Cure tour had come to an end, having sprawled through Australasia, the Far East, America and Canada. Thornally and Anderson were out of the band. Vince Ely, late of the Psychedelic Furs, took up the drum sticks for the rest of the American dates, with Boris Williams, who had been working recently with The Thompson Twins, taking over again when Ely had other commitments to fulfil. Smith, having visited his doctor back in the UK, was given a sick note, which he used to serve two weeks' notice to Severin and Siouxsie. If The Cure were in some shape or form back on track, then he could no longer be slave to two high profile bands. An era came to a close for another incarnation of the band, and a new dawn beckoned for The Cure.

Elsewhere, in a cold and rainy land far, far away, The Smiths had taken on the mantle of Britain's most miserable group. Manchester's finest entertained half the nation, horrified the other half, and set the world alight for anyone with an ear for a finely strummed guitar line. A string of 1984 hits saw Morrissey & Co make the charts with 'What Difference Does It Make?', 'Heaven Knows I'm Miserable Now' and 'William It Was Really Nothing'. Perhaps a good time for The Cure to turn a corner?

*

Autumn 1984 saw the release of *Concert,* a live album set to counter the increasing trade in Cure bootlegs. It was the band's first live release, and was well-received by reviewers. *Sounds* described its "magnificent undertow" and pointed to the lyrical content of Smith's work as its key strength. "A vast factor in what attracts people to a (too big to be a) 'cult' such as The Cure," wrote Chris Roberts, "is *the words.* Why do so few of you grown-up music critics realise this?" The band spent four days mixing the album and – for the cassette version – included 'Curiosity', a selection of Smith-selected tracks from his collection of over 100 Cure gigs from way back when.

"How do you play *Monopoly* with a wizard?" asked *Zig Zag* journo Antonella in an early 1985 piece for the style mag. Antonella found Smith in excellent mood, part-Christopher Robin, part-Uncle Alfred from *Mary Poppins.* She garnered some of the best quotes out of Robert that any interviewer had to date. You have weird hands: "They're *murderer's* hands!" Do you believe in an afterlife? "Today I don't but yesterday I may have ... the idea of an afterlife is just as valid as the idea of a hot dinner – it all depends if you are hungry." Do drugs expand consciousness? "Drugs haven't changed my outlook on anything. But no one particular thing has ... all right. I admit it: my favourite drug is alcohol." Are you a pompous twat? "I'm not pompous at all." Have you ever been involved in bondage? "I'm open to all of these things but I've not really experimented much in the seamier side of sex." Robert comes across as a laid-back, intelligent, articulate, thoughtful man. Not the typical rock star, a dull breed whom the interviewer described as "garrulous tits mesmerized by their airbrushed reflections." Smith had spent a quiet Christmas at the end of the dreadful year of 1984, at least quiet by his standards. "I was in a coma over Christmas," he said. "After the party we had here." Over the yuletide season, Smith played games of bingo with Chris Parry.

The band did not tour until the second half of the next year.

Instead they did what they knew best: started work on yet another album. *The Head On The Door* sessions began in March at Angel studios, with the songs being written in a fortnight. This time Robert was interested in *pop songs*. He told *Uncut* in 2000 how suddenly The Cure felt "like a band" again, like The Beatles, and that he wanted to write catchy pop songs for them. Part of the reason was the return of Simon Gallup to the fold. "Someone had to make a start and say 'Hey – come on now,'" Simon told Germany's *Musikexpress* in 2003. "That was me," was Smith's retort. "Either one of us had to leave, or the band would have fallen apart ... everyone tried to see who could be thick-headed the longest." Gallup was genuinely moved by his return, and of course remains a member of the band still, twenty years on. "I was only in bands to pick up chicks," he laughed. "With The Cure it was suddenly about art." After eighteen months of not talking, Smith decided it was time to get his best friend back into his life, the pair meeting in a Crawley public house. Asked by an interviewer why he returned to the band, Gallup said simply, "we missed each other." "What had you been doing?" asked the US reporter in an interview published in a limited edition picture disk by Baktabak Records. "Drinking a lot!" replied Simon. "I'd been thinking about it for a long time," said Smith. "Because I was going to ask Simon if he wanted to join before Phil did, to do *The Top*, but I didn't think the time was right. It took another year of various nights out ..." Smith played a series of demos to Gallup back at his flat. "It was a bit like the first time around really, like *Seventeen Seconds* – I played the tape and said 'What do you think of these?' and Simon said 'I think they're really good,' and I said, 'How'd you like to play them on the record?'"

Simon was still a member of Fools Dance. "It would have seemed a bit horrible if I'd suddenly said, 'come and join The Cure,' 'cos I knew Simon would say 'yes'. So at first I said, 'We need a bass player to play on the record,' and then I said, 'What about doing a few concerts?' It's just gone on from there really."

It was auspicious that a pub should be the starting point. With drugs banned from the studio, *The Head On The Door* was an album lubricated by beer. The Cure was a hard act to be in, a hard race to run even at the best of times. Ignoring early-bird members like Peter O'Toole or Marc Ceccagno, in the eight years since signing for Hansa, Porl Thompson, Michael Dempsey, Matthieu Hartley, Andy Anderson, Phil Thornally and Simon Gallup had all fallen by the wayside, though several, of course, had not fallen far. When Simon returned, the band was a completely different entity to the one he had left. Porl was back, but they hadn't been in touch for years. Boris Williams, invited to join The Cure permanently at the end of the '84, was a virtual stranger.

Demo sessions started at F2, and the recording sessions were held at Islington's Angel and Shepherd's Bush's Townhouse studios, with mixing at Genetic, near Reading. "From Simon rejoining the band," Smith told *Record Collector* in 2004, "everything was recorded as a potential album track. So the quality definitely goes up." There was a more congenial atmosphere in the studios – Robert told one journalist that he realised it was time to grow up. "I knew that this was the band," he told Bill Crandall.

The sound of the new album would be much more commercial. The first release, the single 'Inbetween Days' was a sublime piece of guitar pop. "I wanted us to become more conspicuous," Robert told *Rolling Stone* in Mexico. "I suppose I liked the taste of glamour. I wanted to make a brilliant album, like the old Beatles records." Williams' drumming and Simon's uncomplicated but lyrical, joyous bass lines build a little bridge across which Robert's new acoustic guitar runs back and forth. I love 'Inbetween Days', it was a heady time for the lover of the well-strummed acoustic, with Johnny Marr's wonderful Smiths work and Roddy Frame's Aztec Camera doing the business, but 'Inbetween Days' is right up there as one of the most exuberant releases of the Eighties. The beautiful Tim Pope video featured the most expressive ultra-violet make-up, and Smith had to lip-sync the lyrics with his eyes shut for four hours. Asked about the increased optimism evident in The Cure's new material, Robert said, "(It's) always been there. I just find it easier to express it now in songs. I never used to be able to put any feelings of optimism or hope or anything into songs – it was always complete despair, even though my actual personality was always quite balanced – or as balanced as it is ..."

Unfortunately, The Cure still struggled to be stable for long. Tension was growing with long-time member and friend Lol. It was nearly always Robert that was interviewed, and nearly always the subject matter turned either to his sleeping, reading or writing habits. Tolhurst's drinking meant that his contribution to the album was much reduced. In *Mojo* in 2003, Lol himself talked about his lack of contribution with admirable and stark honesty: "I'd sit in the studio getting very upset at myself for not being able to play ... unfortunately, as I now know, the most likely thing that's going to happen is you're going to use that as an excuse to drink some more. By the time we got to *The Head On The Door*, it was not funny any more."

By summer The Cure were on tour again, now with a (relatively) stable, five-piece line-up. Simon's first gig in the new band was in Barcelona on June 20, and they then worked in Madrid, Roskilde and Hamburg before heading into Italy and on to their first Greek show. Venues were increasing as the audience did likewise. In the UK they now played Wembley Arena and Birmingham's NEC, and could officially be classed as a 'stadium band'. MTV continued to build the profile of the band in America as Pope's increasingly witty and atmospheric videos received more and more airplay, and as the band began their North American dates in October there was a genuine hunger among the native audience. Sessions for John Peel's radio show premiered songs from the new album back home, while plans were left open for the coming year. "I never think about what we're going to do until we've finished doing what we're doing," Robert told one radio interviewer. "So when we've finished in a couple of

Robert Smith, Torhout,
1981.

Lol Tolhurst
in the spotlight, 1981.

The Cure, 1984: Anderson, Tolhurst, Thompson, Smith.

Always a prolific touring band, here Smith writes
new material on the tour bus, 1986.

The Azzurro Pop Festival, 1987.

Robert Smith in 1989.

The hair at its most vertically challenging, 1992.

Classic Robert Smith, 1996.

In his element, 1997.

Alias Smith and Jones?
Robert and David, Meltdown Festival, London, 2002.

Robert and Simon on stage, 2004.

In Hollywood, 2004: Cooper, Gallup, Smith, O' Donnell and Bamonte.

Simon in the studio, 2004.

Robert Smith, The Cure and wishful thinking: recording *The Cure* in London, 2004.

weeks that'll be the end of *The Head On The Door* year, and then we can think about what we're going to do next. Maybe nothing – maybe I'll take a very long holiday."

The Cure weren't invited to play at Live Aid, incredibly – given the number of their evidently lesser contemporaries who were: Simple Minds, Howard Jones, Spandau Ballet, Nik Kershaw etc. For a different generation, it was Woodstock fever all over again. Like Woodstock, you were either at Live Aid or you remember where you were when you watched it. Paul McCartney recently remembered for the BBC his journey by car to Wembley Stadium, hearing the concert streaming out of what seemed like every household on that hot afternoon. But when Status Quo kicked the afternoon off on July 13, 1985, The Cure were in Milan, Italy. "We weren't asked – but we wouldn't have done it anyway," Robert told *The Face* in October. "If most of the people involved had given a percentage of their personal wealth, like the people who sent money in, then it would probably have doubled the overall total ... the best bit was Bob Dylan, Keith Richards and Ron Wood 'cos it was so embarrassing. It was humiliatingly bad in the extreme! They were brilliant, they were so awful!" While some careers were reignited by Live Aid (Queen, Quo) others were secured (Madonna). What would The Cure have done had they played their increasingly breezy hits in front of the whole world? If their career was really going places on July 12, 1985, would it by July 14 have gone in a different direction? I think Robert probably preferred it the way it was. Me too.

The Head On The Door was released in August to good, if not ecstatic reviews, its cover another sidelong glance into Robert Smith's private world. This time the subject of the gently obscure photograph was Janet, Robert's little sister. *Melody Maker* said "we don't know what to expect any more," and called Smith a "harmless, often hilarious eccentric." "Sometimes I think Smith could write songs like these *in* his sleep, not just *about* it," wrote Steve Sutherland in a witty piece. "*The Head On The Door* is perfection of sorts." For

Record Mirror the album was "beautiful and melodic," while *Smash Hits* noted "unusually brilliant pop songs." Chris Heath of *Smash Hits* joined the tour as it returned to the UK in September, finding Smith in good form. Football matches, tour-bus parties, Ribena and honey: it was rock and roll all the way as one of Robert's brothers' young sons bobbed around the bus. When fans who had shelled out hard-earned cash to see the band passed Smith without recognising him, Robert joked "Nobody thinks I'm me. But then I look less like me than most of the people coming to the concerts." Reviewing the Wembley gig on September 12, Donald McRae wrote for *NME* of "interminable stretches of especially dull mediocrity ... ended suddenly by a song which is sublime in both construction and execution." "No-one knows what to expect – I don't suppose anyone really cares actually," said the writer of the sublime songs himself. Notably, *The Head On The Door* was voted the critics' album of the year at *Melody Maker.*

The collection started with the resplendent 'Inbetween Days', surely one of the greatest opening tracks on any album. 'Kyoto Song' was an understated track with a lilting, Japanese-influenced hook, while the guitar that kicked off 'Blood' (and the articulate solo in the middle of the song) had a Spanish feel to its strumming, a Moorish flavour to the Eastern keyboard motif. 'Six Different Ways' was awash with gentle keyboard textures and jerky piano motifs, string figures and hooky little riffs throughout: a gentle piece that could have been a single release had there been room in the schedule to release it.

The Cure rocked out for one of their longest instrumental introductions on the up-tempo 'Push', with Robert's vocal chords stretching far and wide to accommodate a fantastic performance. There was a great live feel to the track, drums, bass and guitar heavy on the beat. 'Baby Screams', which followed kept the tempo up, and Smith's vocals were heavily echoed across a very new-wave piece built on running, familiar bass lines and unrelenting drum work.

Yet more Cure magic arrived in the form of September's single 'Close To Me', the seventh track on the album. Different again from the last singles, breathless panting introduces the simplest little organ and keyboard phrases ... but catchy? So catchy it got stuck on the way up the chart (only making a still-healthy number twenty-four), 'Close To Me' is another piece of perfectly arranged chart material: articulate, intriguing, fun, with stabs of horn and old-fashioned hand clap rhythms.

'A Night Like This' was a darker, more sober rocker, with a sax solo from Ron Howe – one of Robert's songs of dysfunctional love. 'Screw' was a looser but more edgy, nervy performance, reminiscent of other mid-Eighties chart acts like Blancmange. 'Sinking' changed the mood again, bass-driven, with resounding piano figures against broad keyboard washes, a grand song in the *Faith* tradition.

'Close To Me' was all over MTV in the States through autumn 1985 and the album outsold all previous US Cure releases to date to reach number 59 on the *Billboard* chart. The band's visual image became so instantly recognisable that Robert responded by cutting his hair short. Ironically, of course, this created even more publicity, and MTV included updates on the barnet business in their hourly news updates. Back home, *HOTD* made number seven in the album chart. France took The Cure to its heart perhaps more than any other country, and they retain a vast audience there to this day, but it was *The Head On The Door* that really broke them in that territory. According to *Debrett's*, the album sold half a million copies more than the previous best-selling Cure album *The Top*.

The tour took up much of the rest of the year, through Britain and the rest of the world. Robert became more and more playful with his interviewers. Variously, he was recording a selection of Frank Sinatra covers, had written an autobiography and was engaged in writing a collection of short stories. Audience size increased, as did Robert's hair, and, exponentially, that of the fans who started to ape the

Robert Smith look more and more. "I consider our fans to be my friends," Robert told Dutch magazine *Hitkrant*. "I like it when I can talk to them after a concert. But that's getting harder and harder." In the beginning, said Robert, there were five fans waiting. "Now there are five hundred of them. They don't expect us to behave like stars. I want to keep that personal contact alive. We've managed to make friends all over the world that way."

By spring the following year, the band had a number of new projects on board. First there was a re-recording and remix of 'Boys Don't Cry', which was re-released in April, this time reaching number twenty two. Still, the obvious number one single failed to really hit hard in the chart. The band played a Greenpeace benefit at London's Royal Albert Hall in April, after which they played at the Pink Pop festival in Holland.

Also in April, put together by Smith and Tim Pope, came *Staring At The Sea*, the band's first video compilation. The release was perfectly timed to coincide with the commercially successful previous year, and presented a neat timeline of the band. The Cure had grown up at the same rate that the pop video had evolved, so as their act becomes more sophisticated and articulate, so their representation on screen develops stylistically too. Pope had directed ten of the seventeen tracks included, and the 'extra bits' were provided by Smith and the band.

Staring At The Sea contains an interesting series of off-guard moments in the history of The Cure. The collection opens with the sounds of The Easy Cure warming up in the bandstand at Crawley, a summer's day with attendant teenagers and shoppers outside a local electric store, the footage shot by Alex Smith and showing the long-haired band in flares thrashing away for the people of West Sussex. Tim Pope's 1986 clip for 'Killing An Arab' features the character whose face is shown on the album sleeve, wandering the flat wastes of a snow and ice-bound seashore watching three unresolved horse riders approach. '10:15

Saturday Night' is a studio set 'live' affair directed by Piers Bedford in 1978 – simply showing the boys playing, focusing on little more than their fingers, drum sticks and volume knobs for dramatic effect.

'Boys Don't Cry' is similar in nature to 'Arab', as three school boys take the parts of the band members while the latter's silhouettes fall on the backdrop – Robert dancing enthusiastically in the background. Day-glo graphics punctuate the near-monotone set, The Cure's eyes highlighted with glowing orange spots – a perfect Pope repackage for a perfect song. For a few seconds we are back to grainy hand-held cine world, this time at 1979's Reading Festival, with Motorhead flags waving in the breeze and a general air of pogo and fist-punching in the pit below the stage. 'Jumping Someone Else's Train' is a low-budget affair, one of those 'camera stuck on the front of a train and speeded up' jobbies. High jinks in the tour bus (waiting to board a ferry to Europe?) and close-ups of Lol's unshaven chin – more home movies – lead us on to the more polished 'A Forest', another mixture of studio band performance and footage of … a forest. Robert's presentation to camera is classic early Cure though, emotionless, straight-faced plainsong, but the literal interpretation of the song is quite comical. We're still in the forest – an outdoor gig somewhere in Europe? – for the next clip of archive, which shows the threesome playing 'A Reflection' live.

More studio performance for 'Play For Today', straight to camera. Next we're on tour again – footage of the band grasping cartons of milk and duty free bags as they board a small prop-driven plane for another overseas trip. For 'Primary' the studio footage is more energetic than previously, but there are still endless cuts to fingers throbbing over chunky bass strings and cuts away from Lol's drum kit. Interspersed between are shots of children rummaging through a dressing up box, trying on clothes and hats. The band are conspicuously more 'made-up,' in the clip – lipstick, rouge and eyeliner: by the end of the video so are the laughing children.

Before 'Other Voices' we are back on the road with The Cure, presumably at one of the outdoor 'marquee' gigs in Holland in summer 1981 – very much a circus comes to town. Live footage betrays much drama in the lighting department: stark white lighting against a black set. The look is similar to Bowie's 1976 *Station To Station* tour, but front-of-stage up-lighting here eerily illuminates Robert's face. 'Other Voices' is again bestowed with more sophisticated direction, the set transformed with perspective-distorting graphic lines. As on that old Bowie tour, where the only coloured item on a totally black and white set (the band wore all black, David wore a white shirt) was Bowie's incredibly orange hair, so here the only colour really comes from Robert's crimson lipstick.

The next bit of home movie footage shows the band pushing one another around in wheelchairs, their pensionable knees covered in warm plaid blankets, until the majestic tones of 'Charlotte Sometimes' are ushered in. 'Charlotte' – looking like a teenage Catherine Zeta Jones – enters the school at the centre of the novel on which the song is based. If ever The Cure was gothic it was in this video directed by TV pop producer Mike Mansfield, which in tone recalls David Mallet and Bowie's 'Ashes To Ashes' clip. Yes, we have raincoats, yes we have sober expressions, pallid faces and big hair, but the setting is gothic in the same sense that Joy Division's *Closer* sleeve was: medieval imagery, burning candles, mullioned windows ... These themes are picked up immediately in the next track 'Hanging Garden', with its statuary and style. There's a wonderful literal quality to the video again.

'Let's Go To Bed' is splendid. It opens up with a couple of kooky out-takes, but then into a cartoon world of glorious gormlessness and artful dodging. More wonderfully literal interpretations abound. Fantastic. Equally so, but darker and more stylised is 'The Walk', paddling pools, the toys thrown out of the cot, a doll in a Japanese mask, Lol dancing frantically in a little black number straight out of Coco Chanel.

By the video for 'The Walk', the band had progressed visually from a hapless bunch of locals playing in the street to a hugely entertaining video-friendly act. The studio mugging – upright bass, fags dangling from lips over a set of studio vibes – that introduces the 'The Lovecats' video doesn't hint at the wonder about to follow. If you're a die-hard goth, a card-carrying Morrissey fan, a metal freak or a fan of Julio Iglesias, I defy you all to not smile at this wonderful concoction. Robert has always adopted a distracted air on video: he doesn't really care; he's bored; his mind is on other things – there's an air of this in virtually every clip on *Staring At The Sea* so far. But on 'The Lovecats' the mask is off – or, more likely a new mask is on – and Smith is openly funny, teasing the camera with little smiles and glances, throwing his eyes to the ceiling in despair at the campness of it all. Pale of skin, pink of lip, with eyes like Egyptian statues, he looks fantastic … so wonderfully, wonderfully, wonderfully pretty indeed. The rest of the band, including of course the trio of dead cats manfully being thrown around the set, are up for the ride too, and the needlessly Disney-like closing sequence, dressed up like Sylvester the cartoon cat, is just great.

'Caterpillar' is nuts too. Irresistible, after what we have just watched, not to smile gently again at the wobbling piano, smiling band, and daft backing vocals. If Madness have gone down in history as the greatest exponent of the 'entertaining-the-whole-family' pop video, then it's time to find a place just behind them for The Cure. Daft dancing, shirts buttoned up and hanging out, rouge, mascara and lipstick – where else would you want to be?

For those of us wanting to learn the chords to 'Inbetween Days', the next clip of home movie stuff shows Robert trying the song out on his out-of-tune acoustic: easy to pick up the shapes of the chords. Tim Pope's video animates the static studio work of the earlier videos, taking it to a new level of visual interest by strapping a camera to Simon's bass and having him spin around while playing – with Robert chasing behind at a leisurely trot in the background. If anyone who can only remember the purposeless stadium rock of Simple Minds, the inanity of Howard Jones and the cultured gloss of Sade tells you that the Eighties was a crap time for pop – show them this video. And the visual effect of Robert's day-glo face superimposed upon the monochrome shot is wonderful. And – famously – there are dancing socks too …

A weary, bleary, happy-looking Cure mug up frog-chorus-like in the next home movie clip, and the collection starts to wind down with 'Close To Me'. The keyboard lines played on a hair comb, a little menacing puppet show and claustrophobic camera angles make for another intriguing clip. It's only part-way into the song that the viewer realises the band are packed tight into a wardrobe, which is about to topple over the edge of Beachy Head – one of Britain's favourite spots for dramatic suicides. Cartoon capers continue as the wardrobe fills up with water provided by the local fire brigade.

More home movies from the recent Athens shows offer up a very different Cure to the one that began the tape over an hour earlier: a big rock band on stage in a big arena. Big hair, big white boots and a dark suit. The last official clip, 'A Night Like This', returns to more moody tones. Robert's nervous, insecure body language reminds us that – however many comic cuts for the teenage chart audience there might have been – this is a serious band with serious intent. Silhouettes of haunting trees mark the backcloth in a gloomy set. The image fades to black. For those who sat through the credits, a little reminder that 'hits' packages often signal a return to the holiday camp circuit for many bands was offered up by the teasing little question mark at the end of … 'The End?'

Surely not …?

Chapter 9: Kiss Me Quick

In May, 1986 the band's first hits package, *Standing On A Beach*, was released to accompany the video collection. Comprising the majority of their singles to date, there was also a cassette version featuring a similar selection of B-sides. The critical reaction to a decade of Cure releases was almost universally positive. Writing for *Star Hits*, Michael Small put his finger on one issue for the band. Once you present your work as a whole, can you escape the critical response to it in the future? "The only drawback to *Standing On A Beach*," wrote Small, "is the pressure it puts on The Cure. It will be hard for their next album to match the quality of this package." For so many bands the 'hits' compilation has been a means of wrapping up a contract with a record company before moving on. As The Cure's Polydor contract was up, and with several other major labels watching their next move with interest, it made sense to release a compilation.

The album had a major impact on the record-buying public. At the time the distinctive cover, showing the craggy features of fisherman 'Johnny Buttons' struck me as a deliberate riposte to the innocent child shown on U2's 1983 album *War*: one innocent and open, the other withering with experience. Johnny Black, who would later write liner notes for the band's re-release packages that began in spring 2005 called 'Let's Go To Bed' "the greatest single in the history of recorded music." Tom Hibbert was equally smitten: "The Cure remain impervious to criticism, they stand the test of time, they are voices for the Eighties ... etc ... You've probably heard them all before. And here they are again. Hurrah!" Writing for *Melody Maker*, long-time Cure-watcher Steve Sutherland compared Smith to Prince, "shy of the paraphernalia of celebrity, naturally suspicious of its so-called rewards," who "muddles up melodrama with whimsy, dreaming with waking, because *that's the way it is*." "A very great record," was Sutherland's summing up.

Smith was asked by one reviewer about his reaction to the

transition from cult band to stadium rockers. How had it been? "Slow but comfortable," Robert answered. "It's been just how we wanted it really – the same label, exactly the same people, it's just gradually got bigger in very manageable steps which we've controlled all the way along. So it's been good."

The album was the biggest-selling Cure release to date by a country mile, by 1991 having sold over two and a quarter million copies. Robert has talked in interviews about the g rowing audience of The Cure and of how he valued them all: "If one hundred people buy (a record) ... and four hundred join in just because they can dance to it, I would never make the value judgement that those hundred people are worth more than any hundred out of the four hundred." *Top of The Pops* provided a diversion in May. "I'm always bored (with things like *Top of The Pops)*" said Smith, "because just by their nature you have to be bored. You have to be either so desperate for success that you are willing to put up with being treated like an idiot, or you react in one of two ways ... boredom, or we just get drunk!"

In May the band headed out to Europe again for another series of dates. On board the Orient Express they were joined by a gaggle of rock journalists and filmed by the seminal BBC show *The Old Grey Whistle Test*. The whole affair turned into a mini-festival – the band's own newsletter claimed that everyone drank the Orient Express "a carriage shorter." The gig in Verona was cancelled and the band ran up an enormous bar bill coming in somewhere (according to Lol) between a thousand and two thousand pounds. According to Pat Gilbert's 1993 article for *Record Collector*, the whole jaunt may have cost about £15,000, but it did engender some ace publicity.

After demos for an album – called at this point *One Million Virgins* – were recorded in London, and following a string of dates in Germany the band headed for Glastonbury, where for the princely sum of £17 fans could see them alongside The Psychedelic Furs, The Pogues, The Housemartins, Madness,

The Waterboys, Go-Betweens, June Brides, The Nightingales, Dream Syndicate, Half Man Half Biscuit, Microdisney, Level 42, Fuzzbox, Billy Bragg, Simply Red and Ted Chippington ... not many of them still knocking about in 2005.

In America in July there was controversy when a fan clambered on stage and repeatedly stabbed himself, reportedly to the cheers of the crowd. The US gigs were generally received to rave reviews not suicide attempts, although *The New York Times* noted that "on its feet and willing to dance, (the crowd) would get started and then get frustrated again and again ... Mr Smith's misery doesn't thrive in company." During an interview for *Music Connection* in New York, Smith hinted that after the tour – which would go on to include Canada and a series of concerts in Spain and France – the band would be recording another album.

Playing gigs at Roman arenas and bull rings in southern France sounds like a cool thing to do, thus The Cure found themselves in just such venues in Beziers, Frejus and Orange as summer came to an end. The Orange date was famously filmed by Tim Pope and released the following year as *The Cure In Orange*. "It was really spontaneous," Robert told an interviewer in spring '97. "It looks like a Tim Pope film – a very strange live film ..." The band took a holiday in southern France and demo'd tracks in a studio in Draguinan, west of St Raphael, before moving again to actually record the album. Holed up at the hill-top Miraval studios in the south of France, surrounded by vineyards and olive groves, they recorded tracks quickly, and amassed a lot of material. According to Steve Sutherland they recorded a song a day. Lol returned home early after appearing with the rest of the band in make-up and dresses on the French TV show *Champs Elysees*.

Sessions largely complete, and with a new deal with Fiction and Polydor agreed by the turn of the year, Robert headed for even warmer climes in January. The album – now entitled *Kiss Me Kiss Me Kiss Me* rather than *One Million Virgins* – was taken over to Compass Point Studios in the Bahamas, with

Dave Allen to mix the tracks. Completed in Brussells in early 1987 the band then took to Eire for rehearsals for their first, ground-breaking tour of South America.

Dates started in the Ferro Carvil stadium in Buenos Aires in mid-March, followed by eight dates in Brazil, ending on April 2 in Sao Paolo. The band were trailed by the South American version of goths – 'darks' as they were known. "They do the top half properly," Smith told *Smash Hits*, "trying to get their hair right and wearing a black shirt. But then you look down and they've got Bermuda shorts and flip flops on ... but at least they're trying!" Robert talked of his surprise at the reaction the band received: "We knew that we sold records there but we weren't prepared for the bedlam that occurred (in Buenos Aires)," he told one interviewer. "It was really frightening." The Buenos Aires stadium with a capacity of 17,000, was full both nights running, though Robert had had doubts that the band could sell it out even once. There was a riot when disappointed fans couldn't get into the stadium, the local riot police were called to dampen the disquiet, police dogs were killed and a hot dog man suffered a heart attack, before the band delivered a blistering and nervous set. The second night saw more police in attendance, missiles being thrown around the audience and several officers having to take refuge under the stage.

Melody Maker published a hysterically funny three-week diary of the tour, penned by Robert himself, in May. The tour started off with games of 'Name That Tune' on Lol's "nauseating new Casio synth." The football stadium in Buenos Aires reminded Robert uncannily of his beloved Loftus Road. In the Gigantinho stadium, capacity 12,000, Smith described "the most overwhelming (heat and noise) that any of us have ever experienced in our lives." Winning the 'Best Overseas Act' award at the Brazilian Music Awards ("a garish neon statue that doesn't work") was an entertaining diversion, as was Porl's brother Andy being flown out by Polydor to go over artwork for the next album. For one gig, the rented tour bus packed up, and the band were given lifts to the venue by locals in a VW Beetle, a Ford Escort and a Mini.

'Why Can't I Be You?' was released in April, and in the round up of media interviews Robert talked about the promotional drag and the dates in South America, after eight dates in Brazil. "We have to keep getting up in the morning and flying to a diffe rent country," he said. "We don't have to – we are doing it through choice (but) it gets to be a bit of a pain." Of 'Why Can't I Be You?' Robert talked of its "double twist." "Some of the time I just wish I was other people," he told the press. "Not very often – just when I'm being pointed at too much, I wish I could disappear." The 'other meaning' was that fans would often tell Robert they wished they could be him – contrary to his own feelings that he wished he could be more inconspicuous. "It's not a very serious song," he concluded. "None of our pop songs are very serious – we save those for the albums."

In April The Cure were among the acts to appear on the last edition of the ground-breaking UK Channel 4 series *The Tube*. In the same month, *The Cure In Orange* was premiered at the Odeon cinema, Marble Arch in London. Orange (pronounced 'O-ronjh,' not as in the fruit) is one of southern France's most beautiful towns, its flavour and ambience more affected by the Romans than by the EEC: the Roman amphitheatre a perfect venue for a late summer evening rock concert. *The Cure In Orange* caught the band at the absolute top of their game. The first we see of the five-piece band is their bushy mop tops wandering in silhouette through the arches that Roman gladiators would have taken *en route* to the same a rena space that The Cure now entered. As they came onto the stage area, Simon reached forward and tugged tentatively at Robert's hair, only – on a second attempt – to pull off what turns out to be a wig and, as he tosses it away, Robert is shown to have a short, spikey cut.

'Shake Dog Shake' was the opening track, the band clouded in a mist of dry ice, dressed cool in black and white. Glancing left and right, Robert's performance recalled an insouciant

Pete Shelley, his early Buzzcocks idol. In 'Piggy In The Mirror' he gripped the microphone nervously, raising his fingertips to his temples Ziggy-like for the verses. From the start the audience was clearly trying to find a way to dance, and by the third track 'Play For Today' they got their chance. The sound of the film is superb, and the songs played are crystal clear and note perfect – perhaps as neatly presented, despite their increased complexity, as the early threesome Cure delivered their first material. Song after song was trotted out – 'A Strange Day', 'Primary', (a huge Gallic cheer for this) 'Kyoto Song', with Lol picking out the koto sound on keyboard. Singles 'Charlotte Sometimes' (Smith strangely emotional in its brief introduction) and 'Inbetween Days' are resplendent. Robert seems deeply involved in 'Charlotte', and 'Days' is gorgeous, as the lights dim and the night is really underway, dry ice drifting across the stage in great billowing clouds. After half an hour Robert put down his guitar, clutched the buttons of his jacket and the band left the stage for a break, returning for 'Close To Me', Smith dancing awkwardly in excited little jumps around the stage, tugging his mic lead behind him, laughing and mugging those grey-lined eyes to the ceiling. 'Let's Go To Bed' is introduced as "the last chance I'll ever get to learn to dance."

In all, twenty three songs made up the set, ending up on 'Killing An Arab'. 'Three Imaginary Boys' was jaunty, 'Boys Don't Cry' slower in pace than the single version. 'Give Me It' aggressive and all action, '10:15 Saturday Night' reggae-tinged and catchy as ever. Pope's direction is faultless: he shows the mechanics of film making as camera operators roam the stage; he gives only glimpses of the audience, who nevertheless appear to be in some seventh heaven; shots of the amphitheatre are equally discreet, but as the sun disappears from the velvet sky the setting is wonderfully dramatic. The lighting is stark black and white, but with spots of colour lightening the mood. The band are represented as a working unit, concentrated, serious, but rocking. There aren't many great live rock movies. Talking Heads' *Stop*

Making Sense had set a new benchmark in 1980. *The Cure In Orange* is a seriously good film: it doesn't dress the night's entertainment up in anything that it wasn't, and it reflects The Cure at their onstage finest. As the band leave the stage, the cameras drift into the darkness of the arena, up to the statue of Emperor Tiberius where the band congregate at a distance to the strains of The Chiffons' 'Sweet Talking Guy.' Sweet talking guys indeed …

*

Prior its to release, Smith described *Kiss Me Kiss Me Kiss Me* as "a very peculiar album." He also said, "It goes from Booker T & The MGs through to Chic, through to weird eastern music." The band decided to hold off touring until the album had been released to allow fans to get to know the material first. The Cure also wanted to get to know it better for the concert stage – they planned rehearsals for the tour in early summer and started to talk up a new line-up including Psychedelic Fur and ex-Thompson Twin Roger O'Donnell, who joined them in the three-week publicity tour that they undertook.

With the success of the hits compilation in America, in 1982 The Cure were on the verge of something very big. "Everything I'd ever dreamed of doing was coming to fruition," Robert told *Mojo* in 2000. "I suddenly realised that there were an infinite amount of things I could do with the band. Doing *Kiss Me* was probably the happiest time I've ever had."

Released on May 22, 1987, *Kiss Me Kiss Me Kiss Me* showed, appropriately, a close-up of Robert's now trademark red lips on the cover. In a later interview he would discuss his fascination with oral cavities further. "I do find mouths fascinating and kind of repulsive," he told Robert Sandall in *Q* magazine. "They're sort of like a … gaping wound in people! They can be really horrible. It's such an intimate part of your body and yet it's a multi-purpose opening, used for shovelling food and pouring drink into. I find myself sometimes with people I don't know just staring into their mouths." The mighty, double-album affair was the result of honing down a huge bagful of songs to the eighteen that finally made the cut. Opening 'The Kiss' is – according to an interview for *Star Hits*, in which Robert listed the inspirations for each of the songs on the album – "about me ... one of the very few mornings of the year when I've woken up and don't remember what I've done the night before." The track growls in aggressively: distorted guitar slides and heavy-duty d rumming. If the twelve-year-olds who had already bought 'Why Can't I Be You?' were expecting more of the same, then they had a shock, as it was four minutes before Smith's angry vocal yells at an imagined lover, images of death and poison abounding.

'Catch' – released in June as another single from the album – is more of what pop Cure fans would have wanted to find. Unbearably catchy "do-do-do-ed" from the distracted Robert vocal; thin, reedy keyboard sounds. Desperately romantic, lyrically beautiful. 'Catch' is one great song. And so dry, so funny, touching, refreshing, sad but gently joyful ... perfection. Robert himself summed it up perfectly as "a winsome, mystical love song." Dig out *Kiss Me* and play 'Catch' now. Then play it again. Winsome – that's the word. On 'Torture' Smith is back on the darker side of love – torture, darkness, enclosure, bodies cut and broken. The inspiration of the song was reported by some to be bondage – a particular fetish that Robert has categorically denied any interest in himself; his own explanation was that "it's about my preoccupation with the romantic idea of angels." 'If Only Tonight We Could Sleep' is gentler, eastern in flavour again, angels being the key imagery once more after the long instrumental introduction. Gothic, a *Paradise Lost* of economic proportions, the song has a note of hopefulness in its closing words.

'Why Can't I Be You?' is pure dance pop again. The first chart entry for a Cure single since the re-release of 'Boys

Don't Cry', it made it to number twenty-one in the UK. Smith's best strumming fingers are out on 'How Beautiful You Are', a New Order-like sound to one of his most lyrical songs. The clarity of the diction, the escape from symbolic imagery, the song is like a sixteenth century sonnet that offers a conundrum, proffers an answer to it, and then turns the whole argument on its head in a closing statement. The song is based upon a Baudelaire short story, and Robert described the song as "my favourite set of lyrics."

'The Snakepit' recounts what Smith called 'a bitter incident", adding in *Star Hits* that "the words are pretty clear. I was out in a car with a stupid girl." Smith described 'Hey You' as "the sort of thing you'd see if ... you'd had one drink too many." Immediately following is the gorgeous 'Just Like Heaven', a bitter-sweet track reminiscent of 'Inbetween Days' that Robert described as "a perfect single," and the video for which featured Robert's girlfriend Mary. On 'All I Want' Robert sounded like a sexed-up Billy McKenzie, a cry of passion, while 'Hot Hot Hot!!!' opens up with a quote from Charles Aznavour's classic 1974 hit 'She'. 'Hot Hot Hot!!!' was based upon *Earthfasts,* the trilogy of Arthurian novels by British writer William Mayne. The nearest The Cure get to rapping, the track nods to Chic, Talking Heads and Scottish masters of pop Orange Juice in its clipped guitar phrases and Dylan-like apocalyptic images. 'One More Time' pulls two ways, a juxtaposition of a need for release and escape into the sky with a yearning for security wrapped in the arms of another. Musically, the track is a stately piece, at moments funereal while at others beautiful and celebratory – Robert sounds emotional, fragile and on the other side of the safety fence.

'Like Cockatoos' is a dream-like sequence, simultaneously oblique and transparent in its imagery. 'Icing Sugar' is a tasty treat of indulgence, in which, after imaginary boys and boys that don't cry, we are offered a boy who is as empty as can be. A boy who had travelled a long way from home maybe? 'The Perfect Girl' is a simple, jaunty song of love, whereas

'A Thousand Hours' is a gentle, lilting track washed over with keyboard colour and soft guitar. The song belies the lyric, which is loaded with frustration and a sense of wasted time.

'Shiver and Shake' and 'Fight' round the collection off. The song was reported to reflect tensions between Smith and Tolhurst, and is a possible signifier that all was not well in the relationship. 'Fight' was The Cure's attempt to write a fist-punching call to arms, a note of positivism at the end of much self-examination, hatred, despair. "I thought there had to be a song that translates our pride in the album," Robert told journalist Doug Adamson. "That's 'Fight'. It's almost like a Big Country song ... I can just see our audience punching the air now!"

Kiss Me Kiss Me Kiss Me was met with rave reviews in the main. Smith himself told one reporter that he thought it "a million times better than *The Head On The Door* – much better than most of what we've done." *Pulse* described it as "an acquired taste coming from the best whiner in rock and roll." Betty Page, writing for *Record Mirror*, described how the album "steals styles, revamps old ones, has hippy bits, frivolous bits, dark bits ... (it) reminds me of Pink Floyd but always comes out with its credibility intact." *Sounds* called it "a brilliant plateau ... a double-album with very little baggage." For Steve Sutherland in *Melody Maker* it was the band's "richest, most exotic and most accessible album to date." As Pat Gilbert noted in his piece for *Record Collector* in September 1993, this was the first Cure album to lack a definitive, themed sound. The album was so varied that a backward glance at *Pornography* could be juxtaposed with the synthesizer pop of *The Top*. "We knew what we did best," Lol told Gilbert. "Some of the songs are parodies of other bands, some are parodies of The Cure. We felt a lot more comfortable as a band. After *Pornography* I think that *Kiss Me* is my favourite album."

Almost as a Christmas present to their enduring and growing fan base, the publication of *Ten Imaginary Years*, the band's official biography/autobiography was published by London's Zomba books in the fall. It was a lavish affair, credited to Steve Sutherland, Smith and Lydie Barbarian.

After appearances at the Montreux Pop Festival and a breeze through the Cannes Film Festival, July saw the band out on the road again, this time playing some sixty dates from Vancouver and Los Angeles to major stadium venues such as Madison Square Garden in the States. Dates across the breadth of Europe brought the band to Birmingham's NEC and the tour ended with three sell-out nights at London's Wembley Arena. 'Just Like Heaven' was released as a single, and *The Cure In Orange* finally released on video in November. The Cure was a now clearly a global phenomenon, getting bigger and bigger in the UK and USA, the biggest act in France, enormous in Holland, Germany, Belgium, Canada and South America. It would have been easy for Smith & Co to sit back and watch the money roll in, to hop around the tropical islands of the world and trot out pop fancies for the charts. By now though, any keen Cure observer would have noted that Robert repeatedly distanced himself from success. He never made a secret of his unease at the unavoidable clash between commerciality and art. So if everything in the Cure's garden appeared to be rosy, we had been warned …

Chapter 10: Disintegration

By the turn of the year, The Cure had been a touring and recording band for well over a decade. February 1988's release of 'Hot Hot Hot!!!' was the band's eighteenth official single release. Almost for the first time in ten years their work rate suddenly dropped: with few live shows booked, it was time for writing, reflection and rest. In April the Strange Fruit label finally released the early BBC Radio 1 Peel Sessions dating back to 1978. By the summer changes were afoot and the new album was beginning to take shape.

Most importantly for Robert, on August 13 he finally married his long-term girlfriend Mary Poole at Worth Abbey, the Benedictine monastery near Crawley where the young, tentative Malice had played dates back in the early days. The wedding was a private affair – only 150 guests – with Simon as Robert's best man, and the intrusion of fans and press kept at bay. Sporting a red rose on his lapel, a formal dinner suit and white trainers, Robert looked awfully dashing, and Mary wore a beautiful, traditional white wedding dress. *Star Hits* reported that the evening included a trad jazz band, and that Robert himself took control of the turntables for the disco. The couple were to move from their flat in London's Maida Vale to a new home on the south coast of England. Of Mary, Robert summed up their long relationship: "The thing is, we've known each other for so long that I don't have to finish saying things. It's got down to one word, and she knows what I am going to say!"

As well as appearing on the TV show *That Was Then, This is Now*, Robert began writing for the follow-up to *Kiss Me Kiss Me Kiss* Me. The process was intensely internal, often a personal affair rather than a band concept as *Kiss Me* had predominantly been. "At the time I was a very ... difficult person," he told a reporter later. If Robert descended into isolation, the rest of the band might have been forgiven for feeling a little confused. Were they rock superstars at last? Would the follow up to *Kiss Me* propel them even further into the pop stratosphere? The songs for the forthcoming album, to be called *Disintegration*, were clearly more in the mood of *Pornography* than 'Catch' or 'Just Like Heaven', and Smith was increasingly insular.

Yet again, it could well have been the end of The Cure. Robert told MTV that after making the album, and touring it later the following year, the band may well have folded there and then. The title *Disintegration* referred more to Robert's own feelings of interior dislocation than the disintegration of The Cure, and he told *The Face* about how he "wanted to be involved with something with a lot more depth, a lot of emotions, rather than something glib like *Kiss Me Kiss Me Kiss Me* ... this album is a return to the more atmospheric side of The Cure, which we've been neglecting for several years." By December the band had convened at Boris Williams' house and sessions were held at Outside studios in Berkshire, but matters concerning Tolhurst were coming to a head.

Major problems were at hand. Robert was no longer a school kid with a feisty pop band to promote: he was approaching thirty years of age, a married man and a businessman, alongside his role in an increasingly successful international band. The process of getting the new album together was, as he told one Italian newspaper, "a very private matter." The core discontentment was from people hoping Lol would contribute more. There are many reports in the media detailing Smith and Tolhurst's conflicting issues, but suffice to say by this point a sense of impending fracture was upon the band. The difficulty was exacerbated by the fact that they had known each other for so long. Further, Simon and Roger have both been quoted in magazines as saying they were also disappointed.

Shortly after the Christmas break, the prospect of Lol no longer being in The Cure was mooted. Neither side was happy with the situation and there were verbal volleys in the press. Unfortunately, with Lol no longer in The Cure, he would ultimately decide to sue in what was a lengthy and complicated case. Lengthy legal discussions and court activity resulted in the judge not accepting Lol's case. It seemed very unfortunate that after two decades of working together and being friends it had ended up in court, but rock and roll is littered with relationships that have fell apart in this fashion.

In an extensive 1991 interview for *Select* magazine, Robert spoke at length about the whole affair, which shed some light on the increasingly distant relationship they had shared: "From 1985 onwards I never had a conversation with (him) because we disagreed about virtually everything." [For more specific detail on the case, please refer to: *Mojo* August 2003 and a Benedetta Skrufff interview on Levinhurst, June 2004.] After the case, Tolhurst moved to Los Angeles. In 1999 he contacted Robert, and later Smith invited Lol over to meet with him on his forthcoming visit to LA, whereupon the pair spent a whole night talking together. "He's the person I've known longest in my life," said Lol. "(Things) are never going to be the way they were before, but our friendship is still there ... though it has evolved."

With water under the bridge, a new life in California, and a new band – Levinhurst – to occupy him, Lol looked back reflectively at the whole period. "It was a relief. I wasn't too well (physically and mentally)," he told Skrufff, "although the pain it brought was immense." Lol appeared genuinely at ease: "(It) brought me to the stage where I am today, and I have a funny feeling that (if it hadn't happened) I might actually be dead." Legal costs had been very high but there was no note of bitterness: " I was quite a wealthy man, but I was also very unhappy and miserable. Now I am no longer wealthy, but I am definitely a happier person."

*

Disintegration was the first Cure album to be conceived as a CD release and not a vinyl product. The first single, 'Lullaby', was put out just as news was starting to break of Lol's parting of the ways the band. It was the first Cure single in over a year and earned them another *Top Of The Pops* appearance. A pensive, darkly witty piece (Smith told Dutch magazine *Oor* that it was about "the fear of sleeping,") it was accompanied by a Tim Pope video vision of Robert being eaten by a giant spider, and became the highest chart position yet achieved by the band when it crept spider-like to number five in the charts.

Disintegration was released in May 1989, coinciding by chance with Lol's own marriage to girlfriend Lydia. Reviews were mixed. Giving the album three stars, *Q* magazine compared it unfavourably to *Kiss Me* and *The Head On The Door*, effectively marking it up as a Joy Division/New Order pastiche, its mood "a protracted wallow in the misery of love unrequited." In an accompanying article by Robert Sandall, Smith – just turned thirty years old – was referred to endearingly as a "dreamy, dozy melancholic." It was clear that the album bore more than a glance back to the sophisticated darkness of *Pornography*, and Polydor's initial reaction was that Robert had stepped two paces backwards instead of one forward. *The Chicago Tribune*, amongst others, compared the two albums, calling *Disintegration* "stately." "I thought it was my masterpiece," Robert said to *Uncut* in 2000. "They (the record company) thought it was shit." As is often the case, the artist was proved right, however. *Disintegration* was later voted 'Album of the Year' by *Melody Maker*. Robert told an American reporter that "there's only a couple of times ever in an artist's career where you reach a point where you think 'That's perfect. I couldn't do that any better.' *Disintegration* is one of those albums." Later he said "it made me feel very vindicated when people took to it, when it actually started to sell millions. The record company turned to me and said, 'See, we told you it was a fantastic album!'" Reaching number three in the UK album charts, it also ensured their entry in the US major league of bands.

'Plainsong' fires a shot of a cold love across the bows of the listener from the opening moments: icy keyboards and images of death and ageing, claustrophobic and dark. 'Pictures Of You' – released almost a year later as a single –

was described by *Q*'s reviewer as merely "well-crafted."
The song is wonderful, based upon Robert's experience of
destroying a great pile of old home movies, photographs and
documents in an attempt to clean up and break away from
the past. This catharsis is the root of the song. 'Closedown'
was equally spare, synthesizer, bass and guitar over Boris'
teutonic drum beats, but the track had a typically
Cure-romantic feel to its melodic line and Robert's sensitive
guitar phrases.

'Lovesong' – a wedding present to Mary – was a gorgeous
single release in August, a huge hit that finally 'broke' the
band big time in the States, where only Janet Jackson's 'Miss
You Much' kept it from the top of the charts (though oddly in
the UK it managed only number eighteen). As infectious as
'Catch', it bore some of that single's winsome longing, but
had a deeper, more yearning tone – a lovely song. 'Last
Dance' followed, another yearning, dark song with
uncomplicated keyboard washes introducing mighty-but-
simple bass lines and again Robert's aching guitar phrasing.
Across the whole album there is a gravity, an honesty. Robert
has been scathing on the subject of Bono and U2 over the
years, and the album is in no way similar to U2, but the
general air of gravitas throughout is reminiscent of the more
self-opinionated grandeur of the best of the Irish band,
without the air of self-importance and bluster. Smith's lyrical
approach is much more observing, detached, than Bono's and
carries a far more personal note, yet the musicianship
transferred to big venues in a live context as U2's would also.

'Lullaby' – described by Robert as "the sort of lullaby my
Dad used to sing" – came next, followed by 'Fascination
Street', a single for the US top forty on its release there in
April. Funkier by far than the rest of the album, the track is
an insistent, occasionally discordant piece loaded with
a repressed anger and suggested violence. 'Prayers For Rain'
picked up where 'Fascination Street' left off, hopeless and
reflective, cyclical and moody, the lyrics frustrated and irate.
On 'The Same Deep Water As You' the thunderous

atmosphere suggest that the prayers of the previous track have been answered. Romantic with a capital 'R' and gently disturbing, Robert's performance is longing again, maintaining the continued air of optimism against emotional odds that pervades the entire collection.

'Disintegration' took Robert something like ten attempts at the mic over ten sessions before he was happy with the result; according to one interview by Robert, "(It's) my scream against everything falling apart, and my right to quit with it when I want to," as he described it to one European interviewer. 'Homesick' is equally measured, a sombre blend of articulate guitar phrasing and a more sophisticated chord structure than elsewhere. Like most of the songs, the long instrumental introduction sets a very tangible mood – almost always of melancholy in some degree – which builds through each instrument adding a tone and a flavour to the mix before the vocal line confirms the mood. The set closes with the catchily named 'Untitled', another ultra-reflective opening to a song that brings a further note of optimism, of lyrical poppies amongst the carnage. If emotional inadequacy has been trawled to the very depths throughout the album, the song suggests that that search in itself has been the means of expression. If we cannot say what we mean, if we explain what we are trying to find then in some deeper way we a re expressing the truths we think inexpressible. The song is a beautifully simple coda to a staggering array of expressionism, conceived and executed with immense gravitas, emotional truth and tonal depth. It maintains an enormous sense of honesty and veracity: *Disintegration* is a fabulous album. "(It) will probably always be my favourite Cure album," Robert told *The Orange County Register* in 1997.

Although the album may have appeared sombre and dark to the hordes of new fans weaned on poppier themes, in fact much of *Disintegration* is distinctly positive in its conclusions: 'Lovesong', 'Fascination Street' and 'Lullaby' are all inherently optimistic songs. The tour that followed, with Shellyan Orphan in support, would bring huge audiences in to see the band perform songs from it, but Robert appeared less than comfortable with the whole idea of his increasing public profile. "I'm not aware of being successful when I'm sitting in my mum and dad's garden reading a book," Robert told a reporter from the *Boston Globe*. Keen to distance himself from his 'overnight' success in America, Robert declared that the tour for *Disintegration* would be the band's last. Speaking from his parent's house in Crawley, he told Richard Cromelin of the *LA Times* that "it's no big deal. I just don't feel comfortable any more with the kind of attention I am getting." Despite missing their ferry at the first attempt, the band travelled to Denmark for May Day 1989, and the Roskilde festival. The ensuing Prayer tour (apparently Simon observed that audiences might confuse them with Madonna!) took in nearly eighty gigs around the world, including cities such as Budapest and Ljubliana, the band's first outing behind the still extant Iron Curtain. Naming the tour 'Prayer' implied hope and optimism instead of 'disintegration', while it also glanced back to the seriousness of the *Faith* concept. The set, designed by LeRoy Bennett, was a lavish affair that brightened up the dour sonic landscape. After Germany, Holland, Switzerland, Austria, Greece, Italy, France, Spain and Portugal, then two July concerts in Dublin with All About Eve, The Cure were back in the UK for triumphant gigs in Glasgow and Birmingham. The European leg was wound up with three sell-out shows at London's Wembley Arena, including a nearly four-hour set on the last night. These shows were recorded for release on the *Entreat* album the following year.

The band travelled safely to America on the Queen Elizabeth II liner, opening the US leg of the tour at the Giant's stadium in New York on August 20. This time the audiences in America were bigger than they ever had been, thanks in particular to their profile on MTV, on whose *Video Music Awards* The Cure appeared in September. 30,000 tickets for the Giants' Stadium were sold *on the first day*. Robert claimed that the tour was 'a thank you' to the fans who by now had bought more copies of *Disintegration* than they had of even *Kiss Me Kiss Me Kiss Me*. If *Disintegration* had in part been almost an attempt to de-popularise the band, it hadn't worked! Seventy-thousand strong audiences in the States testified bluntly to that. The songs from *Disintegration* worked in large arenas too, with great swathes of guitar drifting over the heads of the crowd. "We throw in a few pop songs, and people forget where they are," Robert joked to one reporter. Because Robert was increasingly unhappy flying (he had come to the conclusion that being so high up in a metal box was nothing more than "absurd"), time restraints had to be imposed upon the tour. Large stadiums were the only way of accommodating the numbers of fans: "Because we refuse to fly, this tour has very finite start and stop points. We can't play two or three nights in one city. It's that simple."

As if on cue, after the tour Roger O'Donnell parted ways with the band, and The Cure's revolving door turned again (he would not be gone forever). The timeless excuse of 'musical differences' was blamed for his exit. The pressures of the tour – and inevitably the co-habiting that it forced upon the group – were enormous. "It was never our intention to become as big as this," Robert told *The Philadelphia Enquire r.* "Most bands that reach our position have a retinue of people trying to keep them propped up so that the money keeps rolling in. We don't have that."

"I left under difficult circumstances," Roger told *Q* magazine in 1996. "I'd decided I wanted a break from touring, and being in a group." Roger, of course, was happily not away for too long, in the interim period releasing *Gray Clouds Red Sky*, an excellent solo jazz project.

Back in the UK, a collection of Robert's lyrics under the title *Songwords* was published. The book was a resounding success: despite Robert's literary leanings and his willingness over the years to credit all the writers who had inspired his own work, his lyrics were often overlooked by reviewers entranced more by the group's atmospheric musical landscapes and overwhelming image. Smith has always, however, been an articulate and enthralling lyricist, as new readers of *Songwords* discovered, and one day hopefully someone will devote a book of this length to his status as one of rock music's finest and most intriguing writers.

1990 was a fairly quiet year for the band. In time for spring gigs, their guitar technician and – more importantly – friend, Perry Bamonte, joined to take on keyboard duties. Perry could have been glimpsed in the wings on *The Cure In Orange* video and it was his long connection with the band that prompted Robert to call him up. As The Cure remains one big evolving family, Perry told the story to one fan of how he was actually at Porl Thompson's house (Porl, of course, being married to Robert's sister!) when the invitation came. "How did it feel to play his first proper gig with the band?" the interviewer asked: "Imagine yourself to be a firework and someone just lit your paper ..." was his graphic reply. For the next fifteen years Perry would be a mainstay of the band, a favourite with many fans, and one of the longest-standing members of The Cure. Left-handed Perry, born of Italian stock in Basildon, Essex, attended the same school as Martin Gore of Depeche Mode, and there is a long and curious connection between them. Perry's brother Daryl made a similar move from technician to band member when he joined Depeche Mode on stage for gigs on the *Devotional* tour. Cure fans will know also, of course, that Daryl was later to come on board The Cure's management.

A new single, 'Pictures Of You', spent six weeks in the UK singles chart on its release in March, after another jolt of recognition pushed the band even further forward in the minds of the record-buying public. At the Brits award ceremony in London, the band won one of the increasingly prestigious awards, 'Lullaby' taking the gong for the 'Best Video'. The ceremony, held at the Dominion Theatre, was a relief following the debacle of the 1989 awards, famously hosted by Sam Fox and Mick Fleetwood. Fine Young Cannibals, Annie Lennox and Phil Collins (each taking two awards home) were among the winners alongside The Cure, and this year's token controversy came about when Premier Margaret Thatcher appeared on video espousing her favourite pop song: 'How Much Is That Doggy In The Window?' At least it wasn't 'The Lovecats'. As a result, The Cannibals returned their award in protest, but The Cure kept hold of theirs, turning up very smart in black suits.

Robert was also asked to guest as guitarist on the forthcoming album by All About Eve, *Touched By Jesus*. He had joined the group to listen to demos and taken the offer very seriously, but eventually had to decline. Responding to questions from a French interviewer it seemed as though the days when he could slip into The Banshees guitar role almost without thinking were well behind him. "I think I'd feel very nervous if I had to play with people I really admire," he told the fanzine.

Perry Bamonte played his first major concert with The Cure in Paris, at La Republique in late June of 1990. Two days later the band, now consisting of Perry, Robert, Simon, Porl and Boris Williams, played the Glastonbury Festival once again, in one of its more controversial years. The 1989 festival saw problems with the various elements of planning that have to be gone through to stage such a large festival, after the previous year's event had not taken place. Glastonbury was becoming a more and more complex event to stage, so hopes were high for the 1990 dates. Unfortunately the twentieth anniversary crowd watched as police and 'travellers' clashed after they were accused of looting the site: £50,000 of damage and over two hundred arrests were the result. For the second time in recent years, the following year's festival was abandoned as a result.

Alongside The Happy Mondays, Sinead O'Connor, World Party and others, The Cure's set was not an entirely happy one either. Robert described the organisation as "leaving an awful lot to be desired," blaming insufficient crash barriers for problems in the crowd. At one point a girl near the stage reportedly had to be revived with the kiss of life, and other reports tell of a helicopter having to land during 'Fascination

Street'. A very concerned Robert repeatedly asked the crowd to move back from the front of the stage, and at one point said, "we will just have to play slower songs so (you'll) fall back." The set, including much of *Disintegration*, also continued The Cure's reflections upon earlier exploits, with 'A Forest', 'Killing An Arab' and '10:15 Saturday Night' all finding places in the show.

After Glastonbury it was back into mainland Europe for festivals at Roskilde, Innsbruck, Leysin, Torhout, Werchter, Prague, Leipzig and Dresden. On August 11 the band wound up their relatively brief concert activity for the year, playing the first rock 'garden party' held at Crystal Palace, London, for ten years. Previous events had featured the likes of Pink Floyd, Lou Reed and The Beach Boys, while Madness had headlined the last one a decade earlier. The affair was marred by the band having a lily-strewn lake separating them from the audience, so that although the crowd could hear the fantastic (and long) set, they couldn't get up close and personal with the band.

Early September saw one of Robert's most audacious acts to date. In the run up to the release of *Mixed UP*, their 'new' album of remixes of established Cure songs, Robert, Chris Parry *et al* instituted Cure FM – a pirate radio station straight out of the Radio Caroline/Radio London pirate radio handbook. The station, set up in the Fiction offices, announced a few days before the big event, that at midnight on Friday Cure FM would broadcast the new album. The project was unluckily troubled with technical difficulties, but by the early hours the station was live and on the airwaves, playing remixes and the new single 'Never Enough', the one new song on the album. A month later, with a version of 'Close To Me' released as another single (both autumn singles reached number thirteen in the UK charts), the radio station – now dubbed Cure 102 – was on the air again, this time more successfully and with few of the teething troubles of the first attempt.

More extra-curricular activity saw The Cure tracks open

and close *Rubaiyat*, an all-star album promoting the fortieth birthday of the Elektra record label, to whom The Cure were signed in America. Later re-released on the *Join The Dots* compilation of B-sides and rarities, The Cure recorded a version of The Doors' 'Hello I Love You', whilst their own 'Inbetween Days' was covered by John Eddie. Elsewhere on the album the results were patchy – the wondrous Sugarcubes covered Sailcat's 'Motorcycle Mama', while The Kronos Quartet, Linda Ronstadt, Jackson Browne and The Happy Mondays were all involved. Smith said in the accompanying booklet to *Join The Dots* that he had originally planned – but canned – a solo acoustic version of Judy Collins' 'Pirate Ships', but that despite not liking the Doors much himself had chosen the track because it reminded him of The Kinks. *Mixed Up*, the much-vaunted album of remixes was released in November to a 'mixed up' reaction.

The concept of a remix album is an excellent one in that it offers a band the chance to plant the daisies on work already released. The Cure chose to pick and mix from their back catalogue for tracks to remix, and apart from that new single 'Never Enough', *Mixed Up* consists of an eclectic selection of recent songs and older material re-worked. Some of it worked better than other parts: the catchy, rhythmic treatment of 'Lullaby' is superb; contemporary shuffles lighten up 'Close To Me' with excellent effect; 'Lovesong' retains the lilting pace of the original, and the minimal, crystalline, and upbeat treatment of 'Fascination Street' is fine too; the claustrophobia of 'A Forest' seemed lost in the increased dance-ability of the track; and the new version of 'Inbetween Days' was not a crowd pleaser either.

In general however, given the nature of its content, *Mixed Up* did extremely well (it would inevitably under-perform in comparison to the sales of a new studio album) The album was a number one hit in the American 'Modern Rock' chart, and entered the *Billboard* 200 Chart at number fourteen, managing one place better in the UK album chart. For some fans the treatment was a defilement of their beloved favourites, while for other more open-minded ones the opportunity to hear variations on a favourite theme was welcomed with open arms. Coming so close on the back of the 'seriousness' of *Disintegration*, it was also a little ray of sunshine on Cure-world. Released on seven- and twelve-inch and on CD, the remix of 'Close To Me' in October was to be the band's last single release in almost two years.

Chapter 11: Wishful Thinking

1991, another year of consolidation rather than empire-building for the band, kicked off with sustained media attention on all things Smith and Cure. In January the band played their four live appearances of the entire year. Despite the clamour of the media and the fans for more Cure following the success of the *Prayer* tour and of *Disintegration* world-wide, this was all we got. The first date, after two days of rehearsals was a 'secret' gig at London's intimate Town & Country Club. In fact it was more of an 'open-secret' gig as the promotion for the event announced 'five imaginary boys.' The band played some old material ('10:15 Saturday Night', 'Arab', Boys Don't Cry', 'Three Imaginary Boys') songs from *Disintegration* and other recent albums. They also premiered new material such as 'Wendy Time' during the soundcheck (it would surface on their next album) and further delighted those present for the soundcheck with The Banshees' 'Mirage' and everyone's favourite Astrid Gilberto track 'Girl From Ipanema.' *NME* reviewed the show ecstatically: "The Cure were flamboyant and dizzying in their impact," wrote the reviewer, describing some of the numbers played as "reports from the knife-edge of unreality where dreams are shattered and helplessness rules." Robert Smith, concluded the magazine, "should be knighted."

Two days later, warmed up and ready for a big gig again, the band headlined The Great British Music Weekend at Wembley Arena in London. In attendance down the order (as The Cure's 'special guests') were current darlings Carter The Unstoppable Sex Machine (replacing The La's who were billed to appear), Ride, Jesus Jones, New Model Army and the redoubtable The Wedding Present. The band played a ten-song set (with 'Three Imaginary Boys', 'Boys Don't Cry' and 'Disintegration' for encores) to a huge wave of affection from the home crowd starved of live Cure since the previous year's appearance at Crystal Palace.

Within the week the activity continued with an appearance

on *The Jonathan Ross TV Show* and – the following day – The Cure filmed an acoustic set for one of the earliest *Unplugged* shows for MTV. Launched in 1989, the series of one-off, electricity-free concerts had become a fantastic stage for bands to promote various elements of themselves not always evident on disc or stage. The Cure demonstrated that behind the make-up and the grandeur was a band of fantastic song-writers whose material stood up to the pared-down nature of *Unplugged*'s all-seeing eye. The band sat around informally on cushions, their instruments including a toy piano and a xylophone. Alongside 'Lullaby', 'Just Like Heaven' and other favourites, the audience were also treated to a new song – 'A Letter To Elise', based upon Kafka's 'Letters to Felice' – and Nick Drake's emotionally draining beauty 'Time Has Told Me'.

Early in February the band were invited to play at The Brit awards. Unaware of whether they were there as winners or not, the band chose to perform 'Never Enough' at the show. As the envelope for the winner of the 'Best British Group' award was opened by Roger Daltrey, The Who singer confessed that he had feared the award might go to a sampler and a drum machine. Relieved, he announced "as it happens the winner is The Cure." After so many years, the band were finally acknowledged by the record industry in their homeland.

*

Typically, just as The Cure and Robert Smith were being accepted into the establishment of the UK, the eyes of the music world were scanning nearly six thousand miles away, to the Pacific north-west coast of America and a new era-defining phenomenon: grunge. Throughout the 1980s, trends in pop music changed radically, from punk to funk and almost back again. By the second half of that decade a new generation of bands – largely from the USA and influenced both by punk and heavy metal – coalesced into what became defined as 'grunge' (a word coined by *Melody Maker* writer Everett True). Mudhoney, Pearl Jam, Soundgarden, Green River, Nirvana: most of the bands had the sharpness of punk, the passion of heavy metal guitar, bass and drums, and a fuck-you attitude that mirrored their punk roots. Within what seemed like a few short months, grunge took over the world, reshaped playlists, MTV schedules, record company policy, radio programming, venue bookings ... everything.

Since those years, abruptly curtailed by Cobain' suicide in 1994, almost everything to do with music has been defined in the context of being 'before' or 'after' grunge. Britpop was a reaction against it, nu-metal a bastard child of it and so on. Any band that has been around for as long as The Cure inevitably begs being placed within some contemporary context when genres as pivotal as grunge emerge. However, for a band like The Cure, grunge was a blessing and a curse: another movement into which they didn't fit, another example of how they lived outside of any movement in pop and subsisted entirely within their own world. Nirvana's genre-defining and genre-breaking hit album *Nevermind,* is indiscernible in The Cure's output that followed it. While the rest of the world trawled the newspapers for Kurt and Courtney's latest misdemeanours, Nirvana were nowhere evident in Robert's world. Somewhere between Kurt Cobain's poppish take on punk and The Cure's post-punk, heavier works, there is a grey area where grunge and Cure might have shook hands stylistically. It never quite happened.

*

The live album, *Entreat* was released and the group decided to donate all their royalties to charities. Less charitable were some of the reviewers. Whilst admitting its strong points ('Prayers For Rain', 'Homesick', and several of the tracks individually) *Sounds* bemoaned the lack of the "pop warmth" of 'Lullaby' and 'Lovesong', and felt the album barely escaped the category of "shabby, perfunctory live recordings." That was unfair criticism – live albums are a record of a complete concert experience, and a huge part of that experience is the audience's responses and reactions within the venue at a given moment. The opportunities to overdub and remix are not always available in producing a live album, and so the album ought really to be considered a document of an event rather than a complete artistic statement in itself. If people wanted that they could always go back to *Disintegration*.

In the summer, another video release completed the comprehensive availability of The Cure's video collection to date. This time *Picture Show* presented a complete Tim Pope collection, with extras added by Robert and Tim between tracks. If ever a relationship between a director, a songwriter and a band worked, *Picture Show* proved that this was it. First up on the collection of ten clips was the twelve-inch version of 'Why Can't I Be You?' In the introduction Robert joked how the band "wanted to be Five Star" – a family of hyperactive pop stars, as light and fluffy as candy floss but with some catchy singles under their belts. The Five Star Cure dance outrageously, hysterically, wonderfully, in a range of costumes from Robert's own fluffy cat suit to kilts, Dracula costumes and sports gear. The whole experience is fantastic, a cross between The Village People, Madness and *The Magic Roundabout*, with the great dancing lips from the *Kiss Me* sleeve in evidence everywhere. Snuck in are extras, including a piece from the French TV show *Champs Elysees*, on which the band had appeared in drag. After the mayhem came the gentle and touching 'Catch', a touch of Mediterranean gothic luxury in the sun: stylish and perfect. For the extended version of 'Hot Hot Hot!!!' the short haired, shades-wearing Smith looks like the cooler cousin of Suggs, dancing with and amongst a series of bizarre puppets. Robert's dancing is great – his bottom half shuffles in style, while his hands are constantly drawn up and down from his face by insecure or surprised gestures, while every so often he throws a graceful rock and roll pose.

So far the selection was a collection of much more sophisticated material than *Staring At The Sea,* the band's last video compilation. 'Just Like Heaven' followed some tour bus and soundcheck footage: fresh fruit, stuffed toys, keyboards and friends in evidence too. The clip for 'Just Like Heaven' picked up the momentum, a glorious pop song and a band performance for the camera that focused on Robert's romantic side: crashing waves, moody darkened clouds, Byronic breezes in Robert's hair and a lovely scene where he dances with a wedding-dressed Mary.

'Lullaby' is the subject of the brief bit of banter between tracks. A stripey-pyjama'd Smith lies in bed as the rest of the band – dressed in French military costumes – play beneath wreaths of ancient spider webs. The video was truly one of the most macabre, inventive and oddly surrealistic examples of the genre ever, a mixture of part-horror tale, part-Buster Keaton; as Robert slowly disappeared between the mandibles of the giant hairy spider the effect was truly creepy. Concert footage and backstage home-movie stuff led on to 'Fascination', said to be one of Robert's least favourite Pope videos. The clip was a pretty literal rendition of the song in a studio set, images fading one into to another of Robert, guitars, drums …

Rehearsals and setting up the 'Lovesong' clip ("Boris – you should be looking at a camera left as well – which is your right-hand side") introduced the gorgeous track itself. The set was a claustrophobic, beautifully-lit underground cavern of stalactites and stalagmites, Robert lip-synching while the band plays along in the background. Reflections shimmered, waterfalls pattered around in the background, and Robert looked great. Roger's home movie shots before 'Pictures Of You' includes footage inside the band's MPV, pool games and snowball fights as The Cure and crew braved the elements in the making of the video itself. Robert hams along to 'Hello I Love You' and Bruno the roadie dresses as a polar bear. The video itself included palm trees that had sprung up in the snow. Robert hugged himself in a thick quilted jacket and white gloves, his pallid face as white as the snow in the background. The snow blew across the set, the palm trees arched in the wind as the whole scene darkened around the lights that illuminated the scene. Naturally, with the wind howling like an out-take from *Scott Of The Antarctic*, the whole thing descends into a snowball fight.

In a short bit of banter between 'Pictures Of You' and 'Never Enough' the band sat on the drum riser, strangled Chris 'Bill' Parry, and discussed their favourite tracks and videos. They settled on 'Never Enough' because "that's the one that's got us all in!" The clip faded into the voice of Chris Parry introducing the track itself – another macabre, *Alice In Wonderland*-like affair, the gigantic band crammed into a tiny, perspective-defying theatre stage. Like performers in some Edwardian end-of-the-pier show, Robert appeared more panda-eyed than ever, crawling to a trap door only to tumble towards the waves below before dangling precariously upside down. Before 'Close To Me' closed the collection, live footage of the band at a variety of venues, lugging gear around at soundchecks, communing with donkeys and broadcasting from the Fiction offices on Cure FM gave further glimpses of the inner life of the band. 'Close To Me' was, of course, one of the band's best-known videos with the aforementioned the wardrobe falling from Beachy Head, the plastic ducks and giant octopus, plus Robert's wonderfully florid shirt!

Picture Show allowed a secret little door to be opened into the world of the band, allowing them to work quietly away on the next project, and was the band's last official release of the year.

1992 was another pivotal year for the band. If the success of their work to date suggested that they had reached a high point, there was more to come. Early signs of new material came in the form of the March release of 'High', a single from the forthcoming album *Wish*. 'High' was a melodic, guitar-driven ballad in the mould of so many chart successes to date: dancing melodic bass lines and one of Robert's loveliest melodies. The single was a top ten hit, and the remix version also made the UK top fifty, reaching a creditable number forty four. *Melody Maker* called the single "a happy-go-lucky skip down Desolation Avenue." *Wish* followed in April, a beautifully packaged album recorded at The Manor, Richard Branson's pile in Oxfordshire. Writing had started the previous summer, but by the time Robert had brought the band together, the forty-odd songs that were available were quickly whittled down. *Melody Maker* visited the studios in March, and found a happy crew: Perry Bamonte's caricatures of the band littered the studio, along with Emily Dickinson poems and headlines snipped from tabloid newspapers, a clear mix of salacious writing, perfectly formed poetry and madcap humour within the band. "It's been brilliant making this album," Robert told the paper, and the collection of songs certainly reflected a broader musical landscape than *Disintegration*'s focused moodiness.

'Open' was, naturally, the opener – kicking off the album with tentative guitar phrases until crashing drums and bass come in and Robert's lyrics dissect the social whirl around someone who is gradually losing control of the situations around him. Rich in images familiar to long-time Cure listeners, the song was filled with blood, pain, gasping, screaming – and staring at the floor. Claustrophobic and falling in despair, the tone of the album already appeared to be dark and under stress. 'High', however, was the perfect antidote as track two. 'Apart' was the third consecutive track with a single word title: conceptual songs about loss of control, elation and emotional dislocation. Mood-full, reflective, the song is another of Robert's most beautifully realised lyrics, as he dissects the dysfunction of a relationship no longer working, its only visual image that of the girl's eyes, observational writing at its best and most melancholy. 'From The Edge Of The Deep Green Sea' was another love song that initially seems to put right the losses of the previous track, but again it's a regretful song of inevitable partings and tears, unspoken intrusions spoiling the game. The music has a very positive tone, poppy drumming and strum-along acoustics, and Robert's guitar solo is a particular highlight. Robert's vocal delivery is poetic, almost pleading – a lyric to get lost in. 'Wendy Time' was a controversial track on the album, one that Robert tried to leave off a number of times: "It made me realise that when sequencing an album, a better song will get left off for the sake of the album as a whole. Whenever we tried to replace it the album seemed to go soft," he told one interviewer.

'Doing The Unstuck' sounds, for a second or so, like it's going to be a Bowie-influenced song. Mixing unbridled happiness and enthusiasm for a brand new day with a tempering response from a partner, the song is one of The Cure's happiest to date. Robert spoke in the booklet accompanying *Join The Dots* (on which a remix version appeared) of how he had wanted the song to be the single release that 'Letter To Elise' finally was. To this day, he says it still makes him laugh with joy. The video for 'Elise' also marked a break with Tim Pope, as the clip for the single was directed by Aubrey Powell.

Six songs in, the album's opening sense of dislocation gradually builds through the jolly strumming and abandoned vocals to a track that for many defined The Cure *forever*. Robert told *Rolling Stone* in 1997 that "(When I'm recognised by) cab drivers, they'll say 'Oh yeah, you're the guy that did 'Friday I'm In Love!'… I've never had a cab driver who turned to me and said, 'You're the bloke who's the Godfather of Goth – the doom and gloom bloke.'" Even the hardest-hearted Cure-hater will turn on a sixpence and admit that they can't resist 'Friday I'm In Love'.

It's a simple pop song. And the greatest of all pop tunes pull the same trick of apparent simplicity: 'Please Please Me', 'Ever Fallen In Love (With Someone You Shouldn't Have Fallen In Love With)?' 'The Boys Are Back In Town' *et al*. But of course, it's not easy, or every two-bit songwriter on the planet would be a millionaire. 'Friday I'm In Love' is the product of one of pop's most finely-tuned song-writing minds, whose craft and creativity had been evident for all to see for over a decade. If it surprised anyone that The Cure should release such a fantastic little record then the fault lay with the lazy listener. Like the little tremors that come before a mighty earthquake, previous singles like 'Lovesong', 'Catch' or 'Boys Don't Cry' should have warned everyone that The Cure had something mighty up their sleeve.

The song's gentle thunder opens with gorgeous, jangling guitar lines, as hooky as any Johnny Marr riff, and more. The lyric takes a theme popular in pop music from 'Stormy Monday' through to Craig David and Sting's (same title, different songs ...) 'Seven Days', spelling out the course of a relationship through the days of the week. Robert's vocal is gently restrained, the tune irresistible. Little handclaps. Sing-along backing vocals. And perfectly – as all great records know how to start, so they know where to stop. I love the fact that 'Friday I'm In Love' ends on a clear-cut stop-now chord. *Melody Maker* hit the nail on the head when they called it "blissfully and exuberantly carefree."

The perfect progression of the tracks so far insisted that the next track be a quiet, reflective piece, and, on cue, the sober piano lines of 'Trust' introduce a beautiful, haunting song that does what it says on the can. The lengthy introduction, acoustic but for the wash of strings, leads into another lyric on which Robert leaves behind his more histrionic vocal style and 'sings it straight.' If his class as a writer was evident on 'Friday I'm In Love' then it was quietly even more so here. 'A Letter To Elise' followed, a natural successor to 'Trust' – cinematic strings, sobering lyrics of falling sand and clutching hands, and a great sense of resignation throughout. 'Cut', with a Hendrix-like guitar solo, pumps the pace up again, frenetic drums and urgent, desperate vocals, the song filled with bile and frustration. 'To Wish Impossible Things' is another gentle, beautiful song, its lyrics economical and pure, Robert's delivery again muted and reflective. If these wishes have long failed to come true, the romantic viola played by Kate Williamson and grand percussion say 'keep on wishing.'

And so, with the album opening with 'Open', so it ends with 'End', dark arpeggios of Floyd-like guitar. The dreams of the previous song have come true and moved on. The songs are finished, and Robert's imagery is back in a familiar Cure landscape of blood, blackness, and burning fires. *Wish* was the band's most successful album to date, "ranging from the brilliantly shallow to the devastatingly profound," as *Melody Maker* put it. The album was a hit everywhere, reaching number one in the UK and two on the other side of the Atlantic. *Q* magazine's Robert Sandall couldn't bring himself to dislike the album, however hard he tried. "(It) contains several of the best things The Cure have done, as well as one or two items which they should be able to pull off in their sleep – and by the sound of it possibly did." But Sandall couldn't resist the variety of song styles and the raw, rough edge to the album's sound. "The Cure really are waving, not drowning," was his conclusion.

Released in May as a single, 'Friday I'm In Love' became the band's second-highest chart single in the UK, reaching number six and staying in the chart for seven weeks. It topped the *Billboard* Modern Rock chart for four weeks in the States. 'Letter To Elise' fared well too, making a dent in the UK at number twenty eight. In all, the band spent thirteen weeks on the singles chart in 1992, and in the UK alone had four singles reach the top fifty.

Robert appeared unsure about the album in retrospect. In one published interview with Bill Crandall, he claimed it both as his favourite album after *Bloodflowers* and, at the same time, admitted that sometimes he was almost "going through the motions."

After a couple of quiet years as a live band, it was time to get back on the road, and the *Wish* tour is remembered by many of the thousands who witnessed it as one of the best Cure tours of all. The biggest outing for the band for years, it was also the last for the current line-up of The Cure: over one hundred concerts, including their first gigs in Australia and New Zealand for eight years.

In Australia they had the surreal experience of being introduced to their own tribute band who had been filling the Cure-hungry gap since the real band last played there. Smith was royally entertained – his counterpart in the band didn't really look like him, and to Robert's ears the whole band sounded nothing like The Cure: "He said, 'You ask anyone, man ... we sound more like you than *you*.' And I said, 'But *this* is what we sound like ...' He just wouldn't see it!"

The first date on the tour was in the UK, at St George's Hall in Bradford, Yorkshire, then on through dates including Newcastle, Dundee, Glasgow and – before heading for America – a final gig in London on May 3. Accidents and illness occasionally threatened to wreck the tour – at Cambridge in April Robert was taken ill with stomach pains during the gig and the set was cut short. In Milan, Simon was temporarily replaced by Shellyan Orphan bass player Roberto Soave after contracting pleurisy, while a motorcycle accident forced Porl to play with his arm in a plaster cast!

Over the pond the band played East and West coast venues and travelled through Canada to Vancouver and Toronto. By August they were back in Chris Parry's homeland with dates in Auckland and Wellington, then Sydney, Brisbane, Melbourne, Adelaide and Perth. Almost hours rather than days later, Oslo, Helsinki, Stockholm and Copenhagen welcomed The Cure to the Scandinavian and Nordic countries, and familiar towns from early Cure tours like Hamburg and Rotterdam were revisited. France, Italy, Switzerland and Spain were knocked off in the course of ten days (with three consecutive nights in Paris amongst them) until they returned to stadium venues – Birmingham's NEC, Manchester's GMEX, London's Olympia – in the UK. Ready for the Christmas break, the tour wound up at The Point in Dublin on December 3. Apart from one date the following year, it would be The Cure's last live appearance for a year and a half.

As if that wasn't enough, they found the time to release another video collection in September. *The Cure Play Out* was a collection of the band's activities in London in the first eight weeks of 1991. Starting with dressing room antics backstage at the Town and Country Club, and checks for microphone levels, the tape opened up with the then-unreleased 'Wendy Time', the band sounding spookily like that on *Three Imaginary Boys* so many years before. Robert hinted in the interview shown during 'Wendy Time' that some of the new material played had "been recorded," suggesting that the next studio album was already in the making. 'The Big Hand', tentative and beautiful, followed, a song to re-appear as the B-side of 'Letter To Elise' eighteen moths later. The band t h roughout this reduced version of their set seemed at ease, concentrated, Robert's shirt wobbling as he shook in 'Let's Go To Bed'.

After the Town & Country gig came footage from the Great British Music Weekend two nights later. Again, pre-gig antics open the piece as The Happy Mondays' set can be heard in the background. It's a revealing though short insight into the band's off-stage life, garrulous and fun-time, until a few seconds later the camera follows the much-more-nervous-looking fivesome through the backstage corridors of Wembley Arena. The band check their on stage time and quickly review the hand-written set list, and after Robert has applied his make-up, the band have had some mug shots taken, Robert ("the lead singer with 'The Curse'") has been interviewed, it's up onto the stage for the opening bars of 'Pictures Of You', followed by 'Fascination Street', 'Lullaby' and 'A Forest'. Throughout, under dramatic lighting, the band looked and sounded fabulous. Immediately off-stage, with towels on faces and a modest table-full of refreshments, the band wound down, Robert looking emotionally drained, pacing the room silently while the rest of the band mug-up for the cameras.

The next clips show the band preparing for that Jonathon Ross show appearance less than a week later. While the band settle into the dressing room, Smith immediately checks out the day's activity. Rehearsals on the set are noisy and punky as they run through The Doors' 'Hello I Love You', which does sound uncannily like The Kinks' 'All Of The Day And All Of The Night.' Clips from a number of songs are included, giving a further little insight into Cure-world as they effortlessly run through snippets of familiar songs and 'Harold And Joe', a B-side track from 'Never Enough'. Robert smiles sweetly through his blackened eyes as Jonathon Ross closes with the line "if I can help a little band like that fulfil an ambition to be on TV, then I feel I've done something worthwhile, ladies and gentlemen!" Rehearsal sessions ('The Blood' and 'The Walk' acoustically, featuring the little-appreciated kazoo to replicate the synth sounds of the original – later to be played by members of the audience) introduce four songs from the MTV *Unplugged* set after extensive chatting 'in make-up,' followed by rehearsals for and appearances from the Brits ceremony in February.

For Cure fans the world over, the release was a fantastic little peep into Cure life, filling the long gap between studio albums with something genuinely new wrapped around something old and familiar. Like a new baggy jumper.

Stressful times were ahead. After the tour, Porl parted ways with the band – during his time out of The Cure he would work with Jimmy Page and Robert Plant – and Simon took time out too. The new year saw a flurry of releases, but little evidence of the band themselves. A rocking version of Jimi Hendrix's 'Purple Haze' was chosen to launch the new Virgin 1215 radio station, while at the Grammy's in February they were nominated for the award for 'Best Alternative Music Performance' for *Wish*. In a year where Eric Clapton won virtually everything, the band was up against The B52s, Morrissey (for *Your Arsenal*) and XTC for their own sublime little gem *Nonsuch*. One of the more interesting categories at The Grammys, the gong went to Tom Waits for *Bone Machine*. June saw the only Cure gig of the year, as the now four-piece played in Finsbury Park, London, a concert organised by Parry to promote Xfm, the new radio station that boasted Parry and Robert as shareholders. Looking to establish a broadcast licence (which at this attempt it failed to get), the event was designed to raise awareness of the station throughout London, and a live album – *Great Xpectations Live* – was released to celebrate the event. A photo in *Q* magazine showed a rare picture of Robert and his mum at the gig, amidst a flurry of admirers.

September and October saw the release of two Cure live albums. The double album *Show,* released first, spawned a film that enjoyed both a video and cinema release, showing the band live in Detroit the previous July. Alongside it came the EP 'Sideshow', an extra little slice of the shows from the Michigan gig. *Paris,* cunningly, was recorded in the French capital in October the previous year, and released as a limited edition album. A second, wildly eccentric version of 'Purple Haze' appeared on *Stone Free: A Tribute To Jimi Hendrix,* released as a single in the USA. 'Lost Wishes', containing four instrumental tracks from the *Wish* sessions was also released in November, a limited edition release for Cure investors with the proceeds going to charity. However, all this activity masked the fact that The Cure as a group appeared to be in disarray.

Matters involving Lol's legal action came to a head in the New Year. First reports of the case began to appear in the music press in the spring. The case occupied Robert and Tolhurst for six months of 1994, a considerable drain on everyone concerned.

Fortunately, much brighter times were ahead for The Cure's former drummer and keyboard player. His new project Presence released their one and only album, *Inside* in 1993. In 1994, with Presence no longer working together, he moved to California. By 2002 Lol was divorced and remarried to Cindy Levinson, and together had formed the aforementioned band (then just the two of them) Levinhurst, with Cindy on vocals and Lol playing keyboards, the couple sharing the writing duties. Joined later by multi-instrumentalist Californian Dayton Borders, Lol once again found himself a part of a bright, optimistic musical threesome. The band have made some very interesting music together since: Lol told one interviewer that "it is the very first time since The Cure that I have really enjoyed making music again – it reminds me of the time, and (of) my life, at the beginning of The Cure." A father now ("it shifted my perspective on what is really important to me,") Tolhurst comes across as a very interesting and focussed man. Interviewers seem ever-keen to talk with Lol – never straying too far away from the opportunity to discuss The Cure, naturally. "The past... is rather a double edged sword," Lol told Joshua Heinrich in 2004.

"In some respects it's great, as people know who I am and it opens some doors that would be otherwise closed ... (but) it doesn't necessarily mean people are open-minded about Levinhurst, because it doesn't sound very like the past." Their music is contemporary synthesizer music and retro-classic blended together, material compared by some reviewers to early Cure (though not by this listener) – altogether a very charming package. Cindy's vocals are pure and true, and both lyrically and musically there is plenty to interest not just Cure-watchers. Lol reckons that between fifty and seventy-five percent of the people coming to live shows of Levinhurst are Cure fans. Occasionally he has been known to play a Cure song in a Levinhurst set – fans at one gig in March 2004 recognised 'A Forest' as a part of the encore.

Lol is gracious on the subjects of both Robert and The Cure: pressed by one interviewer to comment on the fact that both *Bloodflowers* and *Join The Dots* featured pictures of just Robert on the cover, Lol rightly observed that there were plenty of shots of himself in the *Join The Dots* booklet, talking of his pride in what the version of The Cure he was in had achieved. Lol's Levinhurst website lists 'bands we like' – Eels, Bjork, The Pretenders, Elvis Costello and many more. Touchingly, entertainingly, and honestly, the first band on the list of 'the bands we like' is ... The Cure.

And, of Robert, Lol is happy to admit a settling of old emotional ground. "He's like family," he says. "We are pals again. It's good." Recently-taken photographs of the pair have appeared on the internet – looking older and wiser than they did back in the days of The Easy Cure. But looking happy too. Fans interested in hearing Levinhurst – their CD *Perfect Life* is the ideal starting point – can visit www.levinhurst.com for information and updates.

Chapter 12: Mood Swings

By the autumn of 1994, with the court case behind him, Robert could return to his private and creative life after a long b reak. "(I) was very bitter about having six months hacked out of my life," he told *Details* magazine in 1996. Work began on the next batch of songs for a new studio album, and Robert also took time out for himself, at one point trying his hand at sculpture and spending time in New York and Paris. News that Boris was no longer in the band broke in the early autumn. It certainly didn't appear acrimonious, as Boris was to visit the band during the *Wild Mood Swing* sessions, even playing a two-drum jam with his replacement.

Robert had new material ready for the next studio album, and work started down in England's west country, at St Catherine's Court in Bath. The house – a rolling Tudor mansion set in acres and acres of unbelievable English countryside – was a revelation. It belonged to actress Jane Seymour, who leased it to bands while she was in the USA taping the hugely popular TV show *Dr Quinn, Medicine Woman*, (the manor had actually belonged in the past to Henry VIII himself). Robert had checked the property over before the band moved in, and, in order for recording to start, amendments to some of the rooms were made by a London company specialising in top-level acoustics. The band also brought in a vast array of recording equipment, and the ghosts of the original Jane Seymour and hubby Henry VIII must have watched with amusement as the gear was installed.

With Simon taking occasional sabbaticals from the band, Boris gone, and Porl working as an artist before he joined up with Plant and Page's band, at times The Cure were reduced to Robert and Perry alone. "Sitting under a tree somewhere outside the studio," Bamonte told a journalist, "(I remember thinking) ... this is it. Robert and I *are* The Cure." Perry officially made the move from keyboards to guitar within the group, and, after mailing Robert a copy of his solo album and hinting that he was available if needed, Roger O'Donnell came back on board in the keyboard role. Remarkably, The Cure placed an ad in *Melody Maker,* and began auditioning drummer after drummer. Although early rumours had Wonder Stuff tub-thumper Martin Giles pencilled in for the job, after what some sources quote as over 150 hopefuls were turned down, it was ultimately Jason Cooper – ex-My Life Story – who took up The Cure's drumsticks. Like Boris, Cooper was a very 'musical drummer' having scored film music previous to joining the band. In a 1996 interview Robert told the entertaining story of how Jason – a long-time Cure fan – had kept his love of the band a secret until *after* he got the gig: "He suddenly started playing all the old songs. And I was like, 'Fucking Hell! He knows songs that *I* don't even remember.'"

Holed up *chez* Seymour for months on end through 1995, the gestation of *Wild Mood Swings* was a slow but democratic one, with Robert encouraging input from all the band members, "no matter how silly it was." "There wasn't a deadline," Perry told *Sound On Sound* reporter Nigel Humberstone, who visited the band during the sessions, "so we kept pushing it back." Originally intended to be an acoustic album recorded quickly and with only Perry, Simon and Robert involved, as more ideas came in from band members the original concept of what was still at this point called *Bare* was soon dropped. "On some songs, Robert had specific ideas of what he wanted played," Roger O'Donnell told Humberstone. "For other songs I just played along and it was more creative for me." The sessions became more and more extended. With Smith, Cooper, Bamonte, Gallup and O'Donnell on board, the line-up of The Cure that would last for more than a decade was firmly in place. "I had to feel right about starting the group up again," Robert told John Aizelwood for *Q* in 1995. A number of changes in Cure routine were also made. One was to bring in Steve Lyon to engineer and work on the album's production instead of Dave Allen. Technically, too, the process of recording at

St Catherine's involved changes of habit. Steve Lyon introduced them to various new techniques such as recording on Cubase, a software package designed by German company Steinberg, that allowed almost unlimited attention to detail in digital recording, as well as printing off a score for the string players from anything Robert played.

The recording process was a largely happy one, the house and studio comfortable, and Robert enjoyed early morning walks through the fields after winding up sessions in the early hours. "You can go out and do things," he said of the countryside and the city of Bath, where people like Peter Gabriel were resident, "and no-one gives a shit – it's a different vibe." But the time taken to produce the album threatened a lack of direction, what Chris Parry called "a dizzy ride." Robert would spend time on take after take, trying to get the vocals right, and the band would occupy days searching for drum sounds. "I realised," Robert told *Planet Radio* "that we had sort of turned into everything that I loathed." Smith would on occasion record vocal takes out of the house in a traditional recording studio, finding that the social atmosphere and general bonhomie around St Catherine's was not right for him. If fifty or sixty takes for one vocal seem excessive, Robert did at least realise that he was holding the group back in his own perfectionist's struggle. "I made everyone wait for months and months while I'd get the words exactly as I wanted them," he told *X-Press*. He found it difficult to take the lyric-writing to a place beyond his work on *Disintegration* and *Wish*, and perhaps as a result the album was as diverse as the band had ever sounded. "It was brilliant," Robert told *Rolling Stone*. "The best year of my life."

Recording *Wild Mood Swings* occupied the band for much of 1994 and the following year, with a series of outdoor festivals across Europe representing Robert and Co.'s live work for the latter. One sideline activity was that the soundtrack to the newly released *Judge Dredd* movie in June included The Cure's 'Dredd Song', later to be included in the *Join The Dots*

179

compilation. In early June, Jason played his first date with the band ("He was really amazed," said Robert, "that the audience really wanted to listen to us. He had never been in a band (where) the audience was really seriously into what the band were doing ...") With Perry now confirmed as the band's second guitarist alongside Robert, and with Roger on keyboards, they pulled serious weight onstage in Italy, Germany, Denmark, Belgium, France, Portugal, Switzerland and Spain, where they replaced REM on the bill in Madrid. Being festival dates, The Cure shared the stage with many other bands, including (variously) PJ Harvey, REM, Suede, The Cranberries, Elvis Costello and others. Amongst their regular neighbours on the tour were Page and Plant, with whom Robert's brother-in-law Porl Thompson was now engaged, and Porl joined The Cure on stage on a number of occasions reminding everyone that there was no bad blood between him and the band, who were of course temporarily extended to a six-piece with his contributions. Midway through the summer festival season they yet again played the biggest gig of the year at Glastonbury, and Porl played with them there too.

Released in May 1996, *Wild Mood Swings* reflected as much about the changing nature of pop at the time as it did about The Cure. For the first time, it sold fewer copies than its predecessor, despite Chris Parry's optimism that the album would be the band's biggest ever. Much of the blame for this has been put on the vogue-ish intrusion of 'Britpop' in the UK market, and the fact that it had been four years since the last Cure studio album. Had the home market, at least, grown out of the band? Certainly in the long term this was not the case – the reception of later albums proved this succinctly – but at the time, and for the first time, The Cure were perhaps unfashionable. This was wholly ironic: the best of the Britpop bands included Blur, Sleeper, Elastica, Echobelly and the not-so-new Pulp. Most of these bands had an arch, guitar-driven pop psyche going on, and derived much of their influence from bands such as The Kinks and The Jam. But anyone with an open ear to Damon Albarn's acerbic ditties or Jarvis Cocker's throwaway vocal style would surely have detected a sidelong glance at the equally arch, equally left-of-centre early pop of The Cure. Britpop's visual image centred very much on mod and other fashions from the sixties: The Small Faces, The Who, the *Revolver*-period Beatles. While the mighty Oasis admittedly plundered The Beatles, T Rex and Slade for their inspiration, a band still considered as 'Eighties' as The Cure would perhaps be inevitably side-tracked, but the early Cure sound was most definitely in there amongst the Paul Weller or Steve Marriot influences.

The new year kicked off with a couple of major January gigs in Brazil, and then in April The Cure played on both *Top Of The Pops* and *Later With Jools Holland* for the BBC in the UK, covering both the pop and the more seriously-minded rock end of the audience between the two. They also appeared on *TFI Friday*, an irreverent UK show, promoting the new single 'The 13th', which was released in April. Much of the rest of the spring the band continued to wrap up the album, which appeared in stores on the 17 May. 'The 13th' was in fact The Cure's twenty-fifth chart single in the UK market, reaching number fifteen in May, just over sixteen years since 'A Forest' had first made it into the top fifty.

The album was one of the band's most eclectic, a fair representation of its title. Like *Disintegration*, many of the tracks have single-title, conceptual names, each song a dissection or an observation. The sleeve design itself had a clear duality, the little tin doll's face both charming, naïve and innocent while at the same time kind of spooky. The first track 'Want' is a grand affair, opening on strident, heartfelt guitar phrases repeated over and over until Jason's huge drum sound brings Robert's voice in after a two-and-a-half minute, Phil Spector-like wall of Cure sonic battering. Robert's vocal is desperately needful. 'Want' is the reflection of a soul with much more to do, more to achieve, a burning need to overcome the temporal needs of life and to find more at the core of life itself.

The striking spark that opens 'Club America' introduces another guitar-battering, fuming roar. Lyrically, the song explores the dazzling, after-show ligging of wonderful people living fabulous lives: beautiful women hang out on club doorways, and everyone compliments one another to painful excess. But it is a world of lies, and fraud, the *accoutrements* of beauty are only stuck on, and although people engage in intercourse they never actually listen to one another. Robert's observations are cool and detached, his vocal deeper and more mannered than previously, the falcon's eye of his gaze seeing through the plastic and the passion-less parade amidst Hendrix-like guitar swathes. 'Club America' has always been one of the highlights of the album, for me.

The Cure have always been superb at sequencing an album, and so it's no surprise when the lilting, string-driven waltz 'This Is A Lie' comes as respite after the punishing chords of 'Club America'. With its determined acoustic strumming and string quartet, the track is nevertheless weighty, Lennon-esque minor key stuff. The song answers the opening track's quandary: given more time, given more hope, what will we find out about ourselves? The 'poet laureate of adolescent suffering' picks away at all the given assumptions that we make about our loves and our place in the world; monogamy, direction, hell and heaven, dreams and pretence. If the lies lived in 'Club America' belong to only one group of star-struck attention seekers, the same lies pervade us all in 'This Is A Lie' as we scrabble around for excuses for our failings.

Happy-go-lucky jazz improv kicks off the jaunty-but-spooky Latin single 'The 13th', as the emotional pendulum of *Wild Mood Swings* turns upwards on the album's fourth song. Originally called 'The Two Chord Cool', it features Jason's lounge-lizard percussion and lyrics from Robert apparently about "a sensational dancer in a club in Colombia." 'Strange Attraction' keeps the mood up musically, starting off with a kind of *Hammer Horror* cinematic sweep of strings before heading off into a jaunty world of sound. As the lyrics review a relationship between a fan and her object of love, so little sampled tape-rewind noises keep bringing the listener back to question what that relationship is all about. 'Strange Attraction' is a spooky song: a mixture of joyous, innocent, unresolved relationships and, at the same time, of a desperate need in one person and a morbid curiosity in the other. The adorer finally tells the adored that the infatuation is over, but Robert's lyrics lovingly leave the door open …

Big time optimism opens the second single from the *Wild Mood Swings* collection, 'Mint Car', with an unbridled happiness bubbling under Robert's ecstatic, yelping vocal. Robert happily acknowledged that 'Mint Car' was one of his favourite Cure singles. "That's how I felt last summer," he told MTV in 1996 as he reviewed songs that would appear on the then-forthcoming album. "And how I feel again this summer." Of almost any Cure song, this is one of the most emotionally pure: there's no sidelong glance into another alternative, no suggestion that beneath the joy there is a regret. 'Mint Car' is a lovely, lovely thing. Amazingly, after big hits with pure Cure single material such as 'The Lovecats', 'Friday I'm In Love' or 'Lullaby', 'Mint Car' failed to even scrape the top thirty in the UK, making it only to number thirty one at the end of June. Some of the blame for this may well lie with BBC's Radio One channel, who stubbornly refused to push the single as much as they had played previous Cure singles – another symptom of the changing flavour of pop in the few years since *Wish*?

After four uninhibited and joyful tracks, 'Jupiter Crash' comes as a reflective respite. The song is another of Robert's beautifully poetic lyrics, enjoining the news story of a comet crashing into Jupiter with a little sketch of an emotional equivalent at the edges of a turning tide. Robert has a wonderful ability in his lyrics to represent dialogue within the meter and rhyme of a pop song, and 'Jupiter Crash' is a perfect example of this, as the conversation between the two characters of the song circles around the subject of the comet's fate.

'Round And Round And Round' has always seemed to be

a diversionary track on the album. At only two-and-a-half minutes long it is one of the shortest tracks, and musically it is based upon a riff that seems out of sorts so soon after 'Jupiter Crash'. Robert's Billy McKenzie-mode vocal explores the flip side of stardom that 'Club America' dissected, the responsibilities, the smiles when no smile is there, the glad-handing, back-slapping responsibilities when six months in the garden sounds a better option. Glissando bass and acoustic guitar recall the first, minimal intention of the album on 'Numb', a contemplative dissection of the vagaries of drug use. 'Return' once again examines the dichotomy of love and the two-headed monster that is a part of any relationship. Where 'Mint Car' had no dark side, 'Return' is classic Smith duality lyrically. Robert sings in answer on the next track 'Trap', an intense bark of frustration established again by a grand, guitar-led introduction.

'Treasure', yet another conceptual one-word title, slows the mood down again with some beautifully phrased pieces, romantic piano, strings, articulate percussion from Jason and more of that acoustic feel that pervades so much of the album. Lyrically the song is another regretful, remorseful piece, a sonnet-like clarity to the words that are mirrored in 'Bare', the last song in the set. 'Bare' – as mentioned at one point the title of the album itself – is a stately piece, more gentle piano and acoustic guitar, Robert's vocals intimate and regretful. In observational writing of the highest order, Robert dissects both sides of the emotional equation, both the 'I' and the 'you' of the song, before centring back on the 'I' and the failings and the sense of dreams unfulfilled that pervade so much of his work.

Wild Mood Swings sways gently from the bright and cheerful to the reflective and sober. Never gloomy, the collection is nevertheless a serious piece of work in that it blends so many different elements of The Cure and Robert Smith's concerns in such an eminently listenable way. *NME* suggested that such variety was usually the domain of the compilation or Greatest Hits package – "a grab bag of all The Cure's myriad specialities ... an album that has no place in 1996 (and) all the better for it." *Entertainment Weekly* enjoyed the album, describing Robert as "a self-help guru," and found the overall tone of the album to be "gentle melancholia."

It may have been four years since *Wish*, but it was worth the wait. If not every reviewer and fan liked the album, *Wild Mood Swings* for me was a kind of latter-day *Hunky Dory*: eclectic, eccentrically inconsistent with moments of benign genius and a few occasions where the focus lapses. The difference between the two albums, however, is that *Hunky Dory* marked a door opening for David Bowie, a calling card dropped on the mat to show what he *could* do. *Wild Mood Swings* could so easily have been a door closing on The Cure; we already knew what Robert was capable of writing and what the band was capable of playing. It was clear that The Cure could write a pop masterpiece, or an extended piece of majestic and orchestral rock. Fans were probably expecting a definitive statement of where Robert and The Cure stood in the mid-nineties. Instead they got a scrapbook, and many were disappointed. But – which would you rather do? Leaf through Princess Diana's official public speeches, or leaf through her love letters and postcards? Give *Wild Mood Swings* another listen.

Conversely, the tour that followed the album's release was the band's biggest to date. An invitation-only date in Paris and a gig for an audience of record company executives and personally invited guests at London's Adrenaline venue were followed by more TV appearances in the US and UK. It was the end of May before the band hit the stage at London's mighty Earl's Court hall to launch the 'Swing' tour with The Cure's first major UK date since Glastonbury the previous year, but they nearly didn't make it. Returning from the USA, a minor illness forced Robert to postpone dates in Cardiff, Sheffield, Manchester and Birmingham until the very end of the tour in December. Fortunately, he soon recuperated and admirably soldiered on.

Two big nights out at Earl's Court were followed by a date

at The Point in Dublin, and then it was off to Scandinavia, France, Germany, Canada and the USA again. *Rolling Stone* reported on the Earl's Court concerts, noting Robert's continuous apologies from the stage – for the band's performance, the light show, his own singing. If the band seemed somehow out of sorts, Simon told one US interviewer that across America they were playing disco tapes and dancing their way around the country on the tour bus, not the expected profile of the so-called Godfathers of Gloom. By the time the band hit the USA, *Wild Mood Swings* had been available there for a couple of months, and had entered the *Billboard* chart at number twenty three. Amazingly, from the very next week onwards it fell down the charts rapidly. On September 17, the American dates came to a halt at Radio City in New York, the concert being made available on the internet. A dramatic series of concerts in Europe – the tour's stunning 'broken-down circus' set had again been designed by LeRoy Bennett – brought the band back to the UK for the year end, playing the dates postponed from the spring. One reviewer noted that The Cure's audience, particularly in America, was unusually young for a band that had been treading the boards for so long. If The Cure were growing older, their audience was staying young. They were playing to an audience constantly re-invented, as each generation of listeners found something new in the band.

The last concert in Birmingham was a moving affair on which to finish such a mammoth tour. Robert – seemingly very emotional all night – announced to the crowd that it was twenty years to the day since he had first taken to the stage. Way back then the band were playing for a place in an unwritten future, but the 'Swing' tour was rumoured to have grossed over $7 million and to have played to an average gate of over 6,000 punters a night. It was a long way from Crawley's Rocket pub.

*

One 'release' in the summer of 1996 that was a clear-cut success for The Cure, and remains so to this day, was *www.thecure.com*, the band's official website. Originally and for a long time managed closely by the band themselves, it launched with a homepage featuring images based upon St Catherine's Court and the various 'rooms' contained different elements of the site. The band had high hopes for the new baby: it would include tracks to download, live webcasts, interviews, chat rooms and everything that the internet could offer. "Roger tried to get us into computers back in the late Eighties, but we resisted," Robert told *Billboard* on the site's launch. "By the time he came back ... we all had laptops!" At the same time, Robert and Chris Parry were also awaiting the decision as to whether Xfm would be granted its broadcast licence. Settled now on the south coast of England with Mary, without children of their own, but happily uncle and aunt to an increasing number of nephews and nieces who ranged in age from one to twenty-one, Robert was often found by telephone interviewers to be in his garden, happy to talk about the restorative effect of gardening, reading and writing upon his psyche. Robert told Reuters that he really enjoyed "being (a) kind of slightly deranged uncle ... what everyone else does really, but something I haven't done before now because I've been doing other things."

It was a reflective time. Perhaps more than ever now was a possible sense that The Cure had run its course. Robert talked of a retrospective album for the following year that would effectively summarise the entire history of The Cure and – as he told *People Weekly* magazine – leave him free to "walk away from it quietly." The very phrase is telling: this wasn't a millionaire rock star deciding his luck was running out. Robert seemed to genuinely feel that the journey was now complete. The Cure must have taken an enormous toll on Smith: he may well have been financially successful and accredited the world over as a writer and performer, but The Cure had evidently for some years been a significant artistic process, and not just a day job. Then there was the court case with Lol, the massive time spent on the road and the thousands of interviews. Perhaps the creative uncertainty of *Wild Mood Swings* cast a doubt as to where the Cure could possibly go next. Maybe it *was* finally time to let it go to rest. With various mixes of 'Gone' and 'Strange Attraction' released in seven- and twelve-inch format singles, Robert could look back on a career spanning twenty years, during which his band had released a number of films and videos, some thirty-plus singles, and eighteen albums – including hits packages and live shows. It was a prodigious body of work. The band had had top ten singles all over the world and could pack stadiums that only a handful of other acts – particularly other British acts, bearing in mind that the darlings of the world media, U2, were Irish – could fill.

Times were changing, and a new generation of younger singers and bands was moving in on The Cure's chart territory. At the MTV Video Music Awards for 1996, the winners were acts such as Alanis Morissette, Coolio and The Fugees. At one end of the spectrum R&B was increasingly the flavour of the month, while amongst the bands it was post-Nirvana guitar outfits such as Foo Fighters, Smashing Pumpkins and Bush who took the nominations. At The Grammys it was old-timers like Sinatra, Joni Mitchell, Stevie Wonder, The Chieftains and Van Morrisson who took the gongs, while the American Music Awards listed a similar MOR selection of winners. New kids on the block and sanitized R&B took the lion's share of sales: Mariah Carey, Boyz II Men, Celine Dion and Alanis were huge sellers in 1996. It was almost as if the quiet corner of their own making that The Cure had found for themselves over the years had been spotted by the music media and quietly obliterated. 'The 13th' did only modestly well in The States, a far cry from 1992 when – on the back of 'Friday I'm In Love' and *Wish* – they were, behind Genesis, the biggest-selling British singles band in America. Perhaps this was the time to go and make that solo album and call it quits on The Cure?

Chapter 13: Dancing With The Dame

Late in 1996 Robert received an invitation to play a gig that twenty years earlier would have been unthinkable. David Bowie was to celebrate his fiftieth birthday with a gig at New York's Madison Square Garden, and a number of acts were invited to join him on stage. Robert had, of course, been a fan way back when Ziggy had first flickered across our screens, and for anybody this would have been a fantastic opportunity and a total delight. "It's one of the very few ambitions that I ever had when I was young," said Robert. "It's really like a pipe dream to be on stage with Bowie ... the first album I ever bought was *Ziggy Stardust*." How many of us would have died for the same opportunity? Bowie called Robert and asked him to be a part of the evening's show. "You didn't get a choice of duet," Robert told *NME*. "David rang up and said, 'What song would you like to do?' – so I started reeling off all these songs like 'Drive In Saturday', 'Young Americans'. Then he said, 'How about 'Quicksand?' and I thought, 'You bastard!'" Robert also found that – like many of us have done – he had learned the words to the song phonetically, and Bowie kept putting him right.

Robert apparently presented Bowie with a fossilised chameleon for his birthday (referencing the Bowie lyric from 'The Bewlay Brothers' which had almost defined David's entire career: "chameleon, comedian, Corinthian and caricature") – a thoughtful, entirely appropriate and unique gift. The concert was staged on January 9, 1997, the day after David's actual birthday, and it was announced that the show would be broadcast on pay-per-view TV in March. Robert was of course not the only guest: the opening act for the night was Placebo, and then Bowie and band took the stage with contributions from and duets with Lou Reed, Billy Corgan, Frank Black, Foo Fighters, Sonic Youth and others. Bowie and Reed played four songs together on the trot at the end of the night – from Bowie's Velvet Underground-influenced 'Queen Bitch' to 'White Light White Heat', the VU song that Bowie included in his set for years on end. By all accounts the atmosphere in Madison Square Garden was phenomenal. By the time Robert took the stage to join Bowie on 'The Last Thing You Should Do', from Bowie's soon-to-be-released *Earthling*, the audience were having one of the nights of their lives. This was David's first rendition of this song live on stage anywhere in the world. After that it was back to the classic Bowie of *Hunky Dory* as Robert and David sang 'Quicksand' together accompanied by acoustic guitars – an early favourite of nearly every Bowie-phile. Robert got one of the loudest cheers of the night from the Madison Square Garden crowd.

The after-show party was an even more star-studded affair, Bowie magnificent in an orange, Ziggy-style hair cut and little goatee beard: appropriately suave for the fifty-year-old Spider from Mars. Robert himself was of course slowly edging nearer and nearer towards the age at which life, apparently, begins. But if nearing forty implied a slowing down, at least the idea of closing The Cure down for good wasn't pursued. As in previous years the band did not undertake a major world tour in 1997, rather preferring a selection of international festivals, TV appearances and radio broadcasts to keep themselves in front of an ever-loving fan base. At the influential KROQ Weenie Roast Festival at Irvine Meadows, California, The Cure headlined at short notice ("I only told the others in the band that we were going last week," he told a local reporter) above Britpop brat pack Oasis and Blur, The Chemical Brothers and Echo & The Bunnymen. They came close to winning the award for the 'Most Creative Stage Production' at the Concert Industry Awards in the US in January, but the *Swing* tour was pipped to the post by Kiss, still bravely trawling their comic-book rock around the world. In February, after holidaying in the north of England, Robert worked on mixing live recordings and spent much of the rest of the spring at home, relaxing and writing.

In June a 'new' Cure release was made available exclusively and officially through *www.thecure.com*, the band's own website. Five thousand copies of a new limited edition EP, 'Five Swing Live', were released – a live recording of five *Wild Mood Swing* songs from the previous year's tour. Summer 1997 was the summer of the *Titanic* movie and *that* Celine Dion song, as well as of the death of Diana, Princess of Wales and Elton John's newly re-written version of 'Candle In The Wind.' As the year went by, 'London's Most Wanted' Xfm radio station continued to make progress towards its full broadcast licence and its launch on September 1. A series of gigs were arranged around London venues to promote the new station. Venues ranging from the Jazz Café to the Borderline were booked, with Gene, Echobelly, Headswim, Stereolab and many other bands and performers down to appear. Test broadcasts were promoted in the run up to the official launch – with The Cure, Pulp, Prodigy and Underworld all involved. With Robert, concert promoter Harvey Goldsmith and Chris Parry amongst the shareholders, the station – five years on from its early beginnings as a radio station broadcasting at 1991's Reading Festival, and those early broadcasts from the Fiction offices – would challenge the preconceived ideas of popular radio scheduling and would fuel the careers of many nationally-known DJs, including Mary Anne Hobbs and Steve Lamacq, both involved from the early days. The September launch, aimed at an estimated initial listenership of around half a million people within London's M25 orbital motorway, was threatened by the untimely death of Princess Diana the day before the station was due to go fully functional. "There was a moment where we thought 'perhaps we shouldn't launch?'" co-founder Sammy Jacob told *NME*. "(In the end) we played Radiohead's 'Street Spirit (Fade Out).'" The station dedicated the whole day to Diana's memory, and followed the Radiohead track with the MC5's 'Kick Out The Jams!'

In August there were rumours of a new Cure studio album in the making, but it was to be another year at least before it really seemed to take shape. Robert did discuss new Cure material with interviewers, hinting at collaborations with people from outside the band, but it was to be some time before anything became available. Cinema goers got a blast of pure Cure in the new Mike Leigh movie *Career Girls*, which featured Cure songs throughout, as the story of two college friends revisiting their dysfunctional past used 'The Lovecats', 'The Walk' and others on its soundtrack. Instead of a new album in 1997, *Galore: The Singles 1987–1997* was the much vaunted collection that brought the story of the band's chart career up to date, gathering material from the decade since *Standing On A Beach*. Both the album, the DVD and video, and the new single 'Wrong Number', were released in October, in time for the Christmas market. 'Wrong Number' was the new track on this album of old material, featuring a collaboration with Reeves Gabrels, one of Bowie's favoured guitarists and former member of Tin Machine, and is one of Robert's more psychedelic lyrics, frenetic and ballsy musically. The track was co-produced by Mark Plati, who himself had worked on Bowie's *Earthling* album, and who Robert had met at Bowie's birthday gig in New York. Of course 'Wrong Number' made it into the charts, and was very successful in the USA where it reached number nine on the *Billboard* Modern Rock chart – but this time only reached a disappointing sixty two in the UK, despite featuring the first new Cure/Tim Pope video since 'Friday I'm In Love.'

The inspiration for *Galore* was two-fold. Firstly, The Cure were under regularly-applied pressure to release a career spanning *Greatest Hits* compilation (a subtly different project to a singles collection), yet Robert did not want to do this. "I've always held it in my mind that when the group finishes, the *last* thing that's going to come out (will be a) *Greatest Hits*," he told *Addicted To Noise* in September, just before the release of the album. Another more practical reflection was that Robert spotted that if all the singles since *Standing On A Beach* were lined up sequentially, The Cure had reached the limit of what would fit on a single CD. If the songs were to be 'archived' together on one disk at any point, now was the time. 'Wrong Number' was, naturally, a favourite for Smith at the time. "I think it's one of the best things we've done in the last ten years," Robert told *Music Connection* in the States. "It makes me feel good about what we are doing ... I was really pleased that the last ten years have been as good as they have been."

While promotional activity for *Galore* was in full swing (in LA a mini-riot broke out at the Virgin Megastore on Sunset Boulevard when the band appeared there to sign copies for hundreds of excitable fans), Robert was already working on another new project, this time an extensive B-sides collection, and still talking of the time 'after' the next new Cure album would be released, which according to *Billboard* would be in the spring of the following year. "We have started recording stuff, but it's been very stop-start," Robert told an interviewer at the end of 1997. There were plenty of songs, but Robert had reached the stage where he had then to go away and work on them in private to assess each one, before bringing the project back to the open forum. Much of the work had already been discarded by the end of '97, and Robert's home studio was the testing ground for a new kind of feel, much driven by loops and samples. 'Wrong Number' certainly pointed the way: "It's been influenced by listening to people like Xstatic," said Robert on Jam TV in December 1997. "But it's not really dance music." Ideas bounced around as to what the album actually would consist of – a double album containing twelve songs, one disc in a rock medium, the other in a dance medium – but the same twelve songs? A series of collaborative tracks featuring different artists? "The writing is heavier than what I've been writing over the last five years," Robert told *The Boston Globe*. "Not gloomier ... just taking fewer prisoners."

It would be a while before we got to hear the full results. Robert's collection of B-sides project was already growing to mammoth proportions too; he could foresee at least three discs-worth of material, and it had been decided to release it sufficiently later than *Galore* so as not to confuse the message about what the band were currently about. It would actually be a lot longer than that before the project finally saw the light of day.

Promoting the singles compilation meant a flurry of live appearances, including a club gig in New York at the end of October, and appearances on *The Tonight Show* and K-ROQ Radio. In the UK the band appeared on comedian Jack Docherty's TV show and again on *TFI Friday* with Chris Evans, also playing a session for radio station XFM on Bonfire Night. Through December a series of US radio theatre dates were played, from Philadelphia to Texas, Boston to Portland, Oregon, before the band returned to London to wind up the year in London once again with two dates at Shepherd's Bush Empire in mid-December.

It really seemed as though the end of The Cure might genuinely be not far away. With the band's worldwide contracts coming to a natural close with their next album, Robert started to talk about life beyond forty, and it seemed as though he genuinely felt that The Cure after the year 2000 might not work for him any more. "I decided in 1983 that, walking into the new millennium I should be doing something new," he told *The Orange County Register*. That "something new" would involve film music, "but then we can do the comeback tour in 2002!" he joked.

*

1998 was a year of extra-curricular activity for Robert. Most entertaining, was an appearance in *South Park*, and there was also a contribution to a tribute album, a movie piece, and work on the new album.

South Park was, as it neared the end of its first series in early 1998, *the* cult TV animated show on US television. Launched in 1997, it featured the lives of four third-graders in the Colorado town of South Park – a world somewhere between that of Homer Simpson and Beavis & Butthead. Episode 12 of the first series featured Robert, who had seen some of the early shows when in America. "A script was faxed through with just my lines on it, and I tried desperately to piece together what I thought the story would be – and I was way off. I didn't know I was actually fighting Barbra Streisand for the future of South Park!" In the episode, Cartman finds an ancient triangle that Streisand – transformed into 'Mecha-Streisand' – wants, as it will give her world-dominating powers. Movie critic Leonard Maltin, and actor Sidney Poitier both fail in their attempts to reclaim the gem, and so it is up to Robert (or 'Smithra' as he becomes) to save the planet, and hurl Mecha-Streisand into outer space. Right at the end of the show, Kyle hilariously shouts out "*Disintegration* is the best album ever."

"I was actually as taken aback when I first saw it as anyone else was ..." said Robert. "I suppose I was suspecting they were going to take the piss, but it was nice hearing them say that *Disintegration* was the best album ever made. I thought that was a very sweet moment for me ... as Carlton would say!" As well as joining with them on *South Park*, Robert also contributed a track – 'A Sign From God' – to the *South Park* creators Trey Parker/Matt Stone's film *Orgazmo*, the soundtrack for which was issued in the autumn.

As usual, The Cure undertook a series of festival dates through the summer. They played the Axion Beach Festival in Belgium in July, the Forestglade Festival in Austria, dates in the heat of the Mediterranean summer at Nimes, just down the road from Orange. After that, an Italian festival, a trip back to France to Lyon and the Taubertal Open Air Festival in Germany meant that they had played six major European dates in five different countries in less than ten days. Portugal, Spain, Germany, Switzerland and The Czech Republic, where they played at the Brno Sun Festival, followed in quick succession, until they finally came to some kind of rest in St Tropez on the French Riviera.

Ray Cokes was at the time the host of MTV's show *Most Wanted*. Unbeknown to most of his seventy-five-strong wedding party, he had arranged a little light entertainment for his guests at his St Tropez wedding. Like so many brand new bridegrooms, Cokes took the stage to the delight of friends and family, and partied into an attempt to sing The Cure's 'Just Like Heaven'. As it would be for most of us, it wasn't the greatest success. "Where are The Cure when you need them?" asked Ray, when he forgot the lyrics to the song. Right on cue, having arrived in the tiny French seaside town that afternoon, Robert and the boys walked on stage and took over the evening's entertainment ... some wedding!

The story reminds me also of the 1998 movie *The Wedding Singer*, starring Adam Sandler and Drew Barrymore. Sandler plays the role of a sympathetic wedding singer who falls in love with Barrymore's character despite her being engaged to someone else who is wholly unsuitable. Set in the mid-Eighties, filled with choice Eighties references, rolled-back jacket sleeves and Flock of Seagulls hair-cuts, the movie is extremely likeable, and includes a cameo role from Billy Idol at the end. Sandler's character Robbie lies in the dark one night listening to 'Boys Don't Cry', and at one point plays a savage, bitter and hysterically funny song to Barrymore on his guitar. Introducing the snippet, he mutters words to the effect of 'When I wrote this I'd been listening to The Cure a lot." Happy Days.

A snippet of solo Smith appeared mid-year in the shape of a track that Robert – recorded without the rest of the band – contributed to the *X-Files* album *Fight The Future*. Robert claimed inspiration from a classical dance piece, Khatchaturian's *Gayane Ballet Suite* (which had been used in the movie *Aliens)* for the track. 'More Than This' was sandwiched between tracks by Bjork, Foo Fighters, Sarah McLachlan, Noel Gallagher and Ween amongst others, and was an instrumentally gentle piece, orchestral in tone over a cool dance groove. Lyrically the song was a typically romantic, sensitive piece that managed to encapsulate the 'other worldliness' of the X-Files without being a song about aliens.

Mid-year also saw another extracurricular moment for The Cure as they contributed a track – 'World In My Eyes' – to the

Depeche Mode tribute album *For The Masses*. The bands had a number of connections, not least Perry's having been to school with Martin Gore and his brother Daryl's role with the Mode. Over the years the bands had got to know one another pretty well, and Robert described them as "among our very few showbiz friends" in an interview for 'Rocktropolis.' The Cure – like most of the other bands on the album, which included contributions from Smashing Pumpkins, Deftones, Veruca Salt and Rammstein amongst others – deliberately avoided trying to sound anything like Depeche Mode at all, and theirs was a unique contribution to what turned out to be an interesting collection of tracks. The Cure have themselves been the 'victims' of tribute albums themselves, notably back in 1996 when a bunch of American bands covered Cure songs on the album *Give Me The Cure*. Bands such as Shudder To Think, Chisel, Eggs and Tuscadero covered songs from '10:15 Saturday Night' and 'Killing An Arab' to 'Shake Dog Shake' and 'Piggy In The Mirror', – an eclectic collection. Robert was circumspect himself on the subject when discussing tribute albums in general: "There were bits that I liked about it..." he said. "I wrote to the groups involved, thanking them for their efforts. It's a difficult subject."

As the year wound to a close, work on the follow-up album to *Wild Mood Swings* and *Galore* was well under way. A gig on behalf of Miller Beer in London was another unusual date for the band before they moved back into Jane Seymour's mansion outside Bath. The first night there, Robert listened closely to *Pornography*, and he immediately felt a sense that the band were about to produce something equally weighty, equally "important."

Robert turned forty in April 1999. It was – as it is for most of us – inevitably a time of reflection. Reviewing *Pornography*, Robert was looking back at *Disintegration* too. That album had been enormously personal for Smith: it was, as he told one Italian interviewer in 2000, more than anything "about me", and no other Cure release had been quite so personal. Spending more time having the kind of private life that The

Cure's work rate had denied him throughout the Eighties also meant that Robert had chance to really reflect upon his work: the album needed to 'sound like The Cure' again. As the lyric to 'Out Of This World' suggested, Robert was looking back and re-assessing where he belonged.

Smith made a complete *volte face* with the material that had already been recorded. As he told *Record Collector* in 2004, "I thought, 'This is fucking awful,'" and he ditched a lot of the tracks recorded to date. 'Possession', which appears on *Join The Dots,* was given by Robert as an example – these tracks were not 'The Cure.' Robert described the experience as a 'road to Damascus' moment: as 'Out Of This World' developed, a song that encapsulated everything that he felt the band should be doing, he recognised a rich seam for them to mine. The songs then began to develop the kind of context that *Disintegration* boasted: an emotional intensity that ran throughout the work. With the sessions complete, Robert spent two weeks in London on mixing duties, but after the rural bliss of the Bath countryside he ditched the city and headed out to the new studio-cum-farm opened by Genesis, where the mixing was ultimately completed. The finished album reflected Robert's guitar playing as much as anything: where previously he had written on keyboards, guitar or piano, this album was conceived *entirely* on guitar. Robert formalised a number of elements in the album's creation that kept the flow of mood throughout. He restricted tempo, key and instrumentation throughout, playing many of the guitar parts himself, and even recording his own six-string bass parts too. Most of the tracks were recorded live by Robert, Simon and Jason, with Perry and Roger O'Donnell overdubbing later. "With this album I went back to being the despot," Robert joked when interviewed by *The Chicago Tribune* in 2000. "I knew what I wanted from the start, and didn't listen to or care what anyone else had to say." Like *Wild Mood Swings*, the album was recorded on digital equipment, moving from Cubase to Pro Tools for much of the process.

If Robert had 'gone back' to a purer version of The Cure for his inspiration for *Bloodflowers,* he was also happy to reference Scottish band Mogwai as an influence (though of course they carried their own raft of Cure influence in their own work). "I'm indebted to (Mogwai) for re-awakening the idea of what you can do if you take a simple idea to an extreme," he told *Uncut* in early 2000. But regardless of the influence, this was definitely a Cure album of old. On its release in February 2000, the response from fans and reviewers was a mixture of ecstasy and relief: The Cure were back.

The album's opener, 'Out Of This World', is a beautifully-crafted piece of music, contemplative and ruminant. The melody is one of Robert's most simple, and most affecting. 'Watching Me Fall', maintains the sombre, acoustic tone, but employs a heavier sound, crushingly self-observing as the protagonist of the song slips into someone else's world. Originally conceived as an acoustic guitar and drum-loop demo, the sessions for the album turned this into what Robert called "a Meatloaf classic," until it was pared back down to basics again after a number of takes and edits. It is always worth distancing 'Robert' from the 'I' of his songs: although professing to write about 'me', Smith is far too eclectic and sophisticated a lyricist for listeners to assume that every time he refers to 'I' he actually means himself. To interpret songs in this way often gets more to their root than simply reading Robert's work as an autobiography in progress. 'Watching Me Fall' in particular seems to blur the line between 'self' and otherwise – a fantastic piece of music.

'Where The Birds Always Sing' for some reason always reminds me of The Beatles' *Sergeant Pepper* album. Not any particular track nor any specific moment: maybe it's the choppier rhythms, the ascending chord sequences. Once again, Robert's lyrics look through a doorway into another world where truth and the assumptions we live by are different: there's always another way, where one survives and others die. It's a theme running throughout The Cure. 'Maybe Someday' bares a similar soul, but if the previous track implied life's resolution in another world, this time the song 'walks away' from finding that fulfilment in the here and now: maybe, someday, one day ... but don't look for it here baby.

'The Last Day Of Summer', all acoustic and pensive, is another of Robert's best later-Cure melodies, floating around on minor chords to the themes of belief, existence, truth and dreams. The song has an internal struggle in the image of cold summers and inevitable ageing. The wonderful 'band' feel of the entire album is perhaps nowhere more evident than on this track, the sounds of regret and reflection laid bare for every listener. 'There Is No If ...' is gently funky, and the images of first love, rain and the experiences and conversations of the young lovers are beautifully drawn out as the song rounds back to the major key. The lyric then comes more to the present and questions those first, fleeting moments of young love. Where does it end? What does it mean to love? One of the gifts of Robert's writing is his ability to leave the doors open at the end of a song – however much 'There Is No If ...' appears to answer a question, it inevitably leaves the listener with another series of questions to answer.

'The Loudest Sound' is slow and stately once more, fired by Simon's bass lines and punchy drums from Cooper. The trademark Cure single-note riffs are discrete, a far cry from the big hit singles of the Eighties and early Nineties. If Robert's lyric really means there is nothing left to say then that in itself is said moodfully, artfully and understandingly. The song has a whisper of some of the influences going way back in Robert's career, reminding me in particular of the mood of the second side of Bowie's *Low*: dignified and noble. Once again the writer's eye is on relationships both interpersonal and internal ... a song to take home and figure out for ourselves. '39' – composed originally on Robert's thirty-ninth birthday – typifies a certain element of Robert's creative process at the time. He was able to admit to *X-Press* that while he was "quite morose" in the making of some of the album, he realised that he hadn't had "any major breakdown." On *Disintegration*, Robert had notably thrown away a lot of his personal effects, paring his life down to the 'now.' He did a similar thing for *Bloodflowers* – not literally, but reviewing books and influences that had put together the Robert Smith that he had become by 1998/99 and then discarding them: "It all conspired to become the sort of nostalgic, melancholy album that *Bloodflowers* turned into."

The titular 'Bloodflowers' rounds the collection off: it's a searing song of fading flowers, internal dialogue and goodbyes. One extra track, 'Coming Up', appeared on the Japanese edition of the album and re-surfaced on *Join The Dots*, left off the major release of the album despite Robert's fondness for it. As he told Johnny Black for the *Join The Dots* liner notes, "we could never quite get it to fit." Once again Robert was keen to discuss the solo album that would, perhaps inevitably, follow *Bloodflowers*. But at the same time he admitted that if he did finally get that project up and running, he would probably ask the band members to play on it, and it would, ultimately, turn out to be a Cure album. From early in the life of *Bloodflowers* Robert linked the album to both *Pornography* and *Disintegration*, implying the concept of a trilogy that would ultimately be reflected in the Berlin concerts of 2002.

To promote the album, the *Dream* tour set off around the world, taking one of the world's hardest-touring acts back to France, Belgium, a gig at London's Astoria, and into America of course. Remembered as one of the very best-ever Cure tours, *Dream* took the band back to Australia and New Zealand again, where they finished the series of concerts – some seventy dates in all – in Brisbane in October. They had played to over one million people. Smith, still, could never do anything by halves.

Chapter 14: Cut Here?

In the spring of 2001, *Bloodflowers* was recognised at the Grammy awards as one of the best albums released by any band the previous year, an acknowledgement that reflected both the individual album's remarkable and candid nature and also The Cure's iconic status. After twenty-five years in a band, Robert was still listed in the nominations for 'alternative' albums – but then so was Sir Paul McCartney! The winner of the 'Best Alternative Album' went, unsurprisingly, to Radiohead for *Kid A*, so The Cure remained an alternative to the alternatives. The Grammy nominations and winners pointed again to the split personality of the record business. At one end, multiple nominations went to contemporary R&B acts such as Destiny's Child, to Eminem and Dr Dre. At the other, awards were won by acts from a generation ago – Steely Dan (back from the dead with *Two Against Nature*) took the 'Album Of The Year' and Joni Mitchell won the 'Traditional Pop Vocal' award for *Both Sides Now*. The Cure were where they so often had stood, slightly askew, a little too left of field, while U2, perma-darlings of the world media and virtual contemporaries of The Cure, won a basketful of gongs.

Bloodflowers, as *Record Collector* recorded, also saw the beginning of the end of Robert and The Cure's relationship with Fiction Records as an independent label. Ultimately sold to Universal Records, Fiction had been home to The Cure for over twenty years, and understandably Robert was distressed and angered by the sale. "That was more than a disappointment to me," he told Finnish magazine *Soundi* later. "(It) caused me all kinds of headaches." An understatement: one of Robert's first moves was to try and ensure that he had control of original tapes and recordings from across The Cure's recording history. "I have had to fight very hard to get some of my rights back to the material," Robert told Tero Alanko. "And I think it's been a real shame because we've been with Fiction for over twenty years." For *Record Collector* he was more graphic. "For about a day," he recalled with typical understatement in 2004, "it destroyed me."

Fortunately, the relationship with Universal continued on good terms. The first project, at last, was a Cure *Greatest Hits* package that looked back over their entire career and was the first evidence of Robert's long-term revision of The Cure's back-catalogue. In the wake of *Standing On A Beach* and *Galore*, Robert had always insisted that a *Hits* package would only be appropriate as a farewell to the band. Robert nevertheless got involved, picked the order of the tracks, and realised that if – in the wake of a new record deal – a *Hits* package *was* inevitable, it could actually be a platform to do something new with The Cure yet again.

"It was the first project that The Cure had been involved in that hadn't been instigated by the band", Robert told an interviewer for *AOL*, and yet he was happy that the record label had given him the rightful authority over the running order. For the first time, therefore, with the notion of *Hits* as opposed to *Favourites*, Robert chose to leave off the album singles such as 'Killing An Arab', 'Jumping Someone Else's Train', 'Primary' and 'Catch' amongst others. The eighteen tracks opened up with 'Boys Don't Cry', and finished with two new songs.

'Cut Here', released as a single in October 2001, cunningly signposted the final turfs being laid to rest on the grave of The Cure. Well, at least that is how everyone interpreted it – the title is both an anagram of 'The Cure' and thematically suggested an ending, a separation. The track snuck into the bottom reaches of the UK singles charts, spending a single, lonely week at number fifty four. Such a poor response from the single-buying public was a shame: the track is classic, bright-eyed, riff-friendly Cure, regretful, remorseful, enduringly hopeful. Engagingly conversational – another of Robert's wonderful dialogue songs – was the song really a goodbye to Parry as the rumours put forward? Robert specifically references his own handshake as "English" and lines about being too busy to talk to Billy (Parry had for ever been nicknamed 'Bill' within the Cure camp) suggest maybe. But remember – never assume the identity of the 'I' or the 'you.' Whatever, 'Cut Here' is a classic Cure piece which proved that after the sobriety of *Bloodflowers*, Robert hadn't lost his pop edge.

The other new track, 'Just Say Yes', featured an all-too-rare duet for Robert, this time with the exotic Saffron from Republica. With echoes of 'Wrong Number', and trademark yelps and howls in the intro, 'Just Say Yes' was another cracking new track. One early decision was to include not only new material, but also to put something unusual into the CD package for the millions of worldwide fans still hungry for more from the mighty five. So was born the idea of an acoustic version of the entire CD, mirroring the original songs but recorded especially for the release in the fall of 2001. While most Cure-watchers would probably have the majority of the original recordings of the songs on *Greatest Hits*, the bonus CD would be hugely popular with established fans. The project worked perfectly, and many of the songs sparkled anew in a purely acoustic setting. Perhaps this was because many of them had been composed originally in acoustic format anyway, so there was a natural sense of some of the songs being 'where they should be.' 'Boys Don't Cry' is heroically simple and still one of the catchiest pop songs ever written. 'A Forest' is warmly familiar, 'Inbetween Days' gently sublime.' 'Just Like Heaven' is a lovely arrangement, Robert sounding genuinely glad to be there. 'Lullaby' is comic-book dark, 'Lovesong' works perfectly, touching as an acoustic-only song. Even the two new tracks – not yet familiar with most listeners – sounded good in the 'bride stripped bare' acoustic arrangement.

*

The live Cure in 2001 was largely a series of promotional TV and radio appearances in the wake of the release of the *Greatest*

Hits and the 'Cut Here' single. 2002 saw appearances on the anarchic TV show *This is Dom Joly* and *Re:Covered*, the BBC show in which bands played one of their own songs and covered another artist's work. The Cure played 'Lovesong' to the delight of the Cure-strong audience, and then went on to cover Thin Lizzy's 'Don't Believe A Word', an affectionate nod back to one of Robert's earliest influences. A series of festival dates (as usual) occupied the band over the summer months – in Greece, Switzerland, Italy, Sweden, Germany, France, Hungary, Portugal and Belgium. A major event was the gig in Hyde Park, London in July, with support from Mogwai and The Cranes: to an audience of about 20,000 people the band played a two-hour set, and included a number of old songs such as 'M' and 'The Drowning Man', a gig to which fans travelled from all over the world.

The major dates for 2002 though were two nights in Berlin in November. As the interviews included on the *Trilogy* DVD testify, Robert was inspired to attempt to represent the trilogy of *Pornography/Disintegration/Bloodflowers* in its entirety after having seen Bowie play the entire *Low* album from end to end in concert and feeling that The Cure could say something about elements of their own work in a similar context. The concept also gave Robert the opportunity to document the current line-up of the band live on film formally, as *The Cure In Orange* had done previously. Two nights at the Tempodrom in Berlin were recorded, the film directed by Nick Wickham, with Robert and Daryl Bamonte as Executive Producers. After considering other venues – Barcelona, Moscow, London – Berlin was chosen for largely symbolic and cinematic reasons: the austerity and depth of the three albums' worth of music, would not, Robert felt, bear quite the same weight in a warm Mediterranean climate, and while Berlin was a much more open city than it had been in the days before The Wall came down, it still had a grand and dramatic flavour to add to the shows themselves.

The release of *Trilogy* in the spring of 2003 to some extent put the lid on The Cure's reputation and cemented their profile as one of the most significant bands of their generation. Anyone who had a part-formed opinion on the band who saw the shows on screen must have come to the conclusion that they had missed so much. It confirmed the band musically: *so* focused; *so* involved. The production was greeted with ecstatic reviews from all quarters, a dream come true for Cure fans and – indeed – lovers of all good events in rock. The set ran through the three albums faultlessly, and in the original format of each record's release: opening naturally with *Pornography*, the immediate sense of serious minds at play was created with a quote from Romantic poet John Keats, referring to "veil'd melancholy." Triptych-like images of Berlin introduced the city and the flavour of the show – observational, dramatic, significant. A brief "Hello" from Robert introduced the great, majestic chords of 'One Hundred Years', interspersed with footage of a craning, yearning, emotionally high audience. The hand-held camera work was fantastic, giving a truly unique flavour both of the show at large and the sense of being on-stage, a part of the band itself. Far more than *Orange*, where there was enough to go around then, there is a sense of true emotional involvement. Robert seemed very focused, the band very much 'into' the gig from the first moment, and those crashing guitar chords demonstrated how far The Cure had travelled from those poppy, riff-driven early singles to become truly imposing and regal. Anyone who believed that U2 were the world's premier stadium band would have been forced to look afresh at The Cure in 2003 and agree that they were more than mere contenders for the title. Not goths. Not pop stars. But a mighty machine with the momentum of an army on the move.

'A Short Term Effect' cemented the opening atmosphere with dissonant, Gabrels-style guitar, the take-no-prisoners lighting effects careering around the stage almost as much as Simon, his bass slung low and his pacing around the set aggressively concentrated. Fantastic. Peter Hook eat your heart out. The band were on the money throughout – Robert's playing belligerent and articulate in turn: those late childhood nights listening to Hendrix chord structures and rhythm lines well-spent.

There is little respite throughout the entire set. 'Plainsong' introduced the *Disintegration* pieces, jangling bells ringing spectrally above the audience in the cold Berlin night. The band re-took the stage to an audience clearly deeply involved in the performance, fireworks held aloft, the sparkling of a thousand lights around the arena, and then the grand cataclysm of those funereal opening chords ... Jason's drumming was eloquent and perfectly paced to illustrate the guitar chords that lead up to Robert's vocal, as he let go of the guitar and gripped the microphone emotionally. The end of the world ... track after track achieved near-perfection.

Clearly in any major live production there are going to be bum notes here and there, camera faults and editing disasters. If any of this took place it isn't evident in the movie: this is a band in total command of their instrumentation and of their performance, at one moment head-down and concentrated, the next facing the crowd in a kind of shared delirium. Compared to the whimsical pop of the band's Eighties videos and Tim Pope fictions, this was also an immensely *masculine* performance, no feyness in the rolling of Robert's eyes, a genuine sense of emotional need as he crossed his arms over his guitar and hugged himself protectively. 'Lovesong', with its gentle melody came not as a moment of light relief, but as a huge emotional release, its breezy keyboard lines and swirling guitar licks carrying so much beneath Robert's lyric. Gorgeous. After the crashing waves of 'Last Dance', 'Lullaby' assumed a funky pace and slowed the evening down further, spooky and intriguing, as Robert annotates the lyrics with little gestures and waves of his fingers, illustrating the song for the crowd as though telling a story, a wicked smile and the occasional grimace across his lips.

The process of watching *Trilogy* from start to finish is emotionally draining. *Bloodflowers*, as Robert hoped, fits seamlessly alongside the earlier two albums. The package contained much more than the shows themselves, and the interviews that wrap up the third disc were a gift to the fans always keen to find the nuggets of gold in the flowing rivers of The Cure legend. They tell much about the concerts themselves and about the band's history, but also act as a formal tribute to the thousands and thousand of fans who trek literally thousands of miles to follow The Cure; of how they can look in the front row and recognise individuals gig after gig; how the band specifically think of how they can include the fan-base in what they do; how they meet and greet informally with fans before and after shows and "know fifty percent of the audience by their first name." And how, every time The Cure tours it seems as though there is a new, young audience there to meet them afresh.

Most rewardingly for the committed Cure fan, there was a fire in Robert's eyes during the interviews, a sharpness that confirmed that he was still hugely motivated by The Cure. He was not finished yet, not by a long way.

*

In the spring, The Cure appeared again on Dom Joly's show, playing 'Inbetween Days' and 'A Night Like This', chatting to the irreverent presenter who had been a Smith-lookalike goth in his pre-TV days.

In a move that seemed to guarantee releases of new product for at least the foreseeable future, The Cure signed a new record deal with Ross Robinson's label I AM early in 2003. The three album deal generated a great deal of excitement in the media: Robinson had met The Cure at one of their festival dates in Switzerland back in 2002, and was a long-time fan. "They were instrumental in my approach to production," he told *Billboard* in the media flurry that followed, "...(and) opened me up to a more sensitive, heartfelt type of music." For his part, Robert was equally impressed. "I knew [straight away] that I wanted to work with him," he warmly told *VH1*.

"He re-awakened all the old passion for The Cure that was dormant in me ... reminded me why people love what we do so much."

Robinson's resumé included heavy duty acts such as Slipknot and Korn: hardcore bands with a dense, uncompromising and sepulchral tone to their own music that implied a natural progression for whatever his work with The Cure might turn out to be.

New material would inevitably come from the new relationship with Robinson. At the same time rumours abounded that Robert was again working on *that* solo album, to be frequented by various guest artists as yet unconfirmed by Smith himself, though he did hint in Finnish magazine *Soundi* in July 2003 that solo material could be released as early as 2004. During the summer months studio time was taken up with new material, as the relationship with Robinson pointed towards the release of a new album. In the meantime, with only a handful of appearances live in 2003, Robert returned to his archiving project on the band. Barely six months after the release of *Trilogy*, *Join The Dots* appeared. The collection represented a wander around to the back of the Cure's fictional house to view the edifice from a whole new perspective.

Join The Dots was a lavish production upon which Robert had been working for a long time, emotionally backtracking as well as literally re-assessing the hundreds of tapes and records – released and un-released – that the band had produced over the years. Released in January 2004, the four-CD set was a superbly-presented, matt-laminated set containing 70 Cure B-sides and rarities, with extensive notes from Johnny Black in the accompanying booklet, put together with Robert and Simon, who apparently met up in a pub in Crawley, Hampshire (ie. not Robert's 'home town') to work through the project. The collection also serves as a fantastic visual history of the band, with early shots of the smiling Dempsey/Tolhurst/Smith-Cure transmuting into later pics of the dishevelled, bohemian band of the late Nineties and the black-garbed band of more recent years. The selection opens with obvious early tracks: '10:15 Saturday Night' and 'Plastic Passion', 'Pillbox Tales' and 'Do The Hansa', their paean to their first record label, were from the same period but only released as the B-sides to the re-release of 'Boys Don't Cry' in 1986. Played with vigour and aggression, the 'Hansa' track features spirited backing vocals over a disco beat, and reviews their early and bitter experience at the hands of that first record label so long ago. For those Cure fans who missed out on the *Flexipop* free disc 'Lament', the version was included here, all synth and beat box, washed over with Robert's little wooden flutes. The collection includes new information from Smith on the recording processes of many of the tracks included. The first disc also includes the three tracks that accompanied 'The Walk', including the re-worked version of 'Lament' that had become a favourite of Smith's.

Disc 1 also includes the track 'New Day', which Smith remembers in the accompanying booklet as the last thing he did before Simon rejoined the band. Robert remembers being taking to hospital having collapsed after the session. The vocals are a strange mix – Billy Mackenzie meets The Banshees – and the lyrical mood dark and grim.

Disc 2 opens with 'A Japanese Dream', the B-side of 'Why Can't I Be You?' followed by 'Breathe'. Recorded in France during the *Kiss Me* sessions, 'Breathe', with a gentle mixture of keyboard sounds from synth strings to flute-like textures, is a stately reminder of the reflective side of Robert Smith, his multi-tracked vocals washing in and out of one another. Culled from the same source – the B-side of 'Catch', 'A Chain Of Flowers' was born out of Smith's shortage of lyrical input for the Miraval sessions, and in the liner notes to the collection he remembered for Johnny Black how he had asked the other members of the band to give him some words to work on. Of the unreleased tracks on the collection, three versions of The Doors' 'Hello I Love You' are included. The first one opened up *Rubaiyat*, the Elektra celebration album, overtly influenced by The Kinks. A second thrash-metal version is included, occupying no more than the ten seconds that it originally occupied on the *Rubaiyat* record, while the unreleased version is a dark, slow-tempo, keyboard-led track with water-droplet piano and teutonic drumming that recalls 'The End' more than any other Doors track, including a short trumpet solo reminiscent of Robert Wyatt in jazz mode. On all three, Robert's vocals are more measured, less frenetic than on other Cure tracks of the period: the emotional detachment involved in covering other people's songs seems to have given him a break from forcing his own emotions into the open.

Disc 3 features a number of unreleased tracks, including a dignified twelve-inch remix of 'Scared Of You', during the recording of which Robert was in tears. Also here are two versions of Hendrix's 'Purple Haze'. One, recorded for the 1993 Hendrix tribute album *Stone Free*, is an unusual, funky and atmospheric track, the vocals of which take an age to materialize. Smith plays some lead guitar lines with a gentle nod back to the master. The other version, recorded for broadcast on Virgin Radio's opening night, is an entertaining, literal version of the song with much the same arrangement as Hendrix's original: The Cure as A Big Rock Band. Also included is 'Burn', the song written for the Alex Proyas movie *The Crow,* sounding like a pastiche of David Bowie's 'Panic In Detroit', it soon opens up into Cure territory. Interestingly, it is followed on the compilation by the lilting, jerky version of Bowie's 'Young Americans', recorded for XFM. The track has none of Bowie's driving plastic soul, but instead has a typically Cure-like sense of cautious observation, though Robert handles the machine-gun lyrical rush of the second half of the song really well. 'Dredd Song', from the *Judge Dredd* movie, the *X-Files* track 'More Than This', and 'World In My Eyes', from the Depeche Mode homily *For The Masses* make for interesting listening too.

The collection is a prodigious achievement, a wonderful representation of The Cure that long-time fans had always known: varied, emotional, witty, original, carefully considered and above all a collection of great integrity.

The press were mixed in their reaction to the set. *NME* called it "not so brilliant" (maybe just a *little* bit brilliant then?) while *Q* said "only Cure collectors need apply here," (surely partly the point?) Some reviewers missed the point entirely. Still intent on interpreting the band as gloomful goths (surely by now an outdated stereotype), and perhaps still falling foul of an outdated concept of what the band are about, *Mojo* nevertheless observed that "The Cure are creeping sullenly back into fashion." Over recent years a number of bands with an increasing public profile and voice had name-checked The Cure amongst their big influences. Mogwai had already been connected with The Cure, but younger bands like Interpol and The Rapture were clearly influenced by all stages of The Cure's career to date. But the reviewer missed the point: *Join The Dots* was not intended to be an essential introduction to the band for novices, but a rummage through their history to paint the good and the bad but most importantly the more obscure corners of their extensive catalogue. It was not a collection intended to establish The Cure's credentials (the various compilations and *Trilogy* had surely done that). I don't think even Robert himself would claim that everything in the collection is great, or even essential. If *Mojo* struggled with the three versions of 'Purple Haze', surely they missed the point that to present such a vignette of the band is – good or bad – intrinsically *interesting* for people whose interest is The Cure? And if one's curiosity was only part-formed, then *Join The Dots* was not for you. Yet.

The Cure have always enjoyed a good relationship with the silver screen, and in mid-2004 released the theme music to the French cartoon series *The Dragon Hunters*, the first 'new' release since 2001's 'Just Say Yes'. The series had been extremely successful in France, and hopes were high for its adoption in the US schedules. This quietly released single presaged a flurry of activity in the middle of the year though, as – four years after *Bloodflowers* and eight since *Wild Mood*

Swings – a new Cure album was definitely on the way.

Sessions for what would become the self-titled album *The Cure* were held at Olympic studios in London. The title implied a declaration of intent on behalf of the band: 'this album represents everything that *is* The Cure in 2004.' For the first time since *Three Imaginary Boys*, Robert allowed someone else total control of the production process, handing over to Robinson. "Ross put us in a very confined space," Robert told *VH1*, as he recounted the 'live' atmosphere that the producer sought. Having worked through demos and chosen the tracks for the album – a point of contention as Robinson wanted a 'darker' album, whereas Robert wanted to appeal to 'music' fans, not just Cure fans – towards the end of the sessions the band worked on a track per day facing the studio's control booth. When all the technicalities were worked out and the final recording ready, they would turn away, light candles, and play the track live – with Robert's vocal live too. Ironically giving Robinson control freed the band themselves. "He allowed us the freedom to put what we wanted on the album … (and) it wound up sounding like a Cure record," Robert told *VH1.com*. In short, Robinson had somehow put Robert *back* in the band.

The album evolved into one of the Cure's most eclectic-sounding, yet throughout there is an urgency of spirit and a clarity of attack that came from the band's new-found relationship with their producer. If the band had been written off by a cynical press more times than the insurance policies on the Titanic, and equally so by Robert's own periodic doubts about the band's future, this was the sound of a band who felt they had more than just a future, but a *big* future. Robinson's experience with the style-defining production of the likes of Korn put an honest clarity into the sound. "Ross gave me a confidence to sing," Robert told *XFM*. "It sounds strange that I would be lacking confidence, but … I was the guitarist when we started. I've never been a natural singer … I feel much more comfortable with my head down playing a guitar."

From its first opening scrawl, 'Lost' starts tugging at the listener's lapels, feeling his collar and drawing him into the album. And with that first lyric we are caught. This is a man in his middle years still struggling with the issues that he struggled with as a young man, but in a more mature voice, with a diffe rent set of values in place. It's intriguing – and fascinating. The song had emerged from Robert's solo musings, but as a piece that didn't fit the project. It fitted *The Cure* though, as Robert explained on *XFM*: "There's always *a* song that I write and I think 'if we do another Cure album then *this* is it – this is where it starts.'"

The acoustic, eastern cadences of 'Labyrinth' have a similar pace, a similar needful imagery as the lyric and the riff circle around one another with a kind of frustrated menace, trying to establish some kind of foothold, some permanence. 'Before Three' opens with one of Robert's curious little howls, the major key and the melodic bass line rendering a wonderful vocal from Robert as positive as the song itself. In 'Truth, Goodness and Beauty' the lyric dissects the age-old contradiction between absolute concepts like 'truth' and relative concepts such as beauty and goodness. 'The End Of The World' is musically upbeat, like Cure songs of old, the melody and bass lines are inextricably linked, the guitar sharp and crisp, the pace varying. Released as a single to launch the album, the track is a distinctly 'old-fashioned' Cure statement, fantastically melodic and irresistible, especially the backing vocals. Where on earth do these melodies come from, after so many songs, so many albums?

'Anniversary' is darker, a collection of industrial noises introducing heavily sustained guitar, a track that could have come from any of the *Trilogy* albums. Similarly heavy in content comes 'Us Or Them', one of the very few Cure songs (the only Cure song?) that has a political content. In the wake of the 9/11 atrocities in New York and Washington, Robert's vocal attack is passionate. Interestingly, if this is a rant against political positioning it is not the politics that frustrates, but its intrusion into the singer's own world that hurts, with the reverse holding equally true. The song is deeply passionate, exciting and furious. The terror is not of terrorism itself, but of the politics that it creates intruding into our personal lives.

'alt.end' was released as the second single from the album in October, in the wake of the ensuing tour and festival dates that the band took on over the summer. Readable as a song about endings, the lyric is also clearly one half of a dialogue between the two halves of a relationship. '(I Don't Know What's Going) On' is boldly romantic, some of Robert's most acrobatic singing on the album, chasing a fantastic melody around Jason's groovy drumming, leaping octaves ecstatically. On 'Taking Off' there's more upbeat Cure: optimistic, adoring and buoyant. 'Never' turns back into a darker corner, challenging, abrasive, nestled up against the penultimate track 'The Promise.' Vocally extreme again, 'The Promise' is slowly repetitive, turning a handful of chords over and over to see what's hidden underneath them, promises of healing and forgetting, love and salvation. The last track, 'Going Nowhere' is a gently falling, melodic piece, piano and acoustic guitar wrapping up the collection of songs touchingly melodic and familiarly dark in turns.

Reviews were ecstatic, and the album generally deemed not only a return to form for The Cure but one of their best albums of all. Writing this book a year after its release, I think that *The Cure* is one of the best albums they have ever released. It has everything, but – where it could have lost focus – it maintains a tone throughout that stops it becoming patchy: darkness and anger, melody and poppiness abound, but in the same voice. Robert was very aware of this blend too, and he joked with Zane Lowe at the BBC that "there's lite, and then there's Cure-lite," not quite the same thing. The packaging for the album was intriguing too. Robert had asked nephews and nieces to draw the pictures for him, with three instructions: draw a good dream, draw a bad dream, and include the name of the band somewhere in the picture. The various pieces selected had a wonderful sense of innocence and a kind of surreal eccentricity, lifting the entire concept of the album out of the world of rock and roll and dipping it into some magical river of dreams.

*

The Cure hit the top ten all over the world, debuting at number one in Mexico, number two in Italy, three in Germany, four in France, and five in Spain. UK buyers took the album straight into the chart albeit only at number eight, and it entered the *Billboard* chart one place higher than that. From June onwards The Cure were back on the road (yet) again playing summer festivals across Europe as they had so many times before: three in Italy; three in Germany; three in France; Belgium; Manchester, England; Eire, Denmark, Spain and Portugal. As they hit America, The Cure fulfilled the ambition of many bands big and small. "A dream come true," as Robert described it to BBC Radio 1's Zane Lowe in a charming interview in October of 2004. The *Curiosa* festival was a unique experience for all concerned. In short, based on ideas they had been mulling over for a year, The Cure instigated their own festival with bands of their own choosing to share the bill, and toured the States like a travelling circus rolling into town after town [recently, Perry Farrell's 'Lollapalooza' had redefined the festival circuit, and others such as Ozzy Osbourne had reinforced this newly revitalised style of transient show]. The concept was curiously simple: a bunch of bands on a main stage, and a rotating roster of other bands in support. Initially the selection of co-travellers was to include Polly Harvey and The Pixies, but eventually the list of chosen main bands was limited to Interpol, The Rapture and Mogwai. In rotation were Cooper Temple Clause, Muse, Thursday, Cursive, Melissa Auf Der Maur, Head Automatica and Scarling. The whole experience was perfect almost from start to finish: they even ran the entire series of events without a commercial sponsor – almost unheard of in these days of corporate rock tours – and kept ticket prices relatively low to encourage fans to come along.

The bands became very close to one another on the tour, and Robert told Zane Lowe of how, at the end of the tour, it was like the end of school days with everyone having to say goodbye. And, at a time when major festivals were not making the dimes and big name acts were cancelling shows due to disappointing ticket sales, The Cure bucked the trend.

Reviewing the Atlanta date, *Q* magazine caught Robert in a mood typical of most of the tour. "I'm thoroughly enjoying myself," he told that magazine. "Interpol are a great bunch of blokes, and Mogwai are the best band on the planet." The lifelong QPR fan talked of football matches between the bands ("though I might stay as player-manager. I think I'd be fooling myself if I thought I could magically waltz onto a football pitch at my age") and described Simon Gallup's heavy metal DJ act: "It's not ironic," Robert said. "He actually likes Slayer!" The Cure played for nearly two and a quarter hours, a set comprising almost two dozen songs, to an audience of 19,000. As at many of the shows, older Cure fans were enlightened by some of the younger bands on the set, while fans of Interpol and The Rapture, if they didn't know already, learned a lot about The Cure.

Curiosa played from Tampa, Florida to Carson, California; Dallas to Camden, New Jersey, starting on July 24 and winding up over a month later in Sacramento. Immediately afterwards, The Cure played three nights on the trot in Mexico under the headline *An Evening With The Cure*, selling out the Sports Palace in Mexico City – capacity 17,500 – in two hours flat for the first show. The two extra dates were added and these also sold out. With a hugely successful album, a knock-out tour and the world listening, The Cure played radio sessions, gave extensive and very well-humoured interviews on both sides of the Atlantic and even taped an *Icon* show for MTV. In short, the band and Robert worked extremely hard, apparently enjoying the critical re-appraisal that *The Cure* had brought about.

It was ironic then that a second round of promotions should focus on more 'new' product from The Cure, albeit the first in the re-issue series of original Cure albums from Fiction/Polydor/Universal. *Three Imaginary Boys* was re-released as a two-disc set comprising the original album and a second disc of 'rarities' – live versions, outtakes and demos. It was intended that it would be the first release in a series that would see the entire Cure back catalogue – eventually presumably up to and including *Bloodflowers* – re-packaged in all the original artwork from the fridge, the lamp and the hoover onwards. Beautifully presented in a gatefold sleeve, the album contained a booklet of liner notes by journalist Johnny Black, and was compiled by Robert himself. The concept for the re-issue package had been the record company's, but with Robert's endorsement and involvement the idea appealed to both parties. The result was a resounding success, and of course paved the way for more to come.

It's fascinating to go back and hear what it was that turned everybody on – slowly – in the first place. "Some of the stuff on the extras disc ... is awful," Robert told *Virgin Radio*. "Of necessity it's bad: we weren't that good when we started. Most bands aren't!"

'I Want To Be Old' smacks of Robert's enduring be-the-Buzzcocks fantasy. Eighteen-years-old, Lol thrashing wildly on the drums, 'Heroin Face' live is an entertaining recording. The home demo of '10:15 Saturday Night' is equally charming: it's a world so many of us lived in, plugging guitars into disused record players and rubber-banding microphones onto the hoover, struggling with tape recorders and home-made percussion instruments. But buried beneath Robert's demo are the bones of a song that would live on in The Cure's set for years and years, and we can watch the development of that song over three different versions. By the time the band cut a studio demo, gone was the little-symphony keyboard part, and in its place is a ballsy, gutsy performance. The live performance of the same song, which closes the disc, is different again – frenetic, rushed, and greeted with a well of affection by the babbling crowd. These aren't crap old demos, they're fascinating. Likewise the demo tape of 'Boys Don't Cry' reveals an already-polished songwriter and a song that (to appropriate a bit of David Bowie) "sold its soul to every bedsit room," on one of its first nights out. Like '10:15', it's a song to last forever.

April 2005 saw the simultaneous release of the next three albums. *Seventeen Seconds, Faith* and *Pornography* were equally well-received, and equally fascinating. *Pornography,* of course, had been relatively recently re-assessed in the wake of *Trilogy,* and listening to the bonus disc was like digging through the foundations of a grand country house. All three items contained some gems. Four Cult Hero tracks signal one of the first periods of major change in The Cure's history on the *Seventeen Seconds* rarities disc. Live versions of seminal pieces 'A Forest', 'Play For Today' and 'A Final Sound' are invaluable for the core Cure audience. Home demos of 'Faith' and 'Doubt' open up the *Faith* bonus disc: live versions of four tracks close the collection down before the sprightly step of 'Charlotte' can be heard rounding the album up neatly. But not everything was included. "A lot of things have remained unreleased for very good reasons." Robert told one interviewer in 2005.

The process of putting the albums together has so far been a double-edged sword for Smith. On the one hand he admits that he doesn't like looking back, and prefers to live in the present or the future to wallowing in the past, but nevertheless appears to have enjoyed the opening up of old boxes and unwinding of old tapes. "It's almost like reading your own diary," he told the BBC's Zane Lowe. "You kind of spend the first half of your life writing it and the second half of your life reading it." The critical response to the re-releases was as positive – if not more so – than that for *The Cure. Uncut* gave *Three Imaginary Boys* four stars, while *Rolling Stone* was more circumspect in its response, giving *Pornography* four stars but only two-and-a-half to *Faith. Mojo* gave *Seventeen Seconds* three stars, four to *Faith* and five stars to *Pornography.* In part the reviews simply assessed the original album, and almost overlooked the add-ons, but the general consensus was that this was a noble and valuable series of re-issues.

From *Bloodflowers* in 2000, through the *Greatest Hits* compilation and the single 'Cut Here', *Trilogy, Join The Dots,* 'The End Of The World', *The Cure*, 'alt.end', *Three Imaginary Boys, Seventeen Seconds, Faith* and *Pornography*, The Cure had completed a five year cycle of releases that brings their recording career up to date and begins the thorough process of reviewing it in full. It is a mighty body of work, stretching from 'Killing An Arab' in 1979 to 'alt.end' in 2004 and beyond. Popes and Presidents have been shot, Princesses have died, wars have been fought and cities bombed. But for a glance sideways once in a (beautifully observed) blue moon, you wouldn't know any of this from listening to the collected works of The Cure. While some bands – and U2 and REM spring to mind – have catalogued the politics and the passions of the changing world around them, The Cure have resolutely followed an interior path, dissecting issues of the soul, heart and mind, and largely leaving other matters to other people. Although in their private affairs it is clear that the band have donated large amounts of money to various charities over the years, the plights of those charities have not provided the band with their subject matter, nor have political affairs been a motivation. Instead, Robert Smith has – like Coleridge in his 'Lime Tree Bower' – sat and watched, quietly noted, and passed those notes on to us for us to take them apart in our own time. If half a lifetime has gone by, we have the other half to keep listening.

*

The year 2005 proved to be a fascinating year for Cure watchers. Increasingly connecting or connected with younger acts, in the wake of his duet with Saffron and his generous authentication of Mogwai, Interpol, The Rapture and the other *Curiosa* bands, Robert was linked with relative punk newcomers (and soon-to-be-defunct) Blink-182 when he appeared with them on stage just before the end of 2004, and on the track 'All Of Us' on their latest album. Blink member Mark Hoppus was elated by the link, having been a Cure fan since high school. "'Wouldn't it be awesome if we could get Robert Smith ... to play on this song,'" Hoppus remembered for one interviewer. "So we called him. (It was) like a dream come true."

At the Ivor Novello Awards in London – now snappily re-branded The Ivors – Robert was recognised by the music industry with one of its most prestigious awards. While Britney Spears had the UK's best-selling single with 'Toxic', and U2's powerhouse single 'Vertigo' took the gong for 'International Hit Of The Year'. The recently reformed Duran Duran surprised many when they were credited with an 'Outstanding Contribution To British Music' award. Fittingly, Robert was recognised with the award for 'International Achievement.' While contemporary bands like Coldplay were currently biting big chunks out of the *Billboard* charts, The Cure were one of the very few British bands of their generation who, along with Depeche Mode, really 'cracked' America big time, back when very few British acts could. But they have also built enormous audiences in Europe, South America and all over the world. It's a remarkable achievement, and especially as neither Robert nor the rest of the band have appropriated un-English characteristics. Smith's south-of-London accent has remained intact, he has never penned US AOR-style lyrics, and the band have rarely compromised to meet commercial demands. Their achievement is their own, as recognised by the award late in 2003 from Q magazine, who honoured Robert for his outstanding influence on contemporary rock.

In *Strange Fascination – David Bowie: The Definitive Story* author David Buckley observes that while America 'codified' the various subgenres of pop and rock – defining the protocol for R&B, blues, country etc – it fell to the British to 'stylise' it, blending genres, dressing music up and changing pop music for ever. "Someone such as Bowie," writes Buckley, "or The

Cure's Robert Smith ... could only come from England." But like Bowie, The Cure had escaped Englishness and become a truly worldwide, world-class act.

Still involved in outside projects, Robert also appeared on the release of *The Future Embrace*, ex-Pumpkin Billy Corgan's new solo album, on which the pair sang an unlikely and passionate rendition of the old Bee Gee's song 'To Love Somebody'.

Stranger things were afoot. Over the spring of 2005 something happened in the inner circle of the band and both Perry Bamonte and Roger O'Donnell left The Cure, apparently quite suddenly. The circumstances, as this book goes to press, were still unclear, and both sides have kept a dignified near-silence on the subject. On May 17, Roger posted a message on his website announcing that, after nearly twenty years, he was no longer in the band. A few days later The Cure's own site confirmed that the band's line-up had changed, that Perry and Roger were indeed no longer the band. In an interview at www.music.yahoo.com – an interview directly linked to www.thecure.com – Robert talked of how perhaps "too much shared experience" was the reason for the split. Once again the leader of a trio, Robert explained his view further: "It's like you get older married couples, who eat in silence – sort of how I imagine people who have been together for too long." At the same time the band announced a series of summer dates, including a headline performance at *Live8*, the summer's big rock day out, and in order to meet their commitments an old friend would come back once more.

Live8 was the brainchild of 'Sir' Bob Geldof, Boomtown Rat and latter-day Mother Theresa, with a big conscience and an even bigger influence on some of the most powerful men on earth. Rather than simply celebrate the twentieth anniversary of *Live Aid* by re-hashing the event, Geldof tied the anniversary of 1985's big moment to the G8 summit of world leaders that was to be hosted in Scotland during the summer of 2005. The purpose of the event would be to raise awareness of the 'Make Poverty History' campaign rather than to raise funds, and to try and shame the G8 leaders into taking resolute and effective action to aid African countries crippled by debt and trade inequality. Concerts around the world would reach a global audience measured in billions, and – for the prestigious French concert, to be held at the Palace de Versailles – The Cure would headline. The capacity outside the Palace was 220,000, and tickets were to be obtained via an SMS text lottery, with winners getting priority positions at the front of the crowd.

Within a couple of days it was confirmed that Porl Thompson would be re-joining the band for the live dates due over the summer. After *Live8* The Cure would be appearing in Spain, Belgium, St Malo in France, Avenches in Switzerland, Sicily, Hungary, Berlin, Athens and Istanbul by early September. Porl joined the trio at *Live8* over a decade since he last left the band, contributing to a blistering set consisting of 'Open', 'One Hundred Years', 'End' and the encore crowd-pleasers 'Just Like Heaven' and 'Boys Don't Cry'. The late-night Parisian crowd – for so many years amongst the most passionate supporters of The Cure – went apeshit.

The response to *Live8* was hugely positive around the world, and indeed the G8 leaders did seem to have taken the message of the whole world to heart as they wound up their summit. The news of the week was a staggering series of major stories, however. While *Live8* was still filling column inches and front page stories all over Britain, it was announced in Singapore that London would host the 2012 Olympic Games – a superb accolade for the city that had been overlooked for decades. But while that was fresh in everybody's minds, terrorist bombs exploded over London's transport system, killing over fifty people and badly injuring many more. It was a remarkable few days that Cure fans, Londoners, and people all over Britain would not forget in a hurry, with the suicide bombers acutely putting the triumphant events of the preceding days into sharp and painful perspective.

And so we look forward to more Cure concerts in 2005 and beyond, and hope for more collaborative releases as well as new studio albums. The Cure story started in suburban rooms in Crawley, with Woolworth guitars and homework to do in the evenings. It ends for us as it began, with the line-up of the band changing and familiar faces entering and leaving. In between times, The Cure have played to some of the biggest rock audiences ever seen and made some of the best records we've ever heard. Throughout this period Robert Smith has ploughed a remarkable furrow – resolute, intelligent, articulate, and never dull. It has been a remarkable career, and I don't think we've seen the last of either him or his band of strolling players.

*

So what is it about The Cure that makes us love them so much? Since I began my own love affair with pop music back in July 1972, I've bought hundreds of albums and singles, videos and DVDs. I've had every Rick Wakeman solo album, bought and (quite quickly) sold Tubeway Army and Tin Machine albums by the handful, and – while I've kept an abiding interest in some stuff – a lot more has passed by the wayside, never to be listened to again. The people I have continued to listen to have included David Bowie, who has never failed to surprise and enlighten me; Joni Mitchell, consistently the most articulate solo contributor to modern music over the last fifty years; Leonard Cohen, Robert Wyatt, Dylan, Nick Drake, Nanci Griffith and 'newcomers' like Aimee Mann and Beth Orton. Bands that have endured for me have been Joy Division and The Smiths, XTC, and latter-day discoveries like Teenage Fanclub and Fountains of Wayne.

I guess there's a pattern amongst many of these that leads me to The Cure. Firstly, most of them know a good riff when they write one. From 'Paperback Writer' to 'Hand In Glove', there is nothing so joyous as listening to a guitar line that's never been heard before but which immediately joins the list of greats. The Cure can kick a riff further than almost anyone, and the guitar sound of The Cure is unique throughout their career.

Secondly, in some way or other most of the above are literary-minded coves: Bowie, Joni, Dylan, they all have an eye on literature and art as much as on music as their inspiration, and their writing is in every sense literary too. Robert Smith is an outstanding lyricist in my view: literary, articulate, emotional, elegantly vague yet punishingly observant. Clearly, he is a man who sets himself *very* high standards.

Amongst the groups listed above, there is something of the outsider in all of them. They are all capable of writing *within* a genre, whether it be pop, folk, country or whatever, but their best work sits *outside* genre-classifications and should be judged purely on its own merits. One wouldn't rate a Beatles track by comparing it to Wayne Fontana & The Mindbenders, any more than you would assess Robert Wyatt by comparing him to ... well, anyone! These guys inhabit their own artistic spaces, and on the occasions when those spaces have overlapped with mine our relationships have been long and lasting and fruitful. Venn diagrams of the soul. The Cure have always been outsiders. Hard to assess against their Seventies contemporaries, they have things in common with some of the acts that grew out of the Eighties, but nobody covered the same ground in anything like the same way. As their profile grew to the point where they could fill any major stadium in the world at the drop of a hat, how many other bands who were capable of the same could they genuinely be compared to artistically, who hadn't compromised something of themselves in the process?

The Cure have always been wonderfully visual. Despite Robert's evident shyness, and his own admissions over the years that he has not always been comfortable as a performer *per se*, he is in fact a mesmeric performer, emotional and intense. Like a fine actor, he eschews the grandly theatrical and performs with the most understated of gestures. His emotions are writ large, but his means of conveying them are writ small. A rare skill in an industry where big egos require big performances.

The band's video legacy is wonderfully varied and visually stunning too, whether via the Top Ten-friendly clips of 'The Lovecats' or the emotional battering of *Trilogy*. The Cure have always been a band to *watch* as much as to listen to.

Those critics over the years who have cited The Cure as gloomy are often those who have also missed the wit and the wisdom of Leonard Cohen. For forty years Cohen has been stuck with a label similar to the one dumped on The Cure by many an interviewer and reviewer – glum goth dirge-makers. Those who describe Cohen's music as morbid miss the desperately beautiful love songs, the tongue-in-cheek self-critical asides and the dark humour inherent in his work. So it is with The Cure. They are a serious artistic force: no band could last nearly thirty years on candy-floss pop. But The Cure have always stood outside themselves, as much as outside the music community at large. There are glorious moments of wit and humour, gorgeous, sentimental expressions of love and warmth, calls for help and cool observation. Like the best artists – Leonard Cohen, Joni Mitchell, Mr Bowie – The Cure are so multi-dimensional that the phrase is almost inadequate to describe the breadth of their work.

In Robert Smith we have a writer of instinctive poetic genius, who writes with a rare sensitivity and wit combined. Like Emily Dickinson he has kept a very tight rein on his subject matter, and has explored the labyrinthine variety of a restricted number of themes. Smith's lyrics can be buried under a battery of sound or dissected in a gentle pop song. He is a painter of pictures that look good from the far end of the gallery and at the same bear close scrutiny under the microscope's lens. And while many have followed the band over decades, others come to The Cure anew every year. Recently, playing around with a new version of Cubase on my own computer at home, my eighteen-year-old nephew brought his effects pedals and guitar down to have a play with his ageing uncle. I asked him what he'd like to play to get us warmed up. Without thinking, his first response was immediately "The Cure's 'Boys Don't Cry.'" Not Radiohead, The White Stripes or Coldplay. Not The Bees, Green Day or The Rapture. Jonathan hadn't been born when 'Boys Don't Cry' was first released.

The Cure have been the architects of great musical bridges spanning wide emotional rivers, the masons of colossal public buildings of noise that we wander through at will. At the same time they are the craftsmen of tiny, beautiful jewellery, the makers of toys that children will never tire of. Inevitably there will be more new music from either The Cure or from Robert Smith on his own. I hope it is primarily from The Cure, but at the same time I hope that Robert gets that noodling solo album out one day. Either will undoubtedly be interesting. Much of it will no doubt be fascinating. Some of it will, in all probability, be magnificent. And their audience will be there, whatever. "I don't want it to stop," Robert told Zane Lowe for the BBC in 2004. "I never really have, you know." Thank God for that.

And finally, to The Cure themselves: thanks for 'Catch'. Thanks for *Disintegration*. Thanks for 'Just Like Heaven' and 'Boys Don't Cry' and *Bloodflowers* and 'Lovesong'.

It wouldn't have been the same without you.

Robert Smith

Bibliography

An enormous amount has been written on The Cure over nearly thirty years. It would be impossible to give a complete bibliography that included every book or article about the band, but I have referenced here some of the articles and books that are referenced in the text and others which make good reading.

Books:
Ten Imaginary Years – Barbarian, Sutherland and Smith, Zomba/Fiction, 1988
The Cure: A Visual Documentary – Thompson and Greene, Omnibus Press, 1988
The Cure On Record – Darren Butler, Omnibus Press 1995
21st Century Goth – Mick Mercer, Reynolds & Hearn Ltd, 2002
Gothic Rock Black Book - Mick Mercer, Omnibus Press, 1988
Strange Fascination – David Bowie: The Definitive Story – David Buckley, Virgin Books, 1999
In Session Tonight: The Complete Radio One Recording – Ken Garner, BBC Books, 1993
The Boy Looked At Johnny, Julie Burchill and Tony Parsons, Pluto Press, 1980

Articles:
There is so much available on The Cure in article form across hundreds of magazines and papers. There are some particularly important pieces over the years that have served as signpost features on the band. Here is a selection of some of the most interesting:

Record Collector magazine has published a variety of pieces invaluable to Cure collectors, not only for the informative text but also the discographies included. Most notable is Pat Gilbert's three-part series in issues 167–169 (July–September 1993). Several other articles have appeared over the years.

'B-Sides Themselves,' *Record Collector's* January 2004 article is also excellent.

'Bad Medicine' James Oldham, *Uncut*, February 2000

'Hello/Goodbye: Michael Dempsey and The Cure' – *Uncut*, March 2005

'Timeless Tunesmith' Will Hodgkinson, *The Guardian*, May 30, 2003 (available at www.theguardian.co.uk)

'The Wit And Wisdom Of Robert Smith' Doug Adamson, uncredited 1987 interview (*www.threeimaginaryboys.altavista.org*)

'The Cure: Album by Album' Bill Crandall, *www.rollingstone.com*, June 2004

'The Crack-Up,' Alex Petridis, *Mojo,* August 2003

'Impossible Dreamer,' Robin Gibson, *Sounds*, July 11 1987

'Pictures Of Youth,' The Stud Brothers, *Melody Maker*, March 7 1992

'The Gloom Generation,' Susan Colon, *Details* , July 1997

'All you need is Glove,' Paul Bursche, *No 1* magazine, 1983

'A Momentary Collapse Of Reason,' Jonh Wilde, *Melody Maker*, May 1989

'Three Imaginary Weeks: What We Did On Our Holidays,' Robert Smith, *Melody Maker*, May 1987

'Caught In The Act' *Q*, May 1989

'Wild Mood Swings,' Kevin Raub, *Rolling Stone*, Nov. 6 1997

'Country Cure,' *Sound on Sound*, June 1996

'Guitar Gardens,' Kyle Swenson, *Guitar Player Online*, March 2000

'Robert Smith - The Man Who Changed His Mind,' Tero Alanko, *Soundi*, Finland, July 2003 (available variously online)

'Before & After The Cure,' Benedetta Skrufff, www.trustthedj.com/SKRUFFF for Lol Tolhurst interview.

Please note: in researching this book I have also come across two articles by Steve Sutherland, written for *Melody Maker*, entitled 'A History Of The Cure (Parts 1 & 2)' These are both very interesting and useful pieces, and they are reproduced on the internet a number of times, but with no reference to the publication date in *MM*. Sutherland has been an intelligent and important observer of The Cure over the years; arguably one of the band's staunchest supporters.

Web sites:
www.thecure.com - the official and *best* Cure site
www.levinhurst.com - for what Lol is up to these days.
www.perrybamonte.de - 'the only website dedicated to Perry Bamonte'.
www.rogerodonnell.com - Roger's official site
www.simongallup.com - most definitely not the official Simon Gallup site, but a faithful fan's site.

The following three websites can be the starting point for anyone who wishes to explore The Cure in depth. Between them they have the most incredible range for surfers to wade through, not least almost daily updates on Cure activity, collectibles, traders pages, photo collections par excellence, and more links to other excellent Cure sites. I can recommend them unreservedly:
www.afoolisharrangement.com
www.picturesofyou.us
www.ourworld.compuserve.com/homepages/ChainofFlowers

Also worth a look for various snippets of Cure info:
www.5years.com for everything Ziggy
www.pages.eidosnet.co.uk/johnnymoped/punk/webpunk/webpunkhi storypage_introduction.html - for all things punk.
www.cure-concerts.de - lists almost every fact available on nearly every Cure concert ever! A remarkable archive.

Recorded Interviews:
The Cure – Limited Edition Picture Disk Interview, Baktabak CBAK4003
The Cure: Out Of The Woods – An Unauthorised Documentary DVD - Chrome Dreams, 2004
Interview With Zane Lowe, October 8 2004, BBC Radio One

A Collection Of Dreams interview CD, source unkown, early 1990s

Interview with Razor Cuts, Virgin Radio, October 2004 (www.virginradio.co.uk)

XFM interview with John Kennedy, October 5 2004 (www.xfm.co.uk)

Discography

The Cure's discography is an extensive one, with many regular releases and also many limited edition or special edition releases. The Cure collector's market is very heady and – alongside all the picture discs, limited editions and so on – bootlegs abound. The band also occasionally releases official product in different formats, different track listings in different markets for instance. To cover all this history of Cure releases is the subject of an entire book of its own – as Darren Butler's estimable *The Cure On Record* testifies. For this reason I have necessarily restricted this discography to the major album/single/video releases of The Cure, as a testament to their ongoing work, rather than a detailed list of every Cure record ever.

Singles:

Killing An Arab/10:15 Saturday Night
Single – Fiction Records, June 1979

Boys Don't Cry/Plastic Passion
Single – Fiction Records, June 1979

Jumping Someone Else's Train/I'm Cold
Single – Fiction Records, November 1979

A Forest/Another Journey By Train
Single – Fiction Records, March 1981

Primary/Descent
Single – Fiction Records, April 1980

Charlotte Sometimes/Splintered in Her Head/Faith (live)
Single – Fiction Records, October 1981

The Hanging Garden/One Hundred Years/A Forest (live)/

Killing An Arab (live)
Single – Fiction Records, July 1982

Let's Go To Bed/Just One Kiss
Single – Fiction Records, November 1982

The Walk/Lament/The Upstairs Room/The Dream
Single – Fiction Records, July 1983

The Lovecats/Speak My Language/Mr Pink Eyes
Single – Fiction Records, October 1983

The Caterpillar/Happy The Man/Throw Your Foot
Single – Fiction Records, May 1984

Inbetween Days/The Exploding Boy/A Few Hours After
This
Single – Fiction Records, July 1985

Close To Me/A Man Inside My Mouth/Stop Dead/New Day
Single – Fiction Records, September 1985

Boys Don't Cry/Pillbox Tales/Do The Hansa
Single – Fiction Records, April 1986
Re-mix and re-recorded vocal version

Why Can't I Be You/A Japanese Dream/Six Different Ways
(live)/Push (live)
Single – Fiction Records, April 1987

Catch/Breathe/A Chain Of Flowers/Kyoto Song (live)/A
Night Like This (live)
Single – Fiction Records, June 1987

Just Like Heaven/Snow In Summer/Sugar Girl
Single – Fiction Records, October 1987

Hot Hot Hot!!! (extended remix)/Hot Hot Hot!!! (remix)/Hey You!!! (extended remix)
Single – Fiction Records, February 1988

Lullaby/Babble/Out Of Mind/Lullaby (extended remix)
Single – Fiction Records, April 1989

Fascination Street/Babble/Out Of Mind/Fascination Street (extended remix)
Single – Fiction Records, April 1989

Love Song/2 Late/Fear Of Ghosts/Lovesong (12" Extended mix)
Single – Fiction Records, August 1989

Pictures Of You/Last Dance (Live)/Fascination Street (Live) /Prayers For Rain (Live)/Disintegration (Live)/Pictures Of You (Strange mix)
Single – Fiction Records, March 1990

Never Enough (Big mix)/Harold and Joe /Let's Go To Bed (Milk mix)
Single – Fiction Records, September 1990

Close To Me (Closest mix)/Just Like Heaven (Dizzy mix) /Primary (red mix)/Why Can't I Be You? (extended mix)/Pictures Of You (Strange mix)
Single – Fiction Records, October 1990

High/This Twilight Garden/Play/High (Trip mix)/Open (Fix mix) High (Higher mix)
Single – Fiction Records, March 1992

Friday I'm In Love/Halo/Scared As You/Friday I'm In Love (Strangelove mix)
Single – Fiction Records, May 1992

A Letter To Elise/The Big Hand/A Foolish Arrangement/A Letter To Elise (Blue mix)
Single – Fiction Records, October 1992

Lost Wishes: UYEA Sound/Cloudberry/Off To Sleep/The Three Sisters
EP – Fiction Records, November 1993. Ltd edition mail order cassette.

The 13th (Swing Radio mix)/It Used To Be Me/The 13th (Killer Bee mix)/The 13th (Two Chord Cool mix)/Ocean/Adonais
Single – Fiction Records, April 1996.

Mint Car/Home/Mint Car (Busker's mix)/Mint Car (Electric mix)/Waiting/A Pink Dream
Single – Fiction Records, June 1996

Gone! (Radio Mix)/The 13th (Feels Good mix)/This Is A Lie (Ambient mix)/Strange Attraction (Strange mix)/Gone! (Critter mix)/Gone! (Ultra Living mix)/Gone! (Space mix)
Single – Fiction Records, November 1996

Strange Attraction (Adrian Sherwood album mix)/The 13th (Feels Good mix)/This Is A Lie (Ambient mix)/Gone! (Critter mix)/Strange Attraction (Strange mix)
Single – Fiction Records, November 1996. USA only.

Five Swing Live: Want/Club America/Mint Car/Trap/Treasure
Single – Fiction Records, June 1997. Limited edition CD.

Wrong Number (Single mix)/Wrong Number (Digital Exchange mix)/Wrong Number (Analogue Exchange mix)/Wrong Number (Dub Analogue Exchange mix)/Wrong Number (p2p mix)/Wrong Number (Crossed Line mix)/Wrong Number (Isdn mix)/Wrong Number (Engaged

mix)
Single – Fiction Records, October 1997.

Cut Here/Signal To Noise/Cut Here (Missing remix)/Cut Here (CDROM video)
Single – Fiction Records, October 2001

The End Of The World/This Morning/Fake
Single – Geffen, June 2003

alt.end/Why Can't I Be Me?/Your God Is Fear
Single – Geffen, October 2004

Taking Off/Why Can't I Be Me?/Your God Is Fear/ Taking Off (video)
Single – Geffen, October 2004

Albums:

Three Imaginary Boys –
10:15 Saturday Night/Accuracy/Grinding Halt/Another Day/Object/Subway Song/Foxy Lady/Meathook/So What/Fire In Cairo/It's Not You/Three Imaginary Boys/The Weedy Burton
Album – Fiction Records August 1979

Boys Don't Cry –
Boys Don't Cry/Plastic Passion/10:15 Saturday Night/Accuracy/So What/Jumping Someone Else's Train/Subway Song/Killing an Arab/Fire in Cairo/Another Day/Grinding Halt/Three Imaginary Boys
Album – Fiction Records February 1980

Seventeen Seconds –
A Reflection/Play For Today/Secrets/In Your House/ Three/Final Sound/A Forest/M/At Night/Seventeen

Seconds
Album – Fiction Records, April 1980

Faith –
Holy Hour/Primary/Other Voices/All Cats Are Grey/Funeral Party/Doubt/Drowning Man/Faith
Album – Fiction Records, April 1981

Happily Ever After –
A Reflection/Play for Today/Secrets/In Your House/ Three/Final Sound/A Forest/M/At Night/Seventeen Seconds/Holy Hour/Primary/Other Voices/All Cats Are Grey/Funeral Party/Doubt/Drowning Man/Faith
Album – Fiction Records, September 1981

Pornography –
One Hundred Years/Short Term Effect/Hanging Garden/Siamese Twins/Figurehead/Strange Day/Cold/ Pornography
Album – Fiction Records, May 1982

Japanese Whispers –
Let's Go To Bed/The Dream/Just One Kiss/The Upstairs Room/The Walk/Speak My Language/Lament/The Lovecats
Album – Fiction Records, December 1983

The Top –
Shake Dog Shake/Bird Mad Girl/Wailing Wall/Give Me It/Dressing Up/Caterpillar/Piggy In The Mirror/Empty World/Bananafishbones
Album – Fiction Records, December 1983

Concert: The Cure Live –
Shake Dog Shake/Primary/ Charlotte Sometimes/Hanging Garden/Give Me It/The Walk/One Hundred Years/A

Forest/10:15 Saturday Night/Killing An Arab
Album – Fiction Records, October 1984

The Head On The Door –
Inbetween Days/Kyoto Song/Blood/Six Different
Ways/Push/The Baby Screams/Close To Me/A Night Like
This/Screw/Sinking
Album – Fiction Records, August 1985

Standing On A Beach –
Killing an Arab/10:15 Saturday Night/Boys Don't
Cry/Jumping Someone Else's Train/A Forest/Play For
Today/Primary/Other Voices/Charlotte Sometimes/The
Hanging Garden/Let's Go To Bed/The Walk/The
Lovecats/The Caterpillar/Inbetween Days/Close To Me/A
Night Like This
Album - Fiction Records, May 1986

Kiss Me Kiss Me Kiss Me –
Kiss/Catch/Torture/If Only Tonight We Could Sleep/Why
Can't I Be You?/How Beautiful You Are/Snakepit/Just Like
Heaven/All I Want/Hot Hot Hot!!!/One More Time/Like
Cockatoos/Icing Sugar/The Perfect Girl/A Thousand
Hours/Shiver And Shake/Fight
Album - Fiction Records, May 1987

Disintegration –
Plainsong/Pictures Of You/Closedown/Love Song/Last
Dance/Lullaby/Fascination Street/Prayers For Rain/Same
Deep Water As You/Disintegration/Homesick
Album - Fiction Records, May 1989

Entreat –
Pictures Of You/Closedown/Last Dance/Fascination
Street/Prayers For Rain/Disintegration/Homesick/Untitled
Album - Fiction Records, September 1990

Mixed Up –
Lullaby (Extended mix)/Close to Me (Closer mix)/
Fascination Street (Extended mix)/Walk (Everything
mix)/Lovesong (Extended mix)/Forest (Tree mix)/Pictures of
You (Extended Dub mix)/Hot Hot Hot!!! (Extended
mix)/Caterpillar (Flicker mix)/Inbetween Days (Shiver
mix)/Never Enough (Big mix)
Album - Fiction Records, November 1990

Wish –
Open/High/Apart/From The Edge Of The Deep Green
Sea/Wendy Time/Doing The Unstuck/Friday I'm In
Love/Trust/A Letter To Elise/Cut/To Wish Impossible
Things/End
Album - Fiction Records, April 1992

Show –
Open/High/Pictures Of You/Lullaby/Just Like Heaven/A
Night Like This/Trust/Doing The Unstuck/Friday I'm In
Love/Inbetween Days/From The Edge Of The Deep Green
Sea/Never Enough/Cut/End
Album - Fiction Records, October 1993

Paris –
Figurehead/One Hundred Years/At Night/Play For
Today/Apart/In Your House/Lovesong/Catch/Letter To
Elise/Dressing Up/Charlotte Sometimes/Close To Me
Album - Fiction Records, October 1993

Wild Mood Swings –
Want/Club America/This Is A Lie/The 13th/Strange
Attraction/Mint Car/Jupiter Crash/Round & Round &
Round/Gone/Numb/Return/Trap/Treasure/Bare
Album - Fiction Records, May 1996

Galore: The Videos 1987–1997 –
Why Can't I Be You?/Catch/Just Like Heaven/Hot Hot Hot!!!/Lullaby/Fascination Street/Lovesong/Pictures Of You/Never Enough/Close To Me (Closet remix)/High /Friday I'm In Love/A Letter To Elise/The 13th (Swing Radio mix)/Mint Car (Radio mix)/Strange Attraction (Album mix)/Gone! (Radio mix)/Wrong Number
Album – Fiction Records, October 1987

Bloodflowers –
Out Of This World/Watching Me Fall/Where The Birds Always Sing/Maybe Someday/The Last Day Of Summer/There Is No If.../The Loudest Sound/39 /Bloodflowers
Album - Fiction Records, February 2000

The Cure Greatest Hits –
Boys Don't Cry/A Forest/Let's Go To Bed/The Walk/The Lovecats/Inbetween Days/Close To Me/Why Can't I Be You?/Just Like Heaven/Lullaby/Lovesong/Never Enough/ High/Friday I'm In Love/Mint Car/Wrong Number/Cut Here/Just Say Yes
Album – Polydor/Fiction November 2001
Ltd edition release included the same selection of songs in acoustic format.

Join The Dots - B-sides & Rarities 1978 – 2001: The Fiction Years
Disc One: 10:15 Saturday Night/Plastic Passion/Pillbox Tales/Do The Hansa/I'm Cold/Another Journey By Train/DeScent/Splintered In Her Head/Lament (Flexipop Version)/Just One Kiss/The Dream/The Upstairs Room/Lament/Speak My Language/Mr Pink Eyes/Happy The Man/Throw Your Foot/New Day/The Exploding Boy/A Few Hours After This.../A Man Inside My Mouth/Stop Dead
Disc Two: A Japanese Dream/Breathe/A Chain of Flowers/Snow in Summer/Sugar Girl/Icing Sugar (Weird remix)/Hey You!!! (12" remix)/How Beautiful You Are/To

The Sky/Babble/Out Of Mind /2 Late/Fear Of Ghosts/Hello
I Love You/Hello I Love You/Hello I Love You/Harold And
Joe/Just Like Heaven (Dizzy mix)
Disc Three: This Twilight Garden/Play/Halo/Scared As
You/The Big Hand/A Foolish Arrangement/Doing The
Unstuck (12″ Remix)/Purple Haze (for Virgin Radio)/Purple
Haze/Burn/Young Americans/Dredd Song/It Used To Be
Me/Ocean/Adonais
Disc Four: Home/Waiting/A Pink Dream/This Is A Lie
(Ambient remix)/Wrong Number (P2P remix)/More Than
This/World In My Eyes/Possession/Out Of This World
(Oakenfold mix)/Maybe Someday (Acoustic remix)/Coming
Up/Signal To Noise (Acoustic version)/Signal To Noise/Just
Say Yes (Curve mix)/A Forest (Plati mix)
Album – Fiction/Polydor, January 2004

The Cure –
Lost/Labyrinth/Before Three/Truth Goodness & Beauty/The
End Of The World/Anniversary/Us Or Them/alt.end/(I
Don't Know What's Going) On/Taking Off/Never/The
Promise/Going Nowhere
Album – Geffen Records, June 2004.
Deluxe edition includes link to website, Back On, The Broken
Promise, Someone's Coming and the DVD 'Making The
Cure.'

Three Imaginary Boys (deluxe edition)
Disc one is as the original album (above). Disc two contains
the following various demos, live and unreleased studio
versions: I Want To Be Old/I'm Cold/Heroin Face/I Just
Need Myself/10:15 Saturday Night/The Cocktail
Party/Grinding Halt/Boys Don't Cry/It's Not You/10:15
Saturday Night/Fire In Cairo/Winter/Faded Smiles/Play
With Me/World War/Boys Don't Cry/Jumping Someone
Else's Train/Subway Song/Accuracy/10:15 Saturday Night
Album – Universal, December 2004

Seventeen Seconds (deluxe edition)
Disc one is as the original album (above). Disc two contains the following: I'm A Cult Hero/I Dig You/Another Journey By Train/Secrets/Seventeen Seconds/In Your House/Three/I Dig You/I'm A Cult Hero/M/Final Sound/A Reflection/Play For Today/At Night/A Forest
Album – Universal, April 2005

Faith (deluxe edition)
Disc one is as the original album (above). Disc two contains the following: Carnage Visors/Faith/Doubt/Drowning/Holy Hour/Primary/Going Home Time/Violin Song/Normal Story/All Cats Are Grey/Funeral Party/Other Voices/Drowning Man/Faith/Forever/Charlotte Sometimes
Album – Universal, April 2005

Pornography (deluxe edition)
Disc one is as the original album (above). Disc two contains the following: Break/Demise/Temptation/Figurehead/Hanging Garden/One Hundred Years/Airlock: Soundtrack/Cold/A Strange Day/Pornography/All Mine/A Short Term Effect/Siamese Twins/Temptation Two
Album – Universal, April 2005

Video/DVD

Staring At The Sea: The Images –
Killing an Arab/10:15 Saturday Night/Boys Don't Cry/Jumping Someone Else's Train/A Forest/Play For Today/Primary/Other Voices/Charlotte Sometimes/The Hanging Garden/Let's Go To Bed/The Walk/The Lovecats/The Caterpillar/Inbetween Days/Close To Me/A Night Like This
Video – Fiction Films/Palace Video, May 1986

The Cure In Orange –
Introduction/Shake Dog Shake/Piggy In The Mirror/Play
For Today/A Strange Day/Primary/Kyoto Song/Charlotte
Sometimes/Inbetween Days/The Walk/A Night Like
This/Push/One Hundred Years/A Forest/Sinking/Close To
Me/Let's Go To Bed/Six Different Ways/Three Imaginary
Boys/Boys Don't Cry/Faith/Give Me It/10:15 Saturday
Night/Killing An Arab/Sweet Talking Guy (performed by
The Chiffons)
Video – Fiction Films/Polygram Music Video, February 1988

Picture Show –
Why Can't I Be You?/Catch/Hot Hot Hot!!!/Just Like
Heaven/Lullaby/Fascination Street/Lovesong/Pictures Of
You/Never Enough/Close To Me (Closer mix)
Video – Fiction/Polygram Video, July 1991

The Cure Play Out –
Wendy Time/The Big Hand/Away/Let's Go To Bed/A
Strange Day/Pictures Of You/Fascination Street/Lullaby/A
Forest/(various clips including Hello I Love You/Just Like
Heaven/The Walk/Bland With An Edge/Harold & Joe/The
Blood/The Walk/Just Like Heaven/A Letter To Elise/If Only
Tonight We Could Sleep/Boy's Don't Cry/Never Enough
Video – Fiction/Windsong, September 1992

Show –
Tape/Open/High/Pictures Of You/Lullaby/Just Like
Heaven/Fascination Street/A Night Like This /Trust/Doing
The Unstuck/The Walk/Let's Go To Bed/Friday I'm In
Love/Inbetween Days/From The Edge of the Deep Green
Sea/Never Enough/Cut/End/To Wish Impossible
Things/Primary/Boys Don't Cry/Why Can't I Be You?/A
Forest
Video – Fiction October 1993

Galore: The Videos 1987–1997 –
Why Can't I Be You?/Catch/Just Like Heaven/Hot Hot Hot!!!/Lullaby/Fascination Street/Lovesong/Pictures Of You/Never Enough/Close To Me/High/Friday I'm In Love/A Letter To Elise/The 13th/Mint Car/Gone!/Wrong Number
Video – October 1987. Also available on VCD format.

The Cure Greatest Hits –
Boys Don't Cry/A Forest/Let's Go to Bed/The Walk/The Lovecats/Inbetween Days/Close To Me/Why Can't I Be You?/Just Like Heaven/Lullaby/Lovesong/Never Enough/High/Friday I'm In Love/Mint Car/Wrong Number/Cut Here/Just Say Yes. Includes: A Forest (acoustic)/The Lovecats (acoustic)/Close to Me (acoustic)/Lullaby (acoustic)/Friday I'm In Love (acoustic)/Just Say Yes (acoustic).
DVD video – Polydor/Fiction November 2001

Trilogy –
Disc One: *Pornography* set/*Disintegration* set
Disc Two: *Bloodflowers* set/Encores/Interviews
DVD video - Smith Music Co Ltd/Eagle Rock Entertainment Ltd 2003

Picture Credits:

THE STREETS: TOWER BLOCKS AND TOP TENS
by Jimmy Ramsay

Mike Skinner aka the streets is arguably the most acclaimed new talent to emerge in the UK in recent years. A Birmingham native who later ventured into the murky depths of the capital's garage scene, Skinner was an unlikely nominee for Britain's answer to Eminem. Brought up around tough estates on a diet of cheap beer, hip-hop, house and jungle while working fast food jobs just to get by, Skinner bore witness to a teenage trawl through the lower stratum of society. Eventually he started to record his own tunes, which from the very first – such as the ultra-gritty home-cooked 'Has It Come To This?' – have injected a biting degree of social commentary into an extremely diverse and creative scene. In so doing, Skinner has been able to capture a cross-section of the British public as his fans, from the garage heads who were with him in railway arches at the start to the glossy magazines and broadsheet editors who now feature his every move. S kinner is, without doubt, a phenomenon.

This incisive unauthorised and unofficial biography – the very first on the market – chronicles Skinner's most extraordinary of rises to fame. Further emphasis will be accorded to the claims that Skinner is the 'new Alan Bennett' and the countless other lofty literary claims by a media and public who feel he can do no wrong.

ISBN 0 9539942 8 7 160 Pages Paperback, 8pp b/w pics £8.99 World Rights

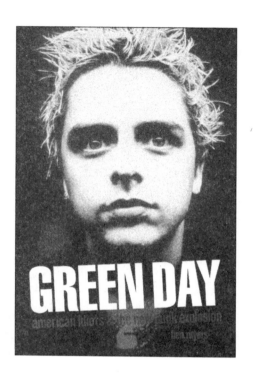

GREEN DAY: AMERICAN IDIOTS AND THE NEW PUNK EXPLOSION
by Ben Myers

The world's first and only full biography of Green Day. Self-confessed latch-key kids from small blue-collar Californian towns, Green Day have gone on to sell 50 million albums and single-handedly redefine the punk and rock genre for an entire generation. Inspired by both the energy of British punk bands as well as cult American groups, Green Day gigged relentlessly across the US underground before eventually signing to Warners and releasing their 1994 major label debut *Dookie*, which was a 10-million-selling worldwide hit album. With the arrival of Green Day, suddenly music was dumb, fun, upbeat and colourful again. Many now credit the band with saving rock from the hands of a hundred grunge-lite acts. In 2004 Green Day reached a career pinnacle with the concept album *American Idiot*, a sophisticated commentary on modern life - not least their dissatisfaction with their president. Myers is an authority on punk and hardcore and in this unauthorised book charts the band members' difficult childhoods and their rise to success, speaking to key members of the punk underground and music industry figures along the way.

ISBN 0 9539942 9 5 208 Pages Paperback, 8pp b/w pics £12.99 World Rights

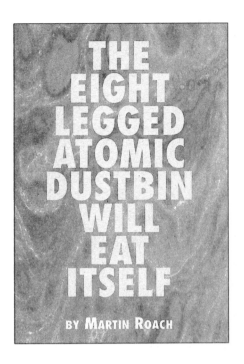

THE EIGHT LEGGED ATOMIC DUSTBIN
WILL EAT ITSELF
by Martin Roach

A fully updated, revised and expanded edition of the book that *Vox* magazine called 'a phenomenon' on its publication in 1992. With all three of the Stourbridge bands – The Wonder Stuff, Pop Will Eat Itself and Ned's Atomic Dustbin – having reformed in 2004, largely due to public demand, this book brings the history of this unique music scene up to date. Extensive interviews with band members reveal what they have been up to throughout the thirteen years since this book's first publication, including writing Hollywood soundtracks and running record companies. A comprehensive chronicle of all their record releases to date and massive histories of each band complete the third edition of this publishing classic. Originally printed in 1992 as I.M.P.'s first ever title, the original 'blue' edition sold over 5,000 copies - predominantly out of carrier bags outside gigs and at festivals! The second 'red' edition was released to the book trade and sold a further 3,000 copies and both are now collectors' items among the fanbase.

ISBN 0 9549704 0 3 176 Pages Paperback, 45pp b/w pics £8.99 World Rights

MUSE: INSIDE THE MUSCLE MUSEUM
by Ben Myers

The first and only biography of one of the most innovative and successful rock bands of recent years. Formed in the mid-1990s in a sleepy sea-side Devonshire town, Muse comprises teenage friends Matt Bellamy, Chris Wolstenholme and Dominic Howard. 2001's *Origin Of Symmetry* album spawned Top 10 hits such as 'Plug-In Baby' and a unique version of Nina Simone's classic, 'Feeling Good'. Their third album, *Absolution*, entered the UK charts at Number 1 in October 2003 – by then, all the signs were there that Muse were on the verge of becoming one of the biggest bands of the new century. Throughout 2004, they won over countless new fans at festivals, including a now-famous headline slot at Glastonbury, which preceded a two-night sell-out of the cavernous Earl's Court and a Brit Award for 'Best Live Act' in early 2005. This book tells that full story right from their inception and includes interviews conducted both with the band and those who have witnessed their climb to the top - a position they show no sign of relinquishing any time soon.

ISBN 0 9539942 6 0 208 Pages Paperback, 8pp b/w pics £12.99 World Rights

JOHN LYDON: THE SEX PISTOLS, PIL & ANTI-CELEBRITY
by Ben Myers

The inimitable ranting voice of John Lydon nee Rotten has graced far more than just the brief yet staggering catalogue of Pistols songs – not least his pivotal post-punk band Public Image Limited, whose full history has never been covered by a book until now. Rising from humble London-Irish beginnings to iconic status by the age of twenty-one, sardonic frontman John Lydon is a constant thorn in the side of the establishment and a true English eccentric. After the Sex Pistols' short career had come to a chaotic and messy demise, Lydon went on to become one of the most influential and talked about stars in rock and roll's incendiary history. This book also contains a full analysis of Lydon's television side projects and, for the very first time, charts his previously undocumented twenty-five years since the demise of the Sex Pistols. Told through exclusive new interviews with associates of Lydon, including members of The Clash, PiL and The Prodigy, this book recounts one of the most incredible stories in modern music.

ISBN 0 9539942 7 9 256 Pages Paperback, 8pp b/w pics £12.99 World Rights

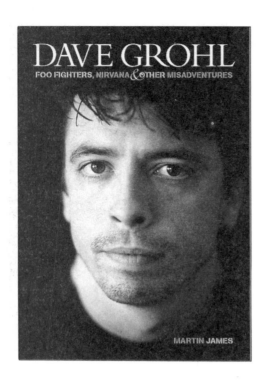

DAVE GROHL: FOO FIGHTERS,
NIRVANA AND OTHER MISADVENTURES
by Martin James

The first biography of one of modern rock's most influential figures. Emerging from the morass of suicide and potent musical legacy that was Nirvana, Foo Fighters established themselves - against all odds - as one of the most popular rock bands in the world. Deflecting early critical disdain, Dave Grohl has single-handedly reinvented himself and cemented his place in the rock pantheon.

This is his story, from his pre-Nirvana days in hardcore band Scream to his current festival-conquering status as a Grammy-winning, platinum-selling grunge legend reborn. Martin James once found himself watching the Prodigy backstage with Grohl, both clambering up a lighting rig to share a better view. With this in-depth book, he pieces together the life story of one of the most remarkable, enigmatic and yet amenable stars in recent music history.

ISBN 0 9539942 4 4 208 Pages Paperback, b/w pics £12.99 World Rights

SENT FROM COVENTRY
TWO TONE'S CHEQUERED PAST
by Richard Eddington

The first detailed analysis and history of the music phenomenon called Two Tone, a movement led by bands such as The Specials, The Selecter, Bad Manners, Madness and The Beat. *Sent From Coventry* examines the early years of the characters central to the embryonic Two Tone scene set in a grainy, monochrome world of pre-Thatcherite Britain. The author was at the heart of the scene and regularly found himself in the company of key individuals, and is therefore perfectly placed to chronicle this most fascinating of movements. Includes previously unseen photographs from the private collections of band members.

ISBN 0 9539942 5 2   256 Pages Paperback, b/w pics £12.99 World Rights

To request a catalogue or find out more about
our other music titles, including books on
The Streets and Mike Skinner, Green Day, Dave Grohl,
John Lydon, Muse, Two Tone, Mick Ronson,
Stereophonics, Shaun Ryder, Prodigy and
numerous subculture classics, please visit:

www.impbooks.com